*Rethinking the Uncanny
in Hoffmann and Tieck*

D1334854

Studies in Modern German Literature

Peter D. G. Brown
General Editor

Vol. 100

PETER LANG
Oxford · Bern · Berlin · Bruxelles · Frankfurt/M. · New York · Wien

Marc Falkenberg

Rethinking the Uncanny in Hoffmann and Tieck

PETER LANG

Oxford · Bern · Berlin · Bruxelles · Frankfurt/M. · New York · Wien

Bibliographic information published by Die Deutsche Bibliothek
Die Deutsche Bibliothek lists this publication in the Deutsche Nationalbibliografie;
detailed bibliographic data is available on the Internet at ‹http://dnb.ddb.de›.

British Library and Library of Congress Cataloguing-in-Publication Data:
A catalogue record for this book is available from *The British Library*, Great
Britain, and from *The Library of Congress*, USA

ISSN 0888-3904
ISBN 3-03910-284-2
US-ISBN 0-8204-7211-5

© Peter Lang AG, European Academic Publishers, Bern 2005
Hochfeldstrasse 32, Postfach 746, CH-3000 Bern 9, Switzerland
info@peterlang.com, www.peterlang.com, www.peterlang.net

Printed in Germany

For my parents

Table of Contents

Preface

While Freud's essay "The 'Uncanny'" (1919h) has been analyzed as an example of Freud repressing his own discoveries, the uncanny as a term in literary criticism still appears largely bound to the Freudian definition. Freud's uncanny has had an enormous influence on readings of Romantic and specifically Fantastic literature, and has led critics to view stock figures like the ghost or the vampire as incarnations of the return of the repressed. Nonetheless, Freud's definition is a polemical rejection of Ernst Jentsch, a psychologist who emphasizes uncertainty for the uncanny. Freud, summarizing Jentsch, calls this uncertainty "intellectual," but a detailed reading of Jentsch's essay reveals that "cognitive uncertainty" more accurately describes the crucial factor in Jentsch's theory of the uncanny. When we revive Jentsch's attention to cognitive uncertainty, we recapture the sense of foreignness and ghastliness in the original meaning of the German word "unheimlich." More importantly, however, we also gain a better understanding of how the German Romantics themselves saw the uncanny. The uncanny effect of the selected examples from Early Modern Fantastic Fiction, Ludwig Tieck's "Der blonde Eckbert" and E.T.A. Hoffmann's "Der Sandmann," depends not only on fantastical events on the plot level and the dramatization of unconscious processes that Freud later termed the "return of the repressed," but also on giving the reader conflicting decoding instructions. The conflict is generated through the "poetical" elements, understood as the formal dimension of the literary text that is realized through such devices as metaphor, irony, or motif. The uncanny effect of these texts is thus enhanced by their lyrical density, which follows a demand by Romantic theorists for a more lyrical prose style. The reliance of the uncanny on "poetical" elements inspires the term poetical uncanny. The poetical uncanny expresses a specifically Romantic insistence on a kernel of reality that is inaccessible to knowledge, and thus prefigures the Modernist vision of an absurdly meaningless universe. In basing the analysis of the uncanny in early modern fantastic fiction on the overlooked component of cognitive uncertainty, we arrive at richer readings of the poetical dimension of these texts and gain a better understanding of the cultural soil that nourishes them.

Acknowledgements

This book began as a dissertation in the Department of Comparative Literature at the University of Chicago. I am grateful to the faculty of that department, not only my thesis advisor, Françoise Meltzer, but also the emeritus professors Kenneth Northcott and Walter R. Johnson.

In addition I would like to thank William Veeder in the English Department of the University of Chicago for his careful and thoughtful editorial suggestions. I want to thank Andreas Gailus (now at the University of Minnesota) for joining the advisory committee and helping during the final stages of the manuscript.

For the conversation, thoughts and comments from friends I am grateful to Mike Syrimis (Washington University St. Louis), Jan Keppler (now at the University of Montpellier) and Kay Schiller (now at Durham University). For their patience, encouragement and support I would like to thank my friends and family.

Abbreviations

EckE Eckbert English (Arabic numerals indicate page numbers). Tieck, Ludwig. "The Fair-Haired Eckbert." *Novellas of Ludwig Tieck and E.T.A. Hoffmann*. Trans. Thomas Carlyle. Ed. Eitel Timm. 1 ed. Studies in German Literature, Linguistics, and Culture, 51. Columbia, SC: Camden House, 1991. 18–42.

EckG Eckbert German (Arabic numerals indicate page and line numbers). Tieck, Ludwig. "Der Blonde Eckbert." *Phantasus*. Ed. Manfred Frank. Vol. 6. Frankfurt am Main: Deutscher Klassiker Verlag, 1985. 126–48.

GW Gesammelte Werke (Roman numerals indicate volume, Arabic numerals indicate page numbers). Freud, Sigmund. *Gesammelte Werke, Chronologisch Geordnet*. Eds. Lilla Veszy-Wagner, *et al.* 18 vols. London and Frankfurt am Main: Imago Publishing Company and S. Fischer Verlag, 1960–1968.

SE Standard Edition (Arabic numerals before the comma indicate volume, Arabic numerals after the comma indicate page and line numbers). Freud, Sigmund. *The Standard Edition of the Complete Psychological Works*. Trans. and ed. James Strachey. 24 vols. London: Hogarth Press/Institute of Psychoanalysis, 1953–1974.

SmE Sandman English (Arabic numerals indicate page and line numbers). Hoffmann, E.T.A. "The Sandman." Trans. and ed. Stanley Appelbaum. *Five Great German Short Stories. Fünf Deutsche Meistererzählungen: A Dual-Language Book*. New York: Dover, 1993. 36–103.

SmG Sandman German (Arabic numerals indicate page and line numbers). Hoffmann, E.T.A. "Der Sandmann." *Fantasie und Nachtstücke*. Ed. Walter Müller Seidel. Darmstadt: Wissenschaftliche Buchgesellschaft, 1971. 331–63.

The gasp of surprise that accompanies the experience of the unusual becomes its name. It fixes the transcendence of the unknown in relation to the known, and therefore terror as sacredness.

Max Horkheimer and Theodor W. Adorno.
Dialectic of Enlightenment.

Chapter 1: Introduction

> I have deliberately touched on what we might refer to
> as the theory of the uncanny [...]. The ideas that are
> probably best known to us are those of Freud. But
> from this rare encounter, this clash between [...] psy-
> choanalysis and aesthetics, springs an argument that
> has gone on to resonate through critical discourse.
>
> Punter, "On Poetry and the Uncanny."

The "uncanny" has become an established term in literary criticism
and is understood as a symptom of the unconscious, based on
Freud's essay "The 'Uncanny'" (1919h).[1] If we follow Freud, we
tend to regard every instance of the uncanny as indicative of
some inner secret that we keep from ourselves, something secretly
familiar. Freud's definition has had an enormous influence on
readings of Romantic prose.[2] Its stock figures coincide with the
prominent examples of any catalogue of uncanny phenomena:
variants of the return of the dead such as ghosts, ghouls, and
vampires, as well as severed limbs, doubles, animated puppets, ro-
bots, and automata.[3] The uncanny in Romantic prose fiction often
erupts from within the crevices of the domestic sphere, which is
explained by Freud's observation that the objects of repression are
frequently "things belonging to the home." Nevertheless, the very
usefulness of Freud's model has obscured its limitations. Freud's
excellent explanation for a certain number of cases has made those
cases the benchmark for what qualifies as uncanny. The misunderstanding about the uncanny has led to a misreading of the
uncanny, frequently reducing the texts to allegories of psychological processes. The Romantics dramatize the uncanny not only
in anticipation of the unconscious as Freud later defined it. They
also employ the inconclusiveness of the poetical dimension of

their texts to recreate a specifically Romantic uncertainty about the epistemological foundations of reality.

The Romantic Uncanny Revisited

The hypothesis of this study is that the component of uncertainty in the uncanny has been too closely associated with Freud's unconscious, and that the uncanny in Romantic fantastic fiction is rooted in aesthetic strategies that create an uncertainty that is separate from repression. This disorienting uncertainty is produced in literary texts on the level of reader–text interaction. Uncertainty is not only represented on the plot level *in* the text, but also re-enacted through the formal elements *of* the text. This formal dimension of the uncanny can be called "poetical," following the notion of the poetical as that dimension of the literary text that calls attention to itself.[4] We can thus speak of a poetical uncanny, which is a result of the aesthetic dimension of the text. As we shall see, the term poetical uncanny is further justified because the German Romantics programmatically recommend a style that mixes poetry and prose. The poetical uncanny is fueled by those qualities in which Romantic prose attempts to achieve the lyrical density of poetry, relying heavily on formal elements, such as symbol, metaphor, and recurring motifs.

When the narrative technique and the metaphorical structure lead the reader to paradoxically ambiguous conclusions, the uncanny world in the text begins to contaminate the reader beyond the identification with the characters. The Romantics coordinate their uncanny subject matter with a textual strategy that purposefully disorients the reader's act of interpretation. The texts also contain implicit poetological programs that call the possibility of interpretation itself into question.

The interpretations presented here will test the hypothesis whether the poetical uncanny can be identified as the defining property of selected examples from Romantic Fantastic fiction, Ludwig Tieck's "Der blonde Eckbert" (1797) and E.T.A. Hoffmann's "Der Sandmann" (1816).[5] When the poetical uncanny becomes the basis of interpretation, the uncanny in these texts is no longer exclusively interpreted as an anticipation of Freud's discoveries. The Romantics lead the reader into interpretative labyrinths to express their sense that reality is itself an ambiguous text, subject to divergent and inconclusive interpretations.

Freud and Jentsch

The psychoanalytic definition of the uncanny that is still largely in use is the outcome of Freud's polemical rejection of an earlier psychological definition by Ernst Jentsch, who was the first to publish a paper on the uncanny in 1906 and emphasizes the role of uncertainty for the uncanny (Jentsch). When we revive Jentsch's attention to uncertainty, we restore a crucial overlooked cognitive aspect of disorientation to the uncanny. In his essay "The 'Uncanny'," Freud defines the uncanny as a fear that can be traced back to repressed, infantile memories, or primitive, superstitious beliefs: "[...] an uncanny experience occurs either when infantile complexes which have been repressed are once more revived by some impression, or when primitive beliefs which have been surmounted seem once more to be confirmed" (SE 17, 249, 13–17). Freud explicitly rejects the thesis put forth earlier by Jentsch, who distinguishes between factors tied to the individual experiencing the uncanny and different kinds of uncanny phenomena in general. His effort to cover the entire spectrum of potentially uncanny experiences reveals his roots in the statistical approach of nineteenth-century psychology, and Jentsch never considers unconscious factors. Nonetheless, Jentsch focuses on the disorienting aspects of the uncanny, and identifies the cause for its effect in the uncertainty that the phenomena create in the observer.

19

Freud claims that, for Jentsch, "intellectual uncertainty" is the central cause for the uncanny (SE 17, 221, 7). Jentsch never uses that exact term, and in fact the disorientation Jentsch describes should more accurately be called "cognitive uncertainty." Jentsch uses the expression "intellectual certainty" ("intellektuelle Sicherheit"), which for him is an insurance against the uncanny: "Intellectual certainty is one of the defenses erected in the battle for survival. When it is lacking, it exposes a vulnerable spot in the fight for survival, both in the life of humans and that of other organisms."[6] Nevertheless, even if "intellectual certainty" prevents the uncanny for Jentsch, its opposite, "intellectual *un*certainty," cannot be inferred as the most accurate description of what constitutes the primary cause of the uncanny for Jentsch. Jentsch in fact refrains from identifying a single cause that could explain all instances of the uncanny. The examples Jentsch discusses suggest that the response to the uncanny is at first intuitive and preconscious. For Jentsch, the uncanny causes a cognitive uncertainty, which at first may not even be fully apprehended intellectually.[7]

Freud's opposition to Jentsch leads Freud to overstate the role of the unconscious in the uncanny in his explanation and to exclude the component of uncertainty altogether. Freud attempts to assign the same role to the uncanny that he has given to jokes and mistakes in everyday life in some of his earlier writings (Freud, *Psychopathology*; Freud, *Jokes*). In Freud's polemical treatment, the uncanny as the repressed familiar becomes more "evidence in favour of the correctness" of psychoanalysis.[8] Freud's relative one-sidedness in ignoring uncertainty as a crucial component of the uncanny is perhaps a symptom of his struggle to establish psychoanalysis as an exact science with status equal to psychology.[9] Furthermore, Freud's emphasis on the familiar that has been repressed in the uncanny is also indicative of his impulse as a doctor to heal his patients and reduce their fear of the uncanny.

In order to recapture the factor of uncertainty and the ensuing disorientation in the observer for the Romantic uncanny, we need to revive Jentsch's definition, which begins with an examination of the roles of uncertainty and threat in conscious experience. Rather than following Freud and searching for sources of the uncanny only in the past, we use Jentsch as a starting point to re-examine the moment in the present when the uncanny is first detected. Jentsch mentions, for example, how the daily rising of the sun could have appeared uncanny to persons not familiar with the scientific explanations of this phenomenon (Jentsch 196, column 1). Uncertainty itself can constitute a threat, because as long as we cannot identify a phenomenon, it constitutes a potential danger.[10] The uncanny is always caused initially by cognitive uncertainty.

Uncertainty plays a role in Freud's uncanny, but an unacknowledged one. The return of the repressed or the revival of surmounted beliefs is initially disorienting because we do not recognize what was repressed or surmounted when it first returns. Our non-recognition itself creates an initial sense of threat, independently of the threat posed by the repressed or the revival of surmounted beliefs. Nonetheless, Freud does not distinguish between the past and present components of the "return of the repressed." He focuses on the past, emphasizing the familiar origins of the uncanny, and overlooks the disorientation in the present caused by the non-recognition of what was once familiar. While specific internal and unconscious or external causes linked to apperception are sufficient causes of the uncanny, uncertainty qualifies as the only necessary cause. Freud's refutation of uncertainty overshoots its aim of refuting psychology and Jentsch because uncertainty is an overlooked factor in every uncanny experience. The older psychological perspective adds an overlooked component to the psychoanalytic perspective.

Critics have pointed out that Freud misunderstood the uncanny and have suggested a reconsideration of Jentsch's earlier emphasis on uncertainty.[11] Nevertheless, Freud's definition has formed the starting point for much of the criticism on the uncanny, and the shortcomings of Freud's refutation of Jentsch have not yet been fully appreciated. The importance of uncertainty for the uncanny remains an overlooked component.[12]

The Theory of the Uncanny in Literary Criticism

Many of the laws governing the unconscious are embodied and incorporated within the works of Romantic prose. Freud comments on the relationship between literature and psychoanalysis in his study of Jensen's *Gradiva*: "[the author] need not state these laws [which the activities of his unconscious must obey], nor even be clearly aware of them; as a result of the tolerance of his intelligence, they are incorporated within his creations."[13] Freud's interpretation of *Gradiva* is beset by the same reduction of a literary work to its psychoanalytically pertinent content that affects his treatment of Hoffmann's "Der Sandmann." Contrary to Freud's claim, we do not know from the start that Gradiva was not a revenant but really a "living German girl."

Romantic prose has proven to be a fertile ground for readings based on Freud's uncanny. It can be understood as a storehouse of observations of the processes that Freud examined scientifically. Yet the exclusive identification of the uncanny with Freud's understanding has led to a restrictive reading of Romantic prose as only a dramatization of repression.

The limitation of interpretations of the uncanny in Romantic prose to Freud's theory is visible in many examples of readings that constitute what Punter calls the "theory of the uncanny."[14] While these studies have been beneficial in revealing how Romantic prose anticipates the psychoanalytic paradigm, they have led to an understanding of the uncanny that is exclusively focused on the psychoanalytic dimension:

> [the] experience of the eerie and the uncanny coincides so closely with Freud's description of the *Unheimliche* (the uncanny) that we are impelled to consider the Freudian derivation. For Freud, the *Un* – this sign of negation

which makes the *heimisch* [sic] into something strange – represents an act of censorship which turns into the weird and uncanny what is in fact too familiar, too close to home: a repressed primal experience. So in *The Monk* [...]. (Brooks 257)

The uncanny becomes synonymous with the repressed. This substitution is problematic because the uncanny does not always originate in the repressed and the home, and the uncanny, literally as the "unhomelike," comes to refer only to the "home" as the place where the family drama is played out. "Home," in the more general sense, however, is the place protected from dangers. Freud emphasizes the familiar in what may return from our past to reduce what is threatening about the uncanny. Jentsch, on the other hand, overlooks the role of the unconscious, but he can help remind us that the uncanny is always initially experienced as threatening.

The dangers inherent in the adaptation of Freud's uncanny become especially visible in a recent study (1995) by Terry Castle. There she describes Romantic prose not only as the embodiment in fiction of the Enlightenment exclusion of the repressed but identifies that age itself as the origin and birthplace of repression and the uncanny:

> [...] it was during the eighteenth century, with its confident rejection of transcendental explanations, compulsive quest for systematic knowledge and self-conscious valorization of "reason" over "superstition," that human beings first experienced that encompassing sense of strangeness and unease Freud finds so characteristic of modern life.[15]

Arguably, important aspects of the processes Freud describes are historically bound to the post-Enlightenment era. Perhaps the structures of socialization that Freud describes become more prominent during the institution of the bourgeois family. The need for repression increases markedly, and a development begins that is characterized by "the unreasonable custom of leaving primary socialization to the nuclear family."[16] Norbert Elias' research into

23

the change of customs (1939) allows us to understand the Enlightenment as the cultural birthplace of repression, because of the heightened demands for the control of the drives during early industrial production. Philip Aries' research (1962) uncovers that childhood becomes increasingly demarcated as a sphere distinct from adulthood, and allegedly free of the need for repression, which amounts to an implicit inscription of repression onto childhood (Elias; Ariès). The fictional productions of the early industrial age dramatize both repression and its uncanny return in the fantastic events of the literary uncanny. Yet Castle limits the uncanny to the Romantic period, because her understanding of the uncanny is determined by Freud's definition. Despite the applicability to Romanticism of the famous theorem that the sleep of reason brings forth monsters, Castle overlooks that, figuratively speaking, not all monsters are brought forth by the sleep of reason. Castle, while recognizing that Freud's uncanny is historically specific, is bound to Freud's definition of the uncanny.

Castle ignores that Freud's own enterprise ambiguously oscillates between Romantic and Enlightenment impulses. The uncanny is historically limited to Romanticism only if it is defined exclusively as the return of the repressed originating in the domestic sphere. Once we re-emphasize the cognitive component of uncertainty in the uncanny, it no longer appears as an exclusively late eighteenth-century phenomenon, but one that predates the enlightenment.

Freud's interpretation of the uncanny has persisted also because of the etymological argument that Freud presents in the first section of his essay, for the significance of the German word "unheimlich." Just as Freud misrepresents Jentsch to strengthen his argument, Freud represents the etymology selectively. A discrepancy has developed between the uncanny in criticism, which is bound to the Freudian sense of the uncanny as having repressed internal causes, and the original meaning of the word "unheimlich," which means "strange," "eerie" or "bizarre."[17] From the late-eighteenth century onward to the present, "unheimlich" expresses a feeling caused by unfamiliarity and ghastliness and a feeling caused by insecurity.[18] While the connection between "unheimlich" and the home indeed exists, the notion of home that "unheimlich" negates is more generally characterized by everything strange and hostile. The uncertainty we experience when we are confronted by something truly unknown is "unheimlich," because it is unclear whether the phenomenon presents a threat.

The etymological portion of Freud's argument is often cited by critics who are non-native speakers of German and who do not realize that they are victims of what is perhaps a misunderstanding on Freud's part, or a pun on words at best:[19]

> [...] the Gothic [...] literalises Freud's point of departure regarding the uncanny: the *Unheimlich* as a presentation of the utterly familiar as strange. The German term declares such things "un-homelike" [...] the nightmarish haunted house as Gothic setting puts into play the anxieties, tensions and imbalances inherent in family structures (Williams 45–6).

The misunderstanding is perpetuated by each consecutive rendition of Freud's argument.[20] The "uncanny" in the English-speaking world has developed a certain dynamic of its own, and the English "uncanny" has become associated with Freud's theory and repression, so that "uncanny" is understood as a mixing of the familiar and unfamiliar.[21] In the German word "unheimlich," on the other hand, the unfamiliar plays a greater role. "Unheimlich" expresses a fear or insecurity when confronted with something strange or ghastly. The German word "unheimlich" never gives up its crucial, overlooked component of cognitive uncertainty.

Freud continuously downplays the aspect of threat and uncertainty in "unheimlich." While Freud rightly points out the connection in German between "unheimlich" and "Heim" (the home), he passes over the meaning of "heimlich" as "cozy." He thus de-emphasizes the component of threat, not only in "unheimlich," but also, by implication, the absence of threat expressed in "heimlich" (cozy). The "cozy" place is a place where all danger is thought to be absent.[22] Coziness itself contains an element of denial and thus also the potential for the unexpected return of the excluded element of threat. Through a more accurate analysis of the etymology, the denial of threat, and by implication threat itself, emerges as a part of the etymology of "unheimlich."[23] "Home" is uncanny, not only because it is the place where the family drama of socialization is played out, but also because "home" in a more universal sense is a secure place. Thus, its opposite is characterized by threat, the element Freud de-emphasizes.

In a recent study of Freud's essay by Lydenberg (1997), Freud's reductive presentation of the etymology is repeated:

> The ambiguity of the uncanny as both familiar and unfamiliar is reinforced by Freud's examination of the German word *unheimlich*: the root, heimlich, carries the primary signification "familiar and agreeable" "des Vertrauten, Behaglichen" [sic] (224),[24] but in its secondary meaning it coincides with its opposite, *unheimlich*, "concealed and kept out of sight [...]" (224–5).[25]

Not surprisingly, German critics do not fall victim to what may be called the etymological fallacy. Kittler writes: "In a pun on words Freud equates the uncanny with the secretive, and the secretive with the home; he thus defines childhood as the location of an original [...] uncanniness."[26] Freud's maneuver is taken by Kittler for what it is, the selective presentation of the etymology to support an opinion rather than a scientifically accurate etymological commentary.[27] Freud's presentation of the etymology thus fosters the misunderstanding of the uncanny that has accompanied its assimilation as a critical term in literary studies.

The Romantic Uncanny

Once we look beyond Freudian theory and its recognized applicability, we discover the importance of uncertainty for the uncanny in the fantastic literature of the Romantic age that has thus far been overlooked. The application of Freud's uncanny to Romantic literature has led to a reductionist image of the period. Romantic fantastic fiction not only dramatizes repression but also expresses an epistemological crisis that originated in Kant's philosophy.

Kant maintains in the *First Critique* (1781) that our thinking can refer only to empirical impressions, and that space and time determine their form, yet the content of these impressions is determined by the senses (Kant). Kant believes that the thing in itself ("das Ding an sich"), the noumenal, cannot be known:

> [...] the possibility of such noumena is quite incomprehensible, and beyond the sphere of phenomena, all is for us a mere void: that is to say, we possess an understanding whose province does problematically extend beyond this sphere [of phenomena], but we do not possess an intuition ["*Anschauung*"] [...] by means of which objects beyond the region of sensibility [noumena] could be given us [...]. (Kant 164–5, Kant's emphasis)

Consequently, Kant allows space for the existence of the noumenal while maintaining that we can know nothing about it. Kant's ideas combine the empiricism and idealism that preceded him into his own transcendental idealism. Kant's *First Critique* was introduced into German Romanticism through F.W.J. Schelling's *System des transzendentalen Idealismus* (1800) (K.W.J. Schelling).

Romanticism is affected by a "Kant crisis," the most obvious example of which is Kleist's letter in which he famously notes:

> If all human beings [...] had green glasses instead of eyes, they would have to believe that the objects they perceive *are* green, and they would never be able to decide whether their eye is showing them things as they are [...] or whether the eye is adding something that is a property of the eyes, not of the things. [...] Since this conviction, namely, that no truth can be found in this world, has clearly presented itself to my soul, I have not touched a book again.

> Wenn alle Menschen [...] statt der Augen grüne Gläser hätten, so würden sie [...] urtheilen müssen, die Gegenstände, welche sie dadurch erblicken, sind grün – und nie würden sie entscheiden können, ob ihr Auge ihnen die Dinge zeigt, wie sie sind, [...] oder ob es nicht etwas zu ihnen hinzuthut, was nicht

ihnen, sondern dem Auge gehört. [...] Seit diese Überzeugung, nämlich, daß hienieden keine Wahrheit zu finden ist, vor meine Seele trat, habe ich nicht wieder ein Buch angerührt.[28]

As will be shown, the earliest of the discussed texts, Tieck's "Der blonde Eckbert" (1797), reproduces this epistemological uncertainty in its formal elements.

The Romantics express their skepticism about the basis of what is knowable by infusing their prose with the formal elements of poetry. These elements are the distinctive trait of the poetical uncanny. The incorporation of poetry into prose is in fact the explicit intention of Friedrich Schlegel's poetological program. Schlegel was the theoretical leader of Early German Romanticism, centered in Jena, which included Tieck, the author of the earlier story discussed here, and also Wackenroder, Novalis, Friedrich Schlegel's brother August Wilhelm, the philosophers Friedrich Schleyermacher, F.W.J. Schelling, and Johann Gottlieb Fichte.[29] Schlegel outlines a program for Romanticism in which poetry ("Poesie") is central:

> Romantic poetry is a progressive universal poetry. It is not only its destiny to unite all separate literary forms and to unite poetry with philosophy and rhetoric. It should be its aim and obligation to unite poetry and prose, genius and criticism, artistic poetry and natural poetry, sometimes mixing them, sometimes amalgamating them, to make poetry vital and communal, and to intermingle communal life and society poetically [...].

> Die romantische Poesie ist eine progressive Universalpoesie. Ihre Bestimmung ist nicht bloß, alle getrennten Gattungen der Poesie wieder zu vereinigen und die Poesie mit der Philosophie und Rhetorik in Berührung zu sehen. Sie will, und soll auch, Poesie und Prosa, Genialität und Kritik, Kunstpoesie und Naturpoesie bald mischen, bald verschmelzen, die Poesie lebendig und gesellig, und das Leben und die Gesellschaft poetisch mischen [...].[30]

When prose begins to draw heavily on such poetic elements as verbal ambiguity, irony, and metaphor, it develops the potential for creating a multiplicity of conflicting interpretations and leads to a reading experience that is constitutive for the poetical uncanny.[31]

The Poetical Uncanny

The notion of conflicting interpretative alternatives, which is constitutive for the poetical uncanny, draws on Shlomith Rimmon's (1977) notion of "paradoxical ambiguity," (Rimmon) which is an extension of William Empson's work (Empson). The Romantics create fictional realities that are constructed like optical illusions. The poetical uncanny contains a particular paradoxical ambiguity that produces a cognitive disorientation structurally similar to an optical illusion:

The uncanny arises at the moment when, figuratively speaking, the outline of the duck begins to look like a rabbit.[32] We observe such ambiguities when the text gives rise to mutually exclusive, yet equally valid interpretations. Rimmon calls this type of indeterminacy "paradoxical ambiguity." Rimmon illustrates the special nature of paradoxical ambiguity by distinguishing two kinds of disjunctions. The first kind is inclusive, such as "Customers who are teachers or students (both) are entitled to a reduction." The second is exclusive, such as: "We are either going to the zoo or the theatre today, not both." She reminds us that Latin uses two different words for the English "or:" "*vel*," which denotes an inclusive disjunction, and "*aut*," which denotes an exclusive one. In mathematical and philosophical logic, the signs corresponding to these types are ∪ (derived from the first letter in *Vel*) and ∩ (derived from *Aut*), respectively. For Rimmon, some texts involve a special ambiguity of the type "∪ AND ∩," where there are "[…]

two separate and complete, strongly contrasted, but equally credible 'realities' simultaneously" (Rimmon 15). It is this type of logically disorienting ambiguity that forms the distinctive feature of the poetical uncanny.

The coexistence of such equally credible realities is a function of the conflicting solutions that the text offers for the interpretative problems it presents to the reader. The plot may suggest one interpretation, while a contrasting and indeed conflicting interpretation may be suggested by the subliminal layers of meaning the reader extracts from the poetical, literary dimension of the text. The reader interacts with poetical elements such as metaphors, motifs and irony. In addition, the reader is guided by poetological programs that the text develops implicitly. To distinguish between plot level and reader-interaction more clearly, we draw on a distinction adapted from narratology, between the diegetic and extradiegetic levels of the text. To speak of an extradiegetic level helps to distinguish between the fictional world that the characters inhabit and those portions of the text to which the reader alone has access.[33] "Diegesis" ("narrative" in Greek) applies generally to the plot, although it also "[...] includes events that are presumed to have occurred, and actions and spaces not shown [...]." Such gaps are described by Genette in his essay on narrative modes: "[...] Each telling of the story [...] involv[es] a series of [...] choices between the elements of the *story* to be retained and the elements to be left out, between various points of view, and so on [...]" (Genette 132, emphasis original). In film criticism, extradiegetic elements "[...] do not 'exist' or 'take place' in the same plane of reality inhabited by the characters."[34] Characters do not hear extradiegetic music, for example, only the audience. Although Genette does not introduce the term extradiegetic in the aforementioned essay, he points out that "physical portraits, descriptions of dress and furniture tend [...] to reveal the psychology of the characters [...]" (Genette 135). While such attributes are part of the diegetic level, they express an opinion of the narrator that lies outside the world inhabited by the characters. Even perceptions recorded by a third-person narrator focalized through a protagonist do not have the same significance on the diegetic level as they do for the reader. For the character, these impressions have meaning as sense impressions, while they have meaning as a sign for the reader.[35]

The poetical uncanny is caused by indeterminacy on the diegetic and extradiegetic levels, as well as the juxtaposition of the two. On the diegetic level, we can be directly affected by representations of uncanny events or phenomena through identification with the characters. The extradiegetic level can add to the disorientation when it leads to conflicting interpretations.

The importance of the extradiegetic or poetical dimension for the disorienting paradoxes that define the poetical uncanny also explains why such texts are more likely to be short stories rather than novels. Short prose is especially suited for bringing the poetic dimension into play, because seemingly unrelated elements are more closely associated through a "lyrical density." Short prose elicits what Poe calls a "unity of impression," which insures that they can develop their poetical attributes fully (Poe 482). Poe writes: "If any literary work is too long to be read at one sitting, we must be content to dispense with the immensely important effect derivable from unity of impression – for, if two sittings be required, the affairs of the world interfere, and everything like totality is at once destroyed."[36] We focus on a type of uncanny effect that is not only a cause of our immersion in the world of the text but is also achieved by the reader's detection of the subliminal signals that are missed if more than "one sitting" is required. The uncanny effect is caused by those elements in a short story that most evoke poetic strategies: "[...] brevity must be in direct ration of the intensity of the intended effect [...]" (Poe 482–3). The reader extracts the "undercurrents" of meaning produced by "some amount of suggestiveness."[37] These are contained in the text's extradiegetic, formal elements, which we also call poetical because their effect depends on a prose style that can be called lyrical.[38] The indeterminacy caused by the extradiegetic level allows us to distinguish a poetical uncanny.

Departure from Todorov

The introduction of uncertainty into Freud's definition will sensitize us to the way in which certain fantastic texts produce an uncanny reading experience.[39] This will require, first, a shift of emphasis, not only from past to present, but also from object to observer. Instead of trying to define what allegedly constitutes the uncanny as an object, and detecting its hidden causes in the repressed past, we will focus on how we experience the uncanny itself at the present moment. The shift from object to observer will also guide our interpretations of literature. We are thus led to hypothetically propose that the texts selected for this study constitute a distinct genre, the poetical uncanny, which depends primarily on the extradiegetic dimension for its effect.

The poetical uncanny is a subgenre within the *fantastic*, a genre defined by Tzvetan Todorov's well-known study (*The Fantastic*). Nevertheless, for Todorov, the uncanny is the "supernatural explained." Todorov cites Freud as the source for his understanding of the uncanny. This is another instance of how Freud's uncanny can lead to an omission of the element of threat in the uncanny, for this explained "uncanny" informs Todorov's fantastic itself.

The poetical uncanny shares a distinctive feature with Todorov's fantastic. Todorov identifies the supernatural component of the fantastic in events that conflict with the laws that we have come to accept as a valid descriptions of reality:[40]

> The fantastic is that hesitation experienced by a person who knows only the laws of nature, confronting an apparently supernatural event. (Todorov, *The Fantastic* 25)

> [...] the text must oblige the reader to consider the world of the characters as a world of living persons and to hesitate between a natural and a supernatural explanation of the events described. (Todorov, *The Fantastic* 33)

We adapt Todorov's functional rather than metaphysical concept of the supernatural. The texts we are considering stage events of this type. The supernatural occurrences in the fantastic are subjected to an indeterminacy that causes the reader to hesitate between conflicting evaluations of their reality status. Nevertheless, Todorov does not take the "hesitation" far enough: "At the story's end, the reader makes a decision even if the character does not; he opts for one solution or the other, and thereby emerges from the fantastic" (Todorov, *The Fantastic* 41). The role of hesitation in Todorov's fantastic is thus less threatening than the ambiguities we will identify as a decisive feature of the poetical uncanny. We shall find that, in the selected texts, the ambiguities of the plot become irresolvable. "Hesitation" in the poetical uncanny persists beyond any resolution the plot may suggest. Todorov bases his analyses exclusively on elements of plot and thus overlooks the added indeterminacy created by the extradiegetic factors. In the poetical uncanny, Todorov's hesitation is no longer only a sufficient factor but a necessary one.

While the poetical uncanny is similar to Todorov's fantastic, because it resides on the same middle ground characterized by the reader's "hesitation," the role of hesitation is more far-reaching than in Todorov's model. Todorov is engaged in a repression of the uncanny that is not only similar to Freud but also derived from Freud. For Todorov, the *fantastic* exists in a space between two genres. On the one side, Todorov identifies what he calls "the uncanny," but he defines it as "the supernatural explained" (Todorov, *The Fantastic* 41). On the other hand, Todorov establishes the genre he calls "the marvelous," which for him is equivalent to "the supernatural accepted" (Todorov, *The Fantastic* 42). In Todorov's "uncanny," the reader is assured that the illusion of a supernatural, fantastical occurrence was achieved either through a technical trick or was a product of the character's delusions; the fantastical was a manifestation of his or her repressed conflicts. In the marvelous, the fantastical does not cause any consternation; it is integrated into what Coleridge calls the suspension of disbelief (Coleridge). The reader understands that the events of fairy tales, for example, are unthinkable in the real world but acceptable as part of the conventions of the genre.[41] While Todorov lets the reader temporarily choose between an explained supernatural and an accepted supernatural, he does not allow for this choice to persist and thus has no place for an unexplained supernatural.[42] Like Freud, Todorov dismisses ambiguity and thus dissolves the uncanny. He too engages in a repression of the uncanny.

Todorov bases his understanding of "the uncanny" as the explained supernatural on Freud's definition (Todorov, *The Fantastic* 49). When Todorov discusses the uncanny, we can detect Freud's demystifying uncanny directly in Todorov's reference to Freud's essay:

> [...] psychoanalytic investigation [...] describes the mechanism [...] of psychic activity [...] [and] [...] it reveals the ultimate meaning of the configuration so described. It answers both the question "how" and the question "what." (Todorov, *The Fantastic* 149)

Todorov's understanding of the uncanny as the "supernatural explained" becomes unacceptable once we view the uncanny as characterized primarily by indeterminacy and uncertainty. Todorov is one of the first critics who accepts Freud's claim to have given a sufficient and exhaustive explication of the uncanny. In 1970, Todorov effectively commences the tradition of applying a misunderstood uncanny to literature with his reductive definition.

The Structure of the Study

This study re-examines the inaccuracies in Freud's 1919 essay on the uncanny and its effect on the "theory of the uncanny," with the aim of detaching the uncanny from its exclusively psychoanalytic context. The commentary on Freud's essay takes up an entire chapter, but such attention to detail is necessary, because Freud's argument is rhetorically seductive and has become the touchstone for all subsequent definitions of the uncanny.[43] Furthermore, the commentary on Freud's essay represents the first comprehensive analysis of Freud's oversights and misrepresentations. When the uncanny is expanded by its disorienting cognitive component, the useful aspects of the psychological observations made by Jentsch are recaptured, and this redefined uncanny can serve as a working hypothesis for the interpretations of selected literary texts. The order of the chapters is structural rather than chronological. Although Ludwig Tieck's "Der blonde Eckbert" (1797) constitutes the historically earlier example discussed here, we begin with Hoffmann's "Der Sandmann" (1816), because it allows us to address text-specific issues not discussed in the Freud chapter. The interpretations test the hypothesis that a pervasive paradoxical ambiguity, regarding not only the fantastical events in the text but also as the dominant aesthetic trait, defines the texts as a whole.[44]

E.T.A. Hoffmann's "Der Sandmann" has an uncanny effect on the reader first because we identify with the characters. When we examine the uncanny on the diegetic level, such as Nathanael's suspicion that Coppola is conspiring against him or the uncanniness of the automaton Olimpia, we can demonstrate that uncanny real-life experiences already contain the disorienting component of uncertainty on the cognitive level that Freud overlooked. Second, we detect a more particular type of uncanniness in the structure of the text itself. Hoffmann's poetological remarks about the limitations of representation as well as Nathanael's precarious position as a double of the author are direct expressions of the problems both the reader and the characters encounter in relation to the distinction between fiction and reality. The poetological clues disorient the reader. While they seem to contain a set of instructions for deciphering the text, they ultimately reinforce the inconclusiveness that the text represents as a whole.

Ludwig Tieck's "Der blonde Eckbert" again presents the disorienting aspect of the uncanny on the diegetic level, when Bertha is perplexed by the ever-changing features of the witch or phantom, or when Eckbert suspects that he is being persecuted by the knight Hugo. The uncanniness of the text as whole is produced by the unfathomable motives for the phantom's cruel revenge. The uncanny appears here as incarnation of a pre-Christian, hostile forces of nature that are opposed to man. Yet the text's overall inconclusiveness not only expresses this uncertainty but also creates it with regard to the reality status of the fantastical events it represents. Once we discover that the phantom's ability to change the reality of the characters is dependent on our interpretative activity, the reality we ourselves inhabit becomes unstable.

In both texts the uncanny effect is supplemented by the text's extradiegetic elements. They produce a pervasive disorientation, which replicates the uncanny's overlooked disorienting cognitive component. The reader's insecurity is produced by a narrative strategy that creates a network of conflicting clues regarding the mysterious events in the text. In addition, we can extract poetological programs from the texts that heighten our awareness of a more pervasive epistemological crisis, expressed in these texts, about the reality status of reality itself. The implicit poetological programs contained in these texts compel us to project the poetical uncanny back onto the texts themselves. This self-reflexive structure has a double consequence. On the diegetic level, the uncanny phenomena become the incarnations of the uncanny *of* the text *in* the text. The single uncanny phenomenon or event, constituting the uncanny in the text, becomes the manifestation of the reader's uncanny relation to the world as well. The indeterminacy of the text as a whole is represented on the plot level in the uncanny phantoms that confront the characters. The conflicting interpretations of the fantastic phenomena confronting the characters can contaminate the reader's own interpreting activity. This contamination is directed by the formal attributes of the stories, and we will explore this dimension in the conclusion as a reader-induced form of textual paranoia.

When we apply a notion of the uncanny that reincorporates the overlooked cognitive element of uncertainty into the selected Romantic texts, we get a better sense of how their formal indeterminacy mirrors a historically specific philosophical crisis. Our sensitivity to the poetical, extradiegetic dimension destabilizes our position as readers and makes us aware of an epistemological insecurity, in which the world is seen as mediated through interpretation. Simultaneously, an expanded attention to the poetical, literary dimension of these texts fulfills one of the central aims of literary criticism, which is to increase our appreciation and enjoyment of the works by identifying the details that contribute to their effect on the reader.

Chapter 2: Freud's "Uncanny" Re-evaluated

The uncanny effect of Romantic fantastic literature relies heavily on the component of cognitive uncertainty, both in the uncanny phenomena that appear in the plot and in the overall aesthetic impression of the text.[1] This attention to the factor of cognitive uncertainty prompts our examination of Freud's seminal essay "The 'Uncanny'" (1919h).[2] To gain a better understanding of the essence of the uncanny we see portrayed and dramatized in Romanticism, we review Freud and the critical dispute surrounding the uncanny that constitutes what Punter calls the "theory of the uncanny" (Punter, "On Poetry and the Uncanny" 194). This will also help explain the relative tenacity of Freud's definition of the uncanny in criticism. While Freud emphasizes the familiar origin of the uncanny in the repressed past, we will not only accentuate non-recognition but also show that the unfamiliar alone can cause the uncanny impression. In fact, cognitive uncertainty can represent an uncanny threat in and of itself.

The Pervasive Influence of Freud's Seminal Essay

Critics have analyzed "The 'Uncanny'" as an occasion where Freud puts up "resistance to his own discovery" and detect symptoms of Freud's own repressive tendencies in the essay (Cixous 541). For example, Cixous (1972) writes: "Everything takes place as if [...] one of Freud's repressions acted as the motor re-presenting at each moment the analysis of the repression which Freud was analyzing [...]."[3] Freud's exclusion of uncertainty can undoubtedly be interpreted as an instance of repression. Nevertheless, this aspect has been sufficiently analyzed in previous studies, and psychoanalyzing Freud's essay does not move us beyond the

Freudian paradigm of repression and its return (Weber; Hertz; Ginsburg; McCaffrey; Lydenberg). While we attempt to move beyond Freud, we should acknowledge that the uncanny thwarts a complete scientific explanation because of limitations inherent in the subject. Cixous, for example, states: "Freud does not come out of the system of the *Unheimliche* because no one comes out of it [...]."[4] The uncanny is not only a manifestation of the unconscious, but also of the unknown. Possibly, the most reliable answers in this field are those that accept and incorporate their limitations.

Instead of acknowledging the role of cognitive uncertainty, Freud treats the uncanny with a rigidity that can in part be explained in the context of the time when "The 'Uncanny'" was published. The essay appeared soon after the end of World War I, in which more soldiers lost their lives than in any previous war in human history. The war also made manifest a disintegration of values that had been occurring for decades. In Freud's work, this time brings with it the shift from the earlier topographical division of the psyche into the unconscious, preconscious and conscious, to the structural division into id, ego and superego, visible in the publication in 1923 of *The Ego and the Id*. The earlier optimism still implicit in Freud's assertion in *The Interpretation of Dreams* (1900) that all dreams express repressed wishes appears to disintegrate in *Beyond the Pleasure Principle* (1920g). "The 'Uncanny'" is possibly an attempt to create a bulwark against fear, and simultaneously a symptom that the topic can no longer be avoided. Freud's emphasis on the familiar is also fueled by his impulse to defuse what is frightening about the uncanny. While a lack of "negative capability" is visible in Freud's treatment of the uncanny, we will more specifically focus on Freud's fervent opposition to Jentsch, which is symptomatic of Freud's struggle for the recognition of psychoanalysis in the scientific community.

The component of cognitive uncertainty appears in some key passages of the essay, but Freud does not account for this aspect explicitly in his explanations:

> [...] [the] uncanny is in reality nothing new or alien, but something which is familiar and old-established in the mind and which has become alienated from it only through the process of repression. (SE 17, 241, 16–19)

"Alienation" means that we do not recognize the repressed when it returns, but Freud never explicitly acknowledges that cognitive uncertainty is contained in his own definition of the uncanny. Freud's rebuttal of Jentsch is aimed at de-emphasizing the role of cognitive uncertainty.

The Meaning of German "unheimlich"

Freud tailors his excerpts from the dictionary entries to benefit his interpretation of the uncanny. It is thus helpful to re-examine the meaning of the original German word for "uncanny," "unheimlich." Freud's representation of "unheimlich" is at odds with the more general, colloquial meaning of the word in German. Already by the end of the 18th century, "unheimlich," describes the "eerie" or "weird" feeling that arises whenever we suspect a hidden threat. A dictionary from 1811 already defines "unheimlich" in the following way:

> *unheimlich* adj. and adv. [...] 1) Possessing or eliciting a feeling contrary to that which is experienced when you are comfortably in the area that constitutes your home [...] 2) An uncanny place, where something is not right, and where it is dangerous [...].[5]

"Unheimlich" as a synonym for "ungeheuer" ("monstrous," "ghastly")[6] had existed since the Middle Ages, but had been pushed into the background during the Enlightenment, and was revived in the Romantic period.[7] The Grimm dictionary states that from the late 18th century onward, "unheimlich" expresses a feeling caused by uncertainty and a feeling of insecurity.[8] The word has preserved the meaning of "something causing an uncertain feeling of fear or horror" until the present day.[9] This occurs when phenomena are difficult to perceive or partially hidden. The current edition of the Duden dictionary gives the following example: "In the dark, he had an 'unheimlich' feeling."[10] The uncanniness associated with darkness constitutes one of the least ambiguous and most convincing examples for the uncanny, and it is symptomatic of the insufficiency of Freud's argument that he ends with this topic but cannot integrate it into his explanation. The importance of darkness as a central feature of the uncanny is crucial also because the Early German Romantics emphasize darkness in their prose fictions, in which night, darkness, and mines appear as recurring motifs.

Freud himself refers to the fear of darkness once in his earlier writings, in an image expressing the function of scientific explanations to allay typical human fears: "The benighted traveller may sing aloud in the dark to deny his own fears; but, for all that, he will not see an inch further beyond his nose."[11] The eerie, uncomfortable expectation of a possible threat when we move through unfamiliar terrain is properly described as "unheimlich."[12] When an animal-size or man-size object like a bush appears in the mist, for example, the object is visible but cannot be clearly identified.[13] An encounter with a double is often cited as an example, as well as the uncertain status of wax figures or automata as living or merely lifelike. The uncanny can arise out of a cognitive ambiguity, which can occur in the field of perception or in the field of cognition.[14] In the field of perception, we may get a "creepy" feeling when we indistinctly perceive an object. In the field of cognition, coincidences are a string of clearly perceived events, but the uncertainty whether they are connected by more than chance often creates an uncanny feeling. The events constitute an unexpected regularity conflicting with the expected randomness of experience. In every instance, the uncanny is a premonition of danger. It occurs when it is difficult to perceive or identify whether or not a danger is present.[15]

When defining the uncanny, it is important to remember the distinction between an indistinct threat and a clearly perceived danger. Freud expresses this distinction clearly in *Inhibitions, Symptoms and Anxiety*:

> Anxiety [*Angst*] has an unmistakable relation to *expectation*: it is anxiety *about* [...] something. It has a quality of *indefiniteness and lack of object*. In precise speech we use the word "fear" [*Furcht*] rather than "anxiety" [*Angst*] if it has found an object.

> Die Angst hat eine unverkennbare Beziehung zur Erwartung; sie ist Angst vor etwas. Es haftet ihr ein Charakter von Unbestimmtheit und Objektlosigkeit an; der korrekte Sprachgebrauch ändert selbst ihren Namen, wenn sie ein Objekt gefunden hat, und ersetzt ihn dann durch Furcht.[16]

The uncanny lies between the two, for it shares the indistinctness of anxiety with the often-external source of the disturbance of fear.

Anxiety can be experienced as uncanny because the cause of the anxiety is unknown. In contrast to anxiety, which always has internal causes, the cause of the uncanny can be both internal and external. The uncanny is different from fear and much more similar to anxiety because of the factor of uncertainty, a quality Freud acknowledges in the above-quoted essay (1926d), but not in "The 'Uncanny'" (1919h). In our redefinition of the uncanny, and in contrast to Freud's emphasis on the familiar origin of the uncanny, we suggest a definition according to which the uncanny object always possesses a "quality of indefiniteness."

Freud does not yet focus on the indistinctness of anxiety in "The Uncanny," although he classifies the uncanny as part of what the Standard Edition translated as "the frightening" ("das Ängstliche"), where the German word is derived from "anxiety" ("Angst"), not fear ("Furcht"):

> [...] then among the instances of frightening things there must be one class in which the frightening element can be shown to be something repressed which recurs. This class would then constitute the uncanny. (SE 17, 241, 7–11, Freud's emphasis)

[...] so muß es unter den Fällen des Ängstlichen eine Gruppe geben, in der sich zeigen läßt, daß dies Ängstliche etwas wiederkehrendes Verdrängtes ist. Diese Art des Ängstlichen wäre eben das Unheimliche [...]. (GW XII, 254, my emphasis)[17]

This is one of the instances in which the topic of cognitive uncertainty enters Freud's discourse on the periphery without being discussed. Again, Freud does not incorporate the indistinct quality expressed in the word he uses into his discussion.

Certain shades of meaning of the English "uncanny" are not very different from the German "unheimlich." The following dictionary entries for "uncanny" show the close affinity to the German counterpart: "[...] seeming to have a supernatural character or origin: *eerie, mysterious* [...] *weird*." [18] The English word is often used to express astonishment about an extraordinary ability, like that of an acrobat, magician or surgeon.[19] The German term includes the connotation "astounding," but it is one among several meanings and not as dominant as in English. We will discuss the discrepancies between the English and the German term in more detail below. The etymological section thus also serves to pre-empt any doubts German readers might have about Freud's redefinition of the word "unheimlich."

The meaning of "unheimlich" in 1919 was no different from the meaning in present-day German.[20] Freud's audience would therefore have received his rejection of uncertainty as at odds with their understanding of the word. Freud thus devotes a third of his essay to showing how etymology supports his emphasis on concealed familiarity. Freud presents his findings in reverse sequence by presenting the etymological study first.[21] Freud arrived at the conviction that repression produces the uncanny and then reviewed the etymology to find confirmation for this hypothesis. While Freud assures us "at once that both courses lead to the same result" (SE 17, 220, 24–5), we shall find that the etymology leads to far more ambiguous results than Freud claims. Freud's play on words, derived from etymology, consequently appears more aimed at convincing the reader that the truths he allegedly discovers are in reality already contained in the long-established development of the word's meaning itself.[22] Freud is aware of the discrepancy between his emphasis on the familiar in the uncanny and the strangeness or lack of familiarity commonly associated with "unheimlich." This may explain why he sets out to show that the general understanding of "unheimlich" as unfamiliar is wrong, and that familiarity is a hidden aspect even of the term that is in general use.

The Rhetorical Function of the Etymological Review

The etymological section demands extensive commentary, first, because Freud misrepresents the knowledge that can be drawn from investigating the colloquial meaning of "unheimlich." He reduces the word to the meaning produced by the negating function of "un," applied to "heimlich" in the sense "familiar." He neglects to acknowledge that the prefix also has a pejorative function, and "*heimlich*" also means "cozy," as well as "secretively." Accordingly, Jentsch's use of the term "psychic uncertainty," commented upon extensively below, is much closer to the term suggested here for "uncanny," namely "cognitive uncertainty," while Freud reduces Jentsch's argument to an identification of the uncanny with the new and unfamiliar.[23] Third, Freud portrays the etymology selectively and ignores the element of threat. Some of the material chosen by the dictionary editors and quoted by Freud supports our perspective. It is unclear whether Freud's omissions are an oversight or a rhetorical maneuver. Possibly, they are a combination of both. Nevertheless, they have led to a misunderstanding about the uncanny in which Freud's excellent explanation for a limited number of cases has made those cases the benchmark for what qualifies as uncanny.

Freud places a three-paragraph introduction before the excerpts from the two German dictionaries, which then comprise the bulk of the etymological survey. Freud begins with what he presents as a simple deduction from the meaning of the German word "unheimlich":

> The German word "*unheimlich*" is obviously the opposite of "*heimlich*" [homely], "*heimisch*" [native] – the opposite of what is familiar; and we are tempted to conclude that what is "uncanny" is frightening precisely because it is *not* known and familiar. (SE 17, 220, 33–7, Freud's emphasis)

> Das deutsche Word "unheimlich" ist offenbar der Gegensatz zu heimlich, heimisch, vertraut und der Schluß liegt nahe, es sei etwas eben darum schreckhaft, weil es *nicht* bekannt und vertraut ist. (GW XII, 231; Freud's emphasis)

This sentence contains two inaccuracies.[24] First, the string of synonyms Freud gives for "heimlich" conceals the prevalent meaning of the word, "secretive." Second, he implies that the prefix "un-" expresses only opposition. We shall show that, in German, the prefix can also have a pejorative connotation not mentioned by Freud. Furthermore, the sentence marks the beginning of a carefully designed rhetorical attack on Jentsch, with the aim of making Jentsch's essay appear simplistic and naïve. We will return to the rhetorical attack on Jentsch after having explained the two inaccuracies in more detail.

The first inaccuracy consists in Freud's omitting the meaning "secretive" at this important point in the essay, although he uses the word in this sense later in the essay. "Heimlich" has two meanings, "belonging to the home, familiar, cozy," and "kept from the eyes of strangers, secretive." The meaning "cozy, familiar" was already obsolete in 1919, as demonstrated by the dictionary entries cited in the following section, and is only contained in the composite "unheimlich," whereas the second meaning, "secretive" (heimlich) was prevalent. Had Freud mentioned the prevalent meaning (secretive) at this point, rather than later in the essay, the reader would have been able to see that "heim(e)lich"[25] means first "cozy," not simply "familiar," and that the important aspect of "coziness" for the uncanny is the absence of threat, "being hidden from the eyes of strangers," which leads to the meaning "secretive."[26] The reader could have recognized that the idea of threat is still contained in "coziness," albeit as an absence rather than a presence of threat. "Unheimlich" is firstly the opposite of "coziness," but the meaning of the German term could be rendered in English as a bad or unfathomable "un-coziness." We will explore the role of threat for the uncanny in more detail later on.

Freud misrepresents the first, obsolete meaning of "heimlich." Freud lists "heimlich" with its synonyms "native" and "familiar," but he does not connect it with "cozy." Freud leaves out an entire range of meaning, indicated by other existing synonyms, namely, "heimelig," (cozy), "behaglich" (comfortable), "gemütlich" (sheltered), and "idyllisch" (idyllic), all of which render "heimlich" as a quality in which threat is noticeably absent.[27] The synonyms "familiar" and "native," singled out by Freud, divert the attention from the feeling of security expressed in "cozy."

The English translation of this sentence ("The German word *'unheimlich'* is obviously the opposite of *'heimlich'* [...]" (SE 17, 220, 33–4)) unintentionally further hinders English readers from seeing Freud's inaccuracies. First, no English reader is aware that the prevalent meaning of "heimlich" is "secretive." Second, the translation leads to an even greater misrepresentation of what "un" negates in "unheimlich." The dominant meaning of "heimlich" as "secretive" will be discussed in more detail below. Nevertheless, in the German original, the exclusion of "heimlich" (in the sense of "secretive") takes place only implicitly, because German readers have the prevalent meaning in mind. They have at least the opportunity to ponder the range of meanings when encountering the word "heimlich" itself. The translation of "heimlich" as "homely" instead of "cozy" exacerbates Freud's misrepresentation for English readers. They are unable to recognize that the meaning of "heimlich" ranges from "familiar" to "cozy." English readers also do not learn about the prevalent meaning, "secretively," until later in the essay. Apart even from its late presentation, they are likely to overlook its significance because of the other definitions Freud has privileged. When "unheimlich" is rendered as "unfamiliar" it leaves out the component of perceived threat. We shall see that the etymological misrepresentation plays a role also in Freud's shift from uncanny feeling on the part of the observer to uncanny object. The neologism "un-cozy" would be a provisional approximation of the German meaning of "unheimlich."[28]

Regardless of Freud's possible reasons, he focuses exclusively on the meaning of "heimlich" as "familiar," because he wants to refute the idea that the uncanny is the opposite of the familiar. He therefore mentions only that "un-" in "unheimlich" negates the meaning of "heimlich" as "familiar", which gives him the opportunity to prove the opposite later ("unheimlich" only seems to be "unfamiliar"). Freud overlooks that "un-" in "unheimlich" also negates the meaning of "heimlich" (cozy). Apparently, Freud's urge to prove the falsity of the popularly held understanding of the word's meaning prevents him, in this case, from representing or comprehending the full meaning himself.

Let us now return to the second inaccuracy in the sentence discussed above. "[U]ncanny" is not "obviously" the opposite of what is familiar (SE 17, 220, 34) because the prefix "un-" also has a pejorative function. In the combination "un-x," the prefix not only negates but also modifies "x," expressing the removal of a quality and even the transgression of what is acceptable or reasonable. Etymologically, the pejorative or improbative function developed out of negation. More specifically, the prefix "un-" can denote the reversal or removal of a quality. The pejorative meaning of the prefix reaches back to the Indo-Germanic origins of both German and English. In Sanskrit, for example, "ávåsa" means "a cow that has lost its usefulness for the community, because of age or sickness."[29] "Un-" can thus express disapprobation, condemnation, blame, and deprivation.[30] In German, however, the meaning of "un-" develops from a pejorative particle to one denoting severe condemnation. Examples of pejorative "un-" still in use in German are "das Unwetter" (literally "un-weather" – very bad weather), "die Untat" ("un-deed" – a heinous crime) or "der Unhold" ("a very bad person"). The translation follows Freud's lead in misrepresenting how "un-" modifies "heimlich." Freud does not mention the pejorative function. German readers may again be aware of it, but this function of "un-" is no longer common in English.[31] Thus, the translation makes matters more difficult for non-German readers in a manner comparable to the aforementioned dominant meaning of "heimlich" (secretive).

The Grimm dictionary describes the development from negation to condemnation in some detail and even suggests an additional quality expressed by the prefix in the section on the prefix "*un-*," which Freud could not have consulted, because it appeared after he wrote the essay:

> Whereas the negating function of "un-" simply called the empirical term into question, the pejorative "un-" does not negate the thing as it is, but as it is supposed to be. [...]. This is how the particle arrives at describing the deviation from the proper way and consistency, from the correct path, from the useful, good, normal, traditional, regular, to characterize inhibition, confusion. [...] it develops into the description of the unnecessary, the unpleasant, the uncanny, unformed, overwhelming, etc. An un-person is clearly a person, but one who lacks everything that constitutes a person as a human being, finer human qualities, humanity.[32]

The prefix comes to express a phenomenon that exceeds the limits of what is acceptable or even imaginable. This dimension of the meaning of "un-" affects "unheimlich" (uncanny).

The connotations expressed by the prefix even include uncanniness itself. This is suggested in a more general section in the Grimm dictionary:

> The wide field of lexical concepts expressing transition and intermediacy was developed on the basis of "un-." These concepts describe the non-definite

properties, those intermediate states, which J.[acob] Grimm (Gr[ammar] 3, 684) compared to the phenomena of dawn and dusk occurring between night and day.[33]

Apparently, the prefix "un-" possesses an uncanny quality all by itself, even when it does not modify the word "heimlich." The word "unheimlich" evokes the notion of a dark region beyond the boundaries of what is acceptable or known. Anything that has not yet been identified and classified represents a threat from beyond the boundaries of knowledge, and its indefiniteness generates associations that encompass all that is unacceptable and unimaginable.

The aspect of threat in "unheimlich" is thus contained not only in the negation of "coziness" but also in the connotations of the prefix "un-" itself. Freud limits the meaning of "un-" to opposition, and thus presents "unheimlich" exclusively as the opposite of "heimlich" throughout the essay: "Thus *heimlich* [...] finally coincides with its opposite, *unheimlich*" (SE 17, 226, 14–16; italics original, my emphasis). The uncanny connotations of "un-" are slight. Nevertheless, they further explain Freud's perhaps exaggerated emphasis on the familiar, because he has to overcome the resistance that German readers will develop against his claim.[34]

Another inaccuracy regarding the etymology of "unheimlich" concerns the relationship between the two meanings of "heimlich." Freud's German readers at least have the opportunity to raise questions, whereas the translation conceals the inaccuracy almost entirely. It is peculiar that Freud mentions only in passing and late in the essay that "heimlich" also means "secretively." As mentioned above, the meaning "secretively" is in fact the predominant one. Equally, the following dictionary entries show that the meaning Freud emphasizes, "familiar," was already obsolete in 1919. This information is contained in both dictionaries Freud consults, but Freud omits the pertinent portion from the Grimm dictionary, and thus it appears in his essay only once, in the quotation from Sanders, and without comment: "[heimlich] [...] (a) (Obsolete) belonging to the house or the family, or regarded as so belonging [...]" (SE 17, 222, 6–7, my emphasis). The Grimm entry, dating to 1871 in its first printing, contains the same information, in a passage not reprinted by Freud:

> 3) the idea of the familiar, friendly, intimate develops from the meaning of things belonging to the home. Of a place, a time, or a thing and the feelings associated with them, a meaning which is predominantly developed in Bavaria and South West Germany.[35]

This oldest meaning of "heimlich," "familiar," survives only in the south of Germany. However, even when this older meaning appears in those dialects, it does so, at least in Swabian (Alemanic), in the form "heimelig" (cozy), most likely to avoid confusion with the word "heimlich" (secretive), ubiquitous even among the speakers of the dialect, who use "heimelig" alongside the word "heimlich," "secretive." Considering Austrian German shows many similarities to Bavarian and southern German dialects, Freud perhaps did not view "heimlich" (cozy) as obsolete because he had the dialectal meaning in mind.

In fact, the meaning "secretive" already began its ascent in the 12th century, according to a more recent etymological dictionary:

> "heimlich" – The original meaning has been preserved until the present day, but is now completely obsolete. [...] Already in the 12th century *heimlich* appears as "hidden from the eyes of strangers" [...].[36]

Freud himself uses "heimlich" in the prevalent sense (secretive) in the essay, and these instances point to the aspect of a hidden threat that he excludes from his definition.

Freud chooses not to comment on the lexical connection between "unheimlich" and "geheim" (secret). In connection with examples for unexpected coincidences, Freud mentions the recurrence of the number 62 during a journey: "[...] [you] will be tempted to ascribe some secret meaning to the recurrence of this number [...]" (SE 17, 238, 7–8).[37] In this context, the use of "geheim" (secretive), which is derived from "heimlich," indicates that the uncanny sensation is caused by suspicion. It is comparable to being confronted by a secret language. A meaning is suspected, but cannot be deciphered.[38] Freud uses "geheim" a total of four times, as in this example from the third part of the essay: "[...] the uncanny is something which is secretly familiar [*heimlich-heimisch*]" (SE 17, 245, 26–7).[39] This is the only point in the essay where Freud connects the uncanny stemming from repression with secrecy and concealment. He neither develops this idea nor comments upon it. Freud does make explicit that this secret quality of the uncanny plays a role, or that it is related the factor of uncertainty emphasized by Jentsch.[40] The uncanny of the type Freud discusses has a basis in something familiar. However, its familiarity is at first not recognized; it is, in Freud's view, a secret we keep from ourselves. As mentioned in the introduction, this aspect is contained implicitly in Freud's contention that the uncanny "has become alienated from [the mind] only through the process of repression" (SE 17, 241, 16–19). If the uncanny has become "alienated" from the mind, it will appear "new and alien," even if it is in fact familiar and "old established."[41]

Freud excludes the prevalent meaning of "heimlich" (secretly) at the point where we would most expect he would mention it, at the end of his etymological discussion. Instead, he focuses on the occasion when "heimlich" "cozy" is used as an equivalent of "unheimlich." Freud's claim that "*heimlich* [...] develops in the direction of ambivalence, until it [...] coincides with its opposite" (SE 17, 226, 14–16) is a simplification. Grimm and Sanders say only that among the meanings of "heimlich" there is one that coincides with "unheimlich," but they do not say that "heimlich" is the opposite of "unheimlich."[42] In order to explain the inaccuracy of the above quotation, we have to examine the meanings of the pair "heimlich" and "unheimlich" in more detail.[43]

The dictionary entries confirm that "heimlich" develops toward ambivalence, but the entries emphasize the difference between "familiar" and "secretive." The Grimm entry introduces a third meaning for "heimlich," however, one in which "heimlich" (cozy) is used as a synonym for "unheimlich" (uncanny). Freud focuses on this "ambivalence" but again makes it appear as if the ambivalence exists between "uncanny" on the one hand and "familiar" on the other hand, whereas the meaning that comes into play in these examples is the meaning of "heimlich" (secretive) that Freud neglects.

"Unheimlich" is not only the opposite of "heimlich" (familiar), but is also different from the two meanings of "heimlich" we have discussed, "cozy" and "secretive." Setting aside the pejorative meaning of "un-" discussed above for a moment, we can see illustrated in Table 1 that when "heimlich" comes to mean "unheimlich," it occupies a position outside the antithesis constituted by the two meanings of "heimlich." The spectrum of meanings thus involves three positions, whereas Freud makes it appear as if "unheimlich" simply coincides with the extreme point of the alleged antithetical two meanings of the word "heimlich." The three meanings occupy points in a development that moves from safety towards increasing threat:

	"heimlich, heimelig" (cozy)	"heimlich" (secretively)	"unheimlich" (uncanny)
Inside/ Outside	Speaker on the inside	Speaker on the inside, in conflict with outside	Speaker on the outside
Safety/ Threat	Protected, external dangers are set aside	Secret held as potential threat for others	Unprotected, threat suspected
Informed/ Uninformed	Information advantage gives peace of mind	Information advantage useful against outside enemy	Information deficiency

Table 1. Semantics of "heimlich" and "unheimlich."

It has already become clear that "heimlich" has two separate meanings and that "unheimlich" forms a third meaning. These three meanings can be shown to develop on scale from feeling safe from threat to feeling threatened. In the first stage, "heimlich, heim(e)lig" (cozy) denotes concealment and a feeling of security from outside dangers. In the case of "heimlich" (secretly, clandestine), the view is from the inside outwards; the speaker is plotting something against unsuspecting opponents. Finally, in the case of "unheimlich" (uncanny), the speaker is excluded from a secret, or feels that a place thought to be secure appears to be inhabited by an invisible opponent.

This threefold spectrum becomes more complicated when we conceal something from ourselves, as when something is disavowed.[44] When the pressure exerted to withhold the knowledge from consciousness becomes a "secret" kept from ourselves, we could say the unconscious has taken over the agency of keeping the secret. Although the barrier that separates us from the secret is now on the inside, in contrast to the scenario described above, the situation is also uncanny (unheimlich) because we are no longer in possession of the secret.[45] When we are keeping something secret (heimlich) from ourselves, "unheimlich" indicates the concealment of concealment.[46]

A first clue about the relationship between "home" and "secrecy" appears in the short but concise entry of the Heyne dictionary (1906):

> heimlich 1) belonging to the house [...] has become rare in recent times, but still found in Goethe [...] [Werther] and still in use in the southern German dialects. 2) has been turned into the sense of that withdrawn from the eyes of strangers, hidden (compare secretive).[47]

When we feel "cozy," our safety is guaranteed. We thus feel protected enough not to have to worry about possible outside threats. In this scenario the feeling of safety is so great that the possible aggressor or danger can be put out of mind. But the outside danger is a latent portion of the meaning.[48] The meaning of "heimlich" as "cozy" in German implies a protection from dangers and from enemies.[49]

The more advanced meaning of "heimlich," "secretive," implies that we are exploiting our familiarity or concealment to our advantage. The home is a place that is hidden from public view. We can therefore best keep a secret in the secluded space that the home offers. Somebody with whom we are familiar is also the best person to share our secrets with (this is the origin of the word "secretary," German: "geheimer Rat," "Geheimrat"), and it will play a role in the Tieck story. When acting in secrecy (heimlich), we have privileged access to information not available to others.

Once we are on the receiving end of someone else's secretive (heimlich) activities, we become the victim of a hidden, uncanny threat. We are now furthest removed from being protected and secure, the original meaning of "heim(e)lich" (cozy). Our first awareness of this hidden danger is the feeling called "unheimlich." If the word "unheimlich" is an opposite of "heimlich," it is the opposite of the first, obsolete meaning, "cozy." However, the second meaning, "secretive," also contributes to the meaning of "unheimlich," in the hidden activity performed by our antagonist or the hidden nature of the danger.

The potential for misunderstandings does not end with regard to the meaning of "heimlich," however. More problems arise because of the difficulty of translating the German word "unheimlich" into English. This is already stated in the footnote to the title of Freud's essay in the Standard Edition, but the explanation given there for this difficulty is misleading:

> The German word, translated throughout this paper by the English "uncanny", is "*unheimlich*", literally "*unhomely*". The English term is not, of course, an exact equivalent of the German one. (SE 17, 219, footnote 1, quote placement original)

The footnote only exacerbates the potential for the lexical misunderstandings already described for the "etymological fallacy." The cognate "un-homely" for "unheimlich" is wrong for two reasons. First, "homely," as mentioned above, does not adequately render the range of meanings of the German "heimlich," from familiar, to cozy and secretive. "Homely" covers only the first of these, "familiar, belonging to the home," and the English language adds the connotations "simple, not elaborate, unattractive," that is nowhere contained in "heimlich."[50] The editors of the Standard Edition might have been better advised to choose "homey" instead of "homely" as an alternative translation.[51] Second, even if "unheimlich" was more aptly translated as "uncozy" or "unhome-like," Freud overlooks that the prefix "un-" in German, apart from the negating function that it shares with its English counterpart, has an older, pejorative function that still survives into New High German. "Unheimlich" thus has connotations, in German, of primal or prehistoric awe, of a fear of all that is unknown to man, that points to fears existing long before the Enlightenment.

The relation between the English and the German words was briefly touched upon in the Introduction. "Canny" exhibits an ambiguity comparable to that of German "heimlich." Once we expand the uncanny to incorporate the component of perceived uncertainty that aspect also becomes visible in the English word "uncanny," which thus represents the most important aspects of the uncanny quite adequately, even if the pejorative sense of the German prefix is lost. The word "uncanny" is a "comparatively modern word [...] not found before 17th Century" (OED). "Canny" means firstly "knowing, sagacious, prudent," but also "cozy" and "endowed with secret powers." A footnote in the Standard Edition comments on the ambiguity of "canny": "According to the OED, a similar ambiguity attaches to the English 'canny,' which may mean not only 'cozy' but also 'endowed with occult or magical powers'" (SE 17, 225, footnote 1). "Canny" is derived from "can," in the sense of "to know how, be able," which has the same root as "ken" (obsolete), "to make known," "to know." (OED). The Indo-Germanic root of "can," "*ken-,"[52] is still visible in "kin" and "kindred." There are archaic meanings in Scottish, ranging from "supernaturally wise," "endowed with occult or magical power" (*OED*, "canny" meaning 4) to "quiet, easy, snug, comfortable, pleasant, and cozy" (*OED*, "canny" meaning 8). Furthermore, the meanings "skillful" and "wise" are related to those areas that present mysteries to the understanding: "skillful, clever, cunning."[53] Finally, in negated form, "canny" means "not lucky" or "not safe to meddle with." "Canny" exhibits an ambiguity that is comparable to "heimlich."

The first meaning, "cunning," forms a recognizable connection to the German word "heimlich" (secretive). "Canny" can also mean "cozy," however, which forms the counterpart to the obsolete meaning of German "heim(e)lich" (cozy, familiar).[54] Although the prefix "un-" does not carry any pejorative connotations, the English word nonetheless expresses a demonstrable disruption within the realm we have labeled as known, similar to the connotations of German "unheimlich." The threat arises not only because the object is "unknown," in the sense of "un-cozy," where "cozy" signifies a protection from danger, but also because the danger invades the safe sphere secretively. Therefore "uncanny," perhaps rendered best as "cunningly or secretively uncozy," expresses the quality of a threat that can creep unnoticed and secretly into what appeared as a protected and comfortable sphere. Thus, the etymology of "uncanny" implies an absence of knowledge and expresses a cognitive uncertainty similar to its German counterpart. While Freud accentuates the familiar origin of the uncanny, he de-emphasizes both that its origin is unknown and that its return escapes notice.

Freud believes he has found a predecessor for his understanding of the uncanny as the secretly familiar in Schelling, whose remark on the uncanny first appears as one of the examples in the Sanders entry: "'Unheimlich' is the name for everything that ought to have remained [...] secret and hidden but has come to light" (SE 17, 224, 27–8).[55] Freud stresses the Schelling quotation in the Sanders entry (SE 17, 225, 5–9), and he returns to Schelling late in the essay after having explained how the uncanny is caused by the return of the repressed:

> This reference to the factor of repression enables us, furthermore, to understand Schelling's definition [...] of the uncanny as something which ought to have remained hidden but has come to light. (SE 17, 241, 21–3)

For Freud, Schelling becomes one of the often-quoted earlier thinkers who intuitively expressed the truths systematized in psychoanalysis. When we look at the statement in isolation, it appears puzzling. Something that ought to have remained hidden and secret, but has become known will elicit a reaction of shame, embarrassment, and not uncanniness.[56] Once we view the Schelling remark in its original context, however, we will see that Schelling's remark was misunderstood and that it does not support Freud's argument.

Schelling's comment, seen in its original context, confirms the role of an uncertain sense of danger for the uncanny. A longer excerpt from the Schelling lecture in which the comment appears follows because the work is not accessible in translation, and because the context demonstrates that the fear of the unknown plays an important role in Schelling's notion of the uncanny:

> The world of gods created by Homer silently contains a sphere of mystery within itself, a world that has been erected over a mystery, which can be compared to an abyss. This abyss is covered as if by flowers by the world of gods [...] Greece has a Homer precisely because it has mysteries. He was successful in vanquishing this principle of the past, which still reigned in the Oriental systems, and banishing it to the inside, the secret, and the mystery (from which it had originally evolved). The pure sky that hovers above Homer's works cleared above Greece only after the dark and darkening power of this uncanny principle (uncanny being all that was supposed to have remained secret, in concealment, in latency, and has become visible) – this ether, which expands above the world of Homer, could do so only after the power of the uncanny principle, which governed the earlier religions, was banished into mystery [...].[57]

Schelling accentuates the fact that the old beliefs are contained but also concealed within the new religion. The uncanny appears as the governing principle of the earlier religions, but their secret status gives them an uncanny power. The time of earlier religions refers to a time when the demons were not yet defeated. The gods of Greek religion at the time of Homer are no longer inscrutable enemies of man, but, in Homer's epics, come to the aid of the heroes. The gods of the earlier religion are fear-inspiring because they directly express an all-powerful nature, whose threatening powers are directed against man. At this earlier stage, the uncanny rules supreme. The process that Schelling describes, rather than being simply a denial of an unsolved mystery, is one of a partially successful banishment of fear by virtue of man's increasing knowledge.[58]

A brief digression into Horkheimer and Adorno's "Dialectic of Enlightenment" further illuminates Schelling's understanding of Greek religion: "The chthonic gods of the original inhabitants are banished to the hell, to which, according to the sun and light religion of Indra and Zeus, the earth is transformed" (Horkheimer and Adorno 14). In fact, Horkheimer and Adorno continue their explanation with more sentences that clearly echo Schelling:

> The gloomy and indistinct religious principle that was honored as *mana* in the earliest known stages of humanity lives on in the radiant world of Greek religion. Everything unknown and alien is primary and undifferentiated: that which transcends the confines of experience; whatever in things is more than their previously known reality. What the primitive [person] experiences in this regard is not a spiritual as opposed to a material substance, but the intricacy of the Natural in contrast to the individual. The gasp of surprise that accompanies the experience of the unusual becomes its name. It fixes the transcendence of the unknown in relation to the known, and therefore terror as sacredness. (Horkheimer and Adorno 14–15)

Horkheimer and Adorno emphasize the unknown and the unusual as the source of the oldest forms of religion. The chthonic fear is equivalent to the definition of the uncanny developed here. This fear is uncanny because of uncertainty and not, or not only, because of the subsequent containment or the impending revival of what is banished.[59] Instead, chthonic fear is uncanny already at the moment of its original appearance.[60]

Schelling's definition is reprinted in Sanders as if it were an independent sentence by capitalizing the first letter: "'Unheimlich' is the name for everything [...]" (SE 17, 224, 27–8). In the original, the statement is a parenthetical remark.[61] Furthermore, the parenthesis is an ellipsis, leaving out a few words that the reader or listener has to supply to make sense of the statement.[62] Taken literally, Schelling expresses that the uncanny has already been revealed ([...] has become visible again),[63] which is at odds with his image of the chasm covered with flowers. The chasm-image suggests that traces of the earlier religions are latent within the Greek religion of Homer's time.[64] The uncanny is, first, already a part of the earlier religion, which arises out of the fear of the unknown. Second, the fear that the past will somehow be revived produces the uncanny feeling in the present, without the past having in fact become visible. The image and the concept of Schelling's uncanny is that of a hidden threat that can resurface at any moment. The threat itself as well as the unpredictability causes the uncanny impression. If we were to expand the ellipsis into a full sentence, it would read: "*[...] (uncanny being all that was supposed to have remained secret, in concealment, in latency, and of which it is feared that it could become visible again)."[65] The misunderstanding of both the dictionary editors and, consequentially, of Freud has its origin in the inaccurate wording of Schelling's own parenthetical explanation.[66] Schelling is misinterpreted, as if he made the familiar itself responsible for the uncanny sensation. For Schelling, "unheimlich" denotes a fear that something hidden might be revealed again, very much in the traditional sense of the German word. We have shown above that cognitive uncertainty is caused either by the unpredictability of the moment when the return will occur, or by the confrontation with something that is at first not recognized. In Schelling's description of the uncanny, the factor of uncertainty is still present.

Schelling emphasizes the aspect of concealment and estrangement in regard to the uncanny, a few pages later, in the same lecture:

> We can, however, see older models in the features of the Egyptian figures, not exactly of Egyptian art, but rather of an older art altogether, which represents the divine only through disfigured or modified human features so that it is not openly shown, but rather hidden. This art surrounds the divine with a certain uncanniness by giving it something extra-human or non-human – something strange.[67]

The difference between Schelling's understanding of the uncanny and the representation in the dictionary and later by Freud lies in the role of the observer. For Schelling, the uncanny is caused by cognitive uncertainty, whereas Freud emphasizes the repressed familiar. In Freud's interpretation, the uncanny exists independently of the observer. We will return to this shift in perspective.

Freud's Rebuttal of Jentsch

Freud misunderstands the German "unheimlich" because of his dissatisfaction with the earlier essay on the uncanny, by Ernst Jentsch, which was published in two installments, on August 25 and September 1 of 1906. Although Jentsch, unlike Freud, does not undertake detailed etymological research of "unheimlich," he begins his essay with the meaning of the word as well. More generally, however, he provides a valuable foundation for any investigation of the uncanny. Jentsch divides his argument into two sections, describing the factors that increase the observer's uncertainty and examining different types of uncanny phenomena. Although Jentsch's essay is much shorter than Freud's, and makes no reference to psychoanalysis, Jentsch's accomplishment lies in his repeated emphasis on such aspects as fatigue, the observer's imaginative abilities and other factors through which the observer contributes to the uncanny experience. Freud devotes three paragraphs to rebutting Jentsch, but an examination of Jentsch's article itself will reveal that Freud misrepresents and oversimplifies Jentsch, and goes too far in his rebuttal.

Jentsch opens his essay with a comment on the etymology of "unheimlich":

> With the word *unheimlich* our German language seems to have produced a rather fortunate creation. The word seems to express without doubt that for persons to whom something appears uncanny [...] they are not quite at home in the matter [*nicht recht 'zu Hause'*], not familiar with the matter [*nicht heimisch*], that the matter is strange to them, or at least appears that way [...].[68]

Although Jentsch emphasizes threat as a factor in the uncanny, he simplifies the meaning of the root morpheme "heim-" (home) in "heimlich." For Jentsch, "unheimlich" expresses lack of familiarity directly. He does not recognize that "unheimlich" in the sense of "cozy" expresses a complete absence of threat, because it invokes threat through exclusion, as discussed above. Nevertheless, Jentsch underscores the role of the perceiving individual, stressing that familiar objects can cause the uncanny sensation when they are not recognized.[69]

Jentsch subsequently names other factors such as fatigue, strong emotions, narcotic substances, mental illness and an active imagination as contributing factors for uncanny impressions, and mentions children as frequent victims of the uncanny because of their lack of experience (Jentsch 196). In contrast to Freud's paraphrase of Jentsch, Jentsch does not simply repeat the common understanding about the uncanny that it is caused by what is new or not familiar. Instead, Jentsch describes incidents in which perception is hampered by internal or external causes. In his view, the ensuing disorientation produces the uncanny.

Freud's attack on Jentsch begins with the sentence "The German word *'unheimlich'* is obviously the opposite of *'heimlich'* [...]" (SE 17, 220, 33–4). The statement is a concealed paraphrase of the sentence just quoted from Jentsch.[70] Freud does not mention Jentsch explicitly in this first paragraph. Instead, he presents and then attacks what he portrays as a common misconception, namely, that the unfamiliar produces the uncanny. Freud implies that Jentsch drew only the most evident, commonplace conclusions. Freud uses Jentsch's starting point, his comment on the etymology of unheimlich, as if it represented Jentsch's entire theory. This enables Freud to contradict Jentsch easily.

When Freud states that "uncanny" (unheimlich) is obviously the opposite of "familiar" (heimlich) (SE 17, 220, 33–4), he expresses something that seems to be generally agreed upon. Freud will show that he objects to this conception, and that he believes there is a familiar element in the uncanny. The second half of the sentence announces Freud's objection: "[...] and we are tempted to conclude that what is 'uncanny' is frightening precisely because it is not known and familiar" (SE 17, 220, 35). Freud will follow this statement with an attack on what he perceives to be a common fallacy, showing how "unheimlich" is only seemingly the opposite of "heimlich" = "familiar."[71] Freud summarizes Jentsch's uncanny as "a thing one does not know one's way about in" (SE 17, 221, 9).[72] The expression indicates another aspect of Freud's discussion, namely, that Freud turns the adjective "unheimlich" into the noun "Das Unheimliche," which corresponds to a shift in perspective from the feelings of the person who experiences the uncanny to the phenomena causing the impression. This shift turns "uncanny" into a thing. When Jentsch also uses the noun "Das Unheimliche" he still focuses on the observer and the experience of non-recognition. Freud, on the other hand, looks only at the triggering events, and not only restricts them to the return of the repressed or the revival of what was surmounted, but loses sight of the observer's cognitive uncertainty.

Freud also conceals how much he disagrees with Jentsch. At the beginning of the rebuttal, in the above-mentioned second paragraph, Freud declares that he wishes simply to "proceed beyond" Jentsch (SE 17, 221, 14): "On the whole, Jentsch did not get beyond this relation of the uncanny to the novel and unfamiliar" (SE 17, 221, 5–6). It is unjustified to extract this allegedly simple deduction from Jentsch because he does not say the uncanny is always caused by something unfamiliar. In addition, the phrase "did not get beyond this relation [...] to the novel and unfamiliar" implies that the uncanny has a relation to what is novel and familiar, even if more can be said about the uncanny. Freud never returns to this "relation," however. In truth, Freud intends to repudiate this relation of the uncanny to what is new and unfamiliar altogether.

Nevertheless, Freud repeats this alleged agreement with Jentsch a short while later: "It is not difficult to see that this definition [that the uncanny is something unfamiliar] is incomplete, we will therefore try to proceed beyond the equation 'uncanny' = 'unfamiliar'" (SE 17, 221, 13–15). The equation of the uncanny with the new also restricts Jentsch's "lack of orientation" to the genuinely new and overlooks the unrecognized familiar. Freud's purported agreement with Jentsch is a way of avoiding an immediate conflict with the reader's basic understanding of the uncanny. Freud never builds an explicit case against the "relation of the uncanny to the novel and unfamiliar" because such a case would be hard to make, even after the role of the repressed familiar has been uncovered in a number of cases.

The equation of the unfamiliar with the unknown is a crucial aspect of Freud's misreading of Jentsch. Jentsch does not argue that the uncanny is caused by what is new or not familiar. Jentsch writes: "[...] the word [unheimlich] seems to suggest that the uncanny impression of a thing or event is connected to a lack of orientation."[73]

Freud does not paraphrase Jentsch accurately. Jentsch uses the expression "lack of orientation" ("Mangel an Orienti[e]rung") (195), while "intellectual uncertainty" (SE 17, 221, 7) "intellektuelle Unsicherheit" (GW XII, 231), the central factor Freud attributes to Jentsch, is Freud's interpretation, not a term used explicitly by Jentsch. It is possible to infer the association of "intellectual uncertainty" with the uncanny from Jentsch because he ends his essay with the passage quoted in the introduction, where he states that the uncanny arises when "intellectual certainty" is absent.[74] Instead, Jentsch focuses on the observer's disorientation: "[...] certain traces of sensing psychic uncertainty develop, especially in cases when either the ignorance is very apparent or when the subjective perception wavers greatly."[75] Jentsch uses the term "psychic uncertainty," which is closer to the term "cognitive uncertainty," suggested here as the best corrective to the restrictions inherent in "intellectual uncertainty."[76] Furthermore, Jentsch includes possible problems of recognition on the part of the observer. Jentsch mentions how the daily rising of the sun can appear uncanny to persons not familiar with the scientific explanations of this phenomenon.[77] Freud misses an important distinction. Something unfamiliar, but clearly visible, may arouse fear, but this fear is not identical with the feeling of uncanniness because the threat is not hidden.[78] Instead, a familiar object that is not immediately recognized, or which appears in a new context, can elicit the uncanny feeling because it is unclear whether it contains some yet-unidentified threat.

Although Jentsch does not claim that the uncanny and the unfamiliar are synonymous, Freud implies this when he writes: "Naturally not everything that is new and unfamiliar is frightening" (SE 17, 220, 37–8). In a strict sense, everything new is frightening. While an object that is merely a new species within a known class of objects is not threatening, an object for which we have not yet established a category is always potentially threatening. In the case of the uncanny phenomena Freud examines, when a fear is connected to something previously repressed, this moment is uncanny, because the connection to the past is hidden.

Freud's rhetorical maneuver of reducing Jentsch's argument to an oversimplified adaptation of the etymology, and the seemingly obvious and necessary opposition to Jentsch, obstructs Freud's perception. Although Jentsch overlooks the ambiguity of "unheimlich," and also does not consider the pejorative function of the prefix "un-," his focus on uncertainty and the role of the observer are contributions worth preserving. The uncanny always has to do with uncertainty.

Freud's exclusion of the uncertainty in the uncanny is connected to a conceptual pitfall of turning the original German adjective "unheimlich" into the noun "das Unheimliche," which was not in use in ordinary German (Grimm and Grimm, "unheimlich").[79] Both Jentsch and Freud use the noun to signal that they are focusing on the uncanny sensation as the object of their investigation. Jentsch is the first to use the noun in print.[80] As mentioned above, the adjective usually appears in sentences such as: "This shape, appearance, or story gives me an 'unheimlich' feeling" or "I feel 'unheimlich'" ("Mir ist unheimlich"). Whether or not something is perceived as uncanny depends on such factors as the constitution and attentiveness of the observer. The uncanny may affect only one particular individual at one particular time. It should be noted that Freud does not ignore this aspect: "[...] Jentsch [...] lays stress on the obstacle presented by the fact that people vary so very greatly in their sensitivity to this quality of feeling" (SE 17, 220, 4–6). Freud sees this difference in responses only as an obstacle, however, whereas Jentsch's attention to individual differences corresponds with his keeping the adjectival origin of the word in mind.

In the third paragraph of the Jentsch rebuttal, Freud uses Jentsch's alleged limitations as the starting point for consulting the foreign language dictionaries. Later, Freud will use the citations from Sanders and Grimm to confirm his own thesis about the uncanny and prove Jentsch's alleged limitations. Critics have been puzzled by Freud's sentence: "Indeed, we get an impression that many languages are without a word for this particular shade of what is frightening" (SE 17, 221, 16–19). They have read it as Freud expressing estrangement from his own mother tongue (Lydenberg 1076; Punter, "On Poetry and the Uncanny" 203). With his reference to the "foreign language," Freud perhaps assumes the perspective of speakers of other languages to whom the German word "unheimlich" must appear "fremd," which means both "strange" and "foreign."[81] Freud thus himself submits an example for something that appears "uncanny" only to some observers, not to others.[82]

In an earlier reference to the uncanny, in *Totem and Taboo* (1913), Freud still uses "uncanny" in the adjectival sense:

Th[e] power [of the taboo] is attached to all special individuals [...] all exceptional states [...] and to all *uncanny* things, such as sickness and death and what is associated with them through their power of infection or contagion.[83]

Die Kraft [des Verbotenen = Tabu] haftet nun an allen Personen, die etwas Besonderes sind, [...] an allen Ausnahmezuständen, [...] an allem *Unheimlichen*, wie Krankheit und Tod, und was kraft der Ansteckungs- und Ausbreitungsfähigkeit damit zusammenhängt. (GW IX, 31; my emphasis)

In this reference, the uncanny still appears as something that has unknown or mysterious causes. Freud writes *Totem and Taboo* untouched by his dispute with Jentsch. In "The Uncanny," Freud not only adapts the nominalization from Jentsch, but he takes it beyond its use as a mental construct.[84] In his essay, the noun "uncanny" and the derivative "uncanniness" have replaced the adjective completely, and this helps to conceal that the uncanny quality does not necessarily lie in the object of perception. Jentsch keeps the observer in mind and avoids this problem, whereas Freud becomes its victim.

Hoffmann's "Der Sandmann" – A Preview

After the etymological investigation, Freud turns to Hoffmann's "Sandmann" (Hoffmann, "Der Sandmann"). His interpretation of the story has become closely linked to the concept of the uncanny, and critics operating with the uncanny as a critical term frequently include a brief summary of Freud's interpretation (Wright 137–50; Huet 233–6). For Freud, the story functions as an illustration of the uncanny caused by repressed castration anxiety, which he deducts from the Oedipal structures he uncovers in the story. Freud explains the appearance of the Sandman as a personification of Nathanael's abnormal sexual development. Freud makes the questionable implicit claim of having solved the riddle of the Sandman. First, there are a number of examples on the plot level in which the uncanny is caused by hidden or suspected dangers, conforming to the semantics of the original German word, as noted above. Second, Freud fails to do justice to the literary attributes of the text.[85] Crucial events in the text are either the result of Nathanael's deranged perceptions or a fictional representation of fantastic occurrences. When such mutually exclusive interpretations coexist, they create a paradoxical ambiguity, as mentioned in the introduction. The interpretation of "Der Sandmann" offered below demonstrates how this paradoxical ambiguity, produced by the reader's interpretative activity, creates an uncanny reading experience.[86]

In this overview of Freud's interpretation of "Der Sandmann," we will consider the following: first, Freud again follows in Jentsch's footsteps in choosing this story, even if it could be argued that Hoffmann was already one of the most popular authors at the turn of the century because of the popularity of Jacques Offenbach's (1819–1880) "The Tales of Hoffmann," which partially incorporates the plot of "Der Sandmann."[87] Second, Freud's opposition to Jentsch drives and governs his argument, leading to inaccuracies, and prevents him from acknowledging the role of the automaton or developing a satisfactory explanation for its uncanny effect. Third, Freud's Oedipal interpretation manipulates the story to make it fit his model.

Freud discusses "Der Sandmann" immediately after the conclusions drawn from the etymological survey. As noted above, Jentsch already mentions Hoffmann's automata, for which Freud again gives Jentsch no credit, just as just as he failed to credit him for defining "unheimlich" as a lead into the topic of the uncanny. When discussing the uncanny caused by doubt about the status of seemingly living creatures, Jentsch mentions E.T.A. Hoffmann as a master of uncanny effect: "Hoffmann has repeatedly employed this psychological artifice [to leave the reader in doubt whether a particular figure is a human being or an automaton] [...] in his fantastic narratives."[88] Jentsch exaggerates when saying that Hoffmann "repeatedly" employed this effect, because there is only one other Hoffmann tale besides "Der Sandmann" featuring an automaton, "Die Automate" (1814).[89] Furthermore, whereas Jentsch makes only this one reference to Hoffmann, Freud offers a full interpretation of "Der Sandmann."

Nevertheless, Freud overlooks a number of textual details, and his interpretative agenda colors his paraphrase. To give just one example, here is Freud's paraphrase of the story's beginning:

> The fantastic tale opens with the childhood recollections of the student Nathaniel. In spite of his present happiness, he cannot banish the memories associated with the mysterious and terrifying death of his beloved father. (SE 17, 227, 29–32)

Freud's oversights include relatively small ones, such as the misspelling of the protagonist's name, "Nathanael" instead of "Nathaniel."[90] More importantly, however, Freud omits that the disruption of Nathanael's life occurs through Coppola's first visit.[91] This visit triggers Nathanael's childhood recollections and prompts the letters, also omitted by Freud, which form the story's beginning. Freud's inaccurate paraphrase of the plot is part of his attempt to portray the appearance of the Sandman as an internal event triggered by Nathanael's unstable psyche.[92] Instead, Coppola's appearance is more than a manifestation of inner events; it is from the very beginning an external event. The characterization of the Sandman affects how we evaluate the quality of the uncanny in the story.

Freud's diminishes the significance of the Olimpia episode and the cognitive uncertainty connected to automata by making the automaton an expression of Nathanael's alleged abnormality. While Freud is right to criticize Jentsch for referring only to the automaton and overlooking the figure of the Sandman, Freud is mistaken in dismissing the effect of Olimpia entirely.[93] The satiric treatment of the Olimpia episode does not reduce the "unparalleled atmosphere of uncanniness evoked by the story" (SE 17, 227, 21–2). In a long footnote, Freud applies the castration complex to the story: "This automatic doll can be nothing else than a materialization of Nathanael's feminine attitude towards his father in his infancy" (SE 17, 232, note 1). Freud combines two ideas in this explanation. The first is the notion that Nathanael is "fixated upon his father by his castration complex" (SE 17, 232, note 1), the second that Olimpia represents Nathanael's double.[94] For Freud, the automaton is a materialization of Nathanael's unconscious wish to protect himself from the threat of castration by being a woman.[95] We can trace the genesis of Freud's interpretation of Olimpia – as a manifestation of Nathanael's repressed femininity – to his interpretations of literary texts containing doubles later in the essay. The double always personifies the repressed for Freud. Apart from the fact that Freud's explanation for Olimpia is entirely contingent on the patriarchal model of castration anxiety, Freud's interpretation of Olimpia does not explain the uncanniness of automata in general.[96] Freud overlooks that automata are uncanny in themselves, regardless of whether they also function as doubles in a specific context.[97]

Let us examine Freud's first idea, that Olimpia is an incarnation of Nathanael's desire to be a woman:

Spalanzani's otherwise incomprehensible statement that the optician has stolen Nathanael's eyes [...] so as to set them in the doll now becomes significant as supplying evidence of the identity of Olympia and Nathaniel. (SE 17, 232, note 1)

For Freud, the alleged theft of eyes creates the parallel between the two characters because it mirrors Coppelius's earlier threat to Nathanael's eyes. Freud also mentions the screwing off of limbs "as a mechanician would on a doll" (SE 17, 232, note 1). In Olimpia's story, the castration equivalent is the scene in Spalanzani's laboratory in which the pair of fathers tear the doll apart. Nonetheless, Spalanzani's remark remains ominous because Nathanael still has his eyes. Spalanzani's remark could be a way of expressing that Nathanael's infatuated gaze gives life to the lifeless puppet. Perhaps the fictional world Nathanael inhabits is constructed in such a way that the Sandman's influence gives Nathanael the power to physically change the world around him. Nathanael animates Olimpia not only figuratively but also literally.[98] Nathanael would then possess what Freud calls the "omnipotence of thoughts," not as a delusive regression to narcissism, but literally as an omnipotence that turns phantasmata into frightening reality. This is uncanny, regardless whether we can fully substantiate the Freudian explanation based on the avoidance of castration anxiety. This will be explored more deeply in the following chapter.

Freud also identifies Olimpia as Nathanael's double. The explanation of Olimpia as a materialization of a "dissociated complex" (SE 17, 232, note 1) does not do full justice to the specific uncanniness of the automaton that differentiates it from the uncanniness of the double. This becomes clear in the passage where Olimpia is explicitly called uncanny. Olimpia not only deceives the infatuated protagonist, but, with her lifelike effect, equally betrays the reader.[99] His best friend, Siegmund, describes the impression he and his circle have of Olimpia in a conversation with Nathanael:

> "Her walk is strangely precise [...]. Her playing and her singing have the unpleasantly accurate, soulless beat of a singing machine, and the same hold for her dancing. We all became quite uneasy about this Olimpia [better: she became *uncanny* to us], we wanted nothing to do with her, we felt as if she were only pretending to be a living being but was really some sort of oddity." (SmE 89, my emphasis)[100]

Nathanael's friends do not yet carry their doubts to the conclusion that Olimpia is an automaton, but the idiosyncrasies constitute the truly revealing difference between the puppet and a human being, namely, that human beings always have some imperfections.[101] We only need to turn to Jentsch to understand why Olimpia's perfection would appear uncanny. Jentsch mentions that when the distinction between animate and inanimate qualities is blurred, an uncanny feeling arises:

> An example that will elicit the uncanny response in a most consistent manner is doubt about the life status of a seemingly living creature, and the reverse, namely, whether a lifeless object may not be endowed with a soul/consciousness (even when this doubt is only intuited). The uncanny feelings persist as long as the doubt cannot be cleared up. (Jentsch 197, my translation)

Moreover, the source of the uncanny sensation is connected to a potential threat. While nature may occasionally become threatening to human beings, the danger usually is openly visible, such as a dark, foreboding sky. Jentsch illustrates the role of uncertainty in the example of people traveling in the jungle, who have an uncanny feeling when they realize that the tree-stump they are sitting on is in reality a giant snake. The uncanny arises at the moment at which the disorientation occurs.[102] In this case, the uncanniness is produced not by uncertainty about the outcome but by disorientation about the degree of animation in the encountered being. This aspect of the automaton has an uncanny effect in Hoffmann's story independent of any explanation linking Olimpia to Nathanael's complexes.

The shortcomings of Freud's reduction of the automaton to a double become visible again when he attempts to connect Olimpia to the role of dolls in childhood: "[...] in their early games children do not distinguish at all sharply between living and inanimate objects [...]" (SE 17, 233, 13–15). Freud disregards that dolls are not automata. Instead, he is puzzled by the fact that "children have no fears of their dolls coming to life, they may even desire it" (SE 17, 233, 23–4). Freud announces that he will attempt to find a better explanation for the fear of automata later. Nonetheless, when Freud mentions children again, in the third part of the essay, he makes the questionable claim that children do not experience the uncanny in response to darkness. Freud never returns to the topic, however, and offers no further explanation for the uncanniness of automata. Nevertheless, this passage illustrates Freud's impulse to link the uncanny in every instance to childhood.

Jentsch reminds us that children are more easily frightened by inexplicable phenomena than adults because of their lack of experience:

> We observe the latter [traces of sensing psychic uncertainty when the ignorance is very apparent] primarily in children: the child still has so little experience that simple things appear inexplicable, and somewhat complicated situations already become dark secrets. This is one of the primary causes why the child is frequently so frightened and has so little self-confidence [...].[103]

Freud does not pursue the idea he expresses himself, namely, that children bring their puppets to life through their own volition ("they desire it"). Children's dolls differ from automata, because androids and automata have an artificial source of life that is hidden from the observer.[104] Children animate dolls not because they perform a "willing suspension of disbelief" but because they project their self-consciousness onto all things, animate and inanimate.[105] Considering that Freud does not do justice to the uncanny effect of automata, his claim that Olimpia is not important for Hoffmann's story loses credibility. In "Der Sandmann" the uncanniness of the story has its main source in textual indeterminacy, so that the indeterminate life-status of Olimpia, although not the central plot element, acts as the counterpart to the indeterminate reality-status of the Sandman.

Freud's application of the Oedipal scenario to Nathanael's experiences is not completely convincing even when taken on its own terms, regardless of the overlooked literary aspects of "Der Sandmann." According to Freud, the Sandman only appears as a "disturber of love" (SE 17, 231, 37), which follows from Freud's interpretation that the Sandman personifies Nathanael's feminine attitude. Freud perceives Nathanael as faced with a pair of fathers, one who is loved and the other from whom castration is feared. Olimpia's "fathers," Spalanzani and Coppola, repeat the split in Nathanael childhood into his actual father and Coppelius:

> Elements in the story like these [the connection of the father's death to anxiety about the eyes, the Sandman as disturber of love] [...] seem arbitrary [unless] we replace the Sand-Man with the dreaded father at whose hands castration is expected. (SE 17, 232, 1–5)

It is true that the Sandman separates Nathanael from Clara, destroys Olimpia, and could be responsible for driving Nathanael to suicide when Nathanael is about to be reunited with Clara, but he also separates Nathanael from his best friend, Lothar, and he appears on other occasions: when selling Nathanael the telescope, for example, to initiate Nathanael's infatuation rather than to disturb it.[106] The Sandman does not appear exclusively as the disturber of love.

It is questionable whether the uncanny associated with the Sandman has anything to do with the threat of castration. Freud calls attention to the centrality of eyes in the story and warns: "[...]

I would not recommend any opponent of the psycho-analytic view to select this particular story of the Sand-Man with which to support his argument [...]" (SE 17, 231, 31–3). To support his own argument, Freud claims that Hoffmann brings the "anxiety about the eyes in [...] intimate connection to the father's death" (SE 17, 231, 35–6). Instead, the father's death occurs months after the Sandman threatens Nathanael's eyes in the laboratory. The eye-penis equation, despite Freud's insistent claims to its validity, has been rightly criticized:

> [...] in the case of Oedipus, both the eyes and the male member may be called "guilty," but this does not obviate the equally weighty fact that for Oedipus the gouging of the eyes may have been punishment for the primary sin – that of seeing too much – and not substitution of the "real" organ to be singled out.[107]

The uncanny, if viewed as a primal response to the unknown, also provokes the Promethean search for knowledge, a fact Jentsch mentions.[108] The eyes are traditionally the "seat of soul," and the fear of losing one's eyes is justified independently of their symbolic phallic significance because of their importance for survival.

Freud mentions a detail from Hoffmann's biography as final proof for the correctness of his interpretation. According to his biographer, Griesebach, Hoffmann was the child of an unhappy marriage, and the relationship to his father was a sensitive issue for Hoffmann. Apart from the fact that these details are not particularly unique, there is no basis in the text for the argument that Hoffmann's biography is reflected in his work.[109] The life of the poet does not deterministically lead to an inevitable creation or structure of the work.

Some critics have used Freud's interpretation of "Der Sandmann" as a starting point and have modified his approach in useful ways. Weber, Meltzer and Kittler, for example, have successfully applied a Lacanian model to the story to expand the interpretation of the Oedipal conflict from the purely sexual connotations to the themes of acculturation and the dissemination of knowledge (Weber; Kittler; Meltzer, "The Uncanny Rendered Canny"). Nathanael's father and Spalanzani try to create an automaton with the help of the Mephistophelean figure Coppelius/Coppola. Apart from an infringement of the divine privilege of giving life, this also constitutes an attempt at appropriating the maternal procreative privilege. Furthermore, Lydenberg has linked the scientific attempts at procreation in Hoffmann's story to the poetological questions raised both by Nathanael's literary ambitions and the narrator's reflections about the possibilities and limitations of literary representation. She and others have argued that the attempts to imitate creation in "Der Sandmann" mean the recasting of the primal scene as an all-male enterprise and that these attempts, both in the realism of science and art, express the desire to appropriate the maternal.[110]

It is our goal, however, to focus on the poetical uncanny and to recapture the aspect of disorientation produced in the text and by the text. Coppelius frightens Nathanael, for example, not only because he is the incarnation of the "bad father" but also because Hoffmann has made him specifically frightening, for protagonist and reader alike. Coppelius's uncanny quality is caused by his superhuman powers, which are expressed both on the plot level and through ambiguities in the text. These aspects have thus far been overlooked, even by Lacanian extensions of the Freudian paradigm, because such interpretations still view the fantastic occurrences as symptoms of the protagonist's unresolved inner conflicts.

As far as the discussion of Hoffmann's "Der Sandmann" itself is concerned, Freud disregards the mediation of the uncanny events in the story through fiction. The fictional medium draws attention to itself and contains ambiguities that contribute to the uncanny effect. For example, Freud fails to mention that the story is divided into an epistolary first half and a narrative second half. The resulting change of perspective makes Nathanael unreliable as a narrator and constitutes one of the story's uncanny textual elements.[111]

Furthermore, Freud's interpretation is affected by his inability to acknowledge poetical ambiguities. Freud overlooks that he himself is induced by the story's ambiguity to come to contradictory diagnoses regarding Nathanael's sanity. One the one hand, the ending convinces Freud that the identity of Coppelius and Coppola is assured. This leads Freud to conclude at the end of his summary that Nathanael's experiences are not the fantastic productions of a madman, "behind which we, with the superiority of our rational minds, are able to detect the sober truth [...]" (SE 17, 230, 33–4). On the other hand, in the long footnote that offers the psychological explanation, Freud speaks of Nathanael's delirium and offers an explanation for Nathanael's madness.[112] We shall find inaccuracies already in the first claim, regarding the identity of Coppelius and Coppola, and also problems with the evaluation of Nathanael as a madman.

The inherent contradiction between granting the fantastic events an independent reality status in the story and reducing them to merely symbolic dramatizations of intrapsychic events becomes visible specifically Freud's commentary on the first laboratory scene. Freud at first rightly points out that the scene has ambiguous reality status. He writes that it could be either a "first delirium of the panic stricken boy" (SE 17, 228, 19) or "a succession of events which are to be regarded in the story as being real" (SE 17, 228, 20–1). He does not put this insight to use, however, and when commenting on the first laboratory scene, he opts for one of the two possibilities, thereby removing the ambiguity: "Those who decide in favor of a rationalistic interpretation of the Sand-Man will not fail to recognize in the child's phantasy the persisting influence of the nurse's story" (SE 17, 228, 28–31). Freud implies that Nathanael only imagines that Coppelius is the Sandman. Freud has thus opted for the "first delirium of the panic stricken boy." The fictional world that Nathanael inhabits can be read as a materialization of Nathanael's hallucinations. Hoffmann transfers part of the narrative agency to Nathanael. Whereas Freud argues that Nathanael's mad imagination signifies a failure of reality testing, Hoffman perhaps gives Nathanael's imagination the power to influence the physical world he inhabits.[113] In Hoffmann's story, the idea contained implicitly in Clara's advice, that Nathanael brings forth monsters only through his imagination, turns into a frightening reality, in which monsters become real because they are imagined.[114]

Freud's acknowledged acceptance of both "rationalistic" and "antirationalistic" reading places his championing of the "rationalistic interpretation" on unstable ground. As we shall see in the next chapters, *uncanny texts* present the reader with a paradoxical ambiguity, in which two readings can coexist simultaneously, even when they are theoretically not only contradictory but mutually exclusive.[115] Both of Freud's contradictory positions regarding Nathanael's sanity are supported by the text. As we shall see in the discussion of the third section of Freud's essay, Freud's difficulty in accepting the ambiguous reality status of events in "Der Sandmann" also hampers his distinctions between the uncanny in fiction and in real life.

Freud retains the centrality of castration anxiety that he extracts from "Der Sandmann" for some further explications of the uncanny. He adds examples that can be divided into two groups, first the uncanniness of "dismembered limbs" (SE 17, 244), which he explains as calling up associations with castration anxiety, and second a group of phenomena he sums up as "womb-phantasies" (SE 17, 248), namely, the "idea of being buried alive" (SE 17, 244) and the uncanniness allegedly associated with the female genitals (SE 17, 245).

Freud claims that the uncanniness of dismembered limbs springs from a proximity to the castration complex. A passage in Freud's late writings calls the primacy of castration into question. In the *New Introductory Lectures* (1933a), Freud relates the desire to be reunited with the mother to the impulse to reverse the trauma of being separated from her at birth, instead of attributing it to infantile sexuality. Although this theory appears more convincing from today's perspective, it calls into question the centrality of castration anxiety in Freud's system.[116]

Nonetheless, severed limbs are uncanny on their own terms, regardless of the psychoanalytic explanations Freud offers. When we encounter a severed limb in reality, an uncanny feeling may arise because the limb appears outside its usual context of a complete body and without the mind that directs its movement. In fiction, this discrepancy is exploited when a dismembered limb acts as if it had an independent consciousness. A hidden force seems to be at work that contradicts the laws of nature. Jentsch's claim thus applies, which states that a phenomenon is uncanny when the distinction between animate and inanimate qualities becomes indistinct.

When discussing the fear of being buried alive, Freud employs argumentation similar to his notion in the *Interpretation of Dreams* that fears in dreams are repressed wishes.[117] Cixous here supports Freud's analysis rather than subjecting it to questions: "The phantasm of the man buried alive represents the confusion of life and death. There is no recourse to an inside/outside."[118] The idea that this state represents neither life nor death is an interpretive exaggeration, because persons buried alive are still alive, although they may fear that they face a certain death. The model Freud uses to explain the uncanniness of premature burial, as a conversion of a repressed wish into anxiety, also applies to Freud's explanation of the anxiety attached to uncanny impressions in general. In Freud's model, the fearful component of the return of the repressed is not only the fear of the return alone but also a remainder of the originally repressed concept. In a much earlier commentary on premature burial, in *Studies in Hysteria*, Freud explains this fear as the unwillingness of Frau Emmy von N. to believe that her deceased husband has died. Her repressed wish that he should come back to life is converted to fear. Freud explains this process as a split in the unconscious at the time when the initial repression occurs. Only the representation of the repressed affect is repressed, whereas its affective cathexis is converted to anxiety (Freud, *Studies in Hysteria* 88).

The doubts we have begun to express regarding Freud's theory of the uncanny are confirmed implicitly by some of Freud's later revisions in the *New Introductory Lectures* (1933a) regarding anxiety, dreams and intra-uterine phantasies. Freud revises the idea that repression causes anxiety because he realizes that it does not make sense to speak of an anxiety in the Id.[119] Freud claims instead that the anxiety begins with the urge to be united with the mother, but that the fear of castration is external. The fear of this external event is now seen as the cause of repression:

> [...] we have learnt two things: first, that anxiety makes repression and not, as we used to think, the other way round, and [secondly] that the instinctual situation which is feared goes back ultimately to an external situation of danger.[120]

Freud also revises his hypothesis that dreams are wish-fulfilments. He distinguishes wishful-, anxiety- and punishment dreams.[121] Freud now recognizes the importance of the dreams of war veterans, who relive a traumatic situation in their dreams as failed attempts at wish fulfillment.[122] Nevertheless, Freud adheres to the idea that the fear of being buried alive represents a transformation of the phantasy of intra-uterine existence. As mentioned above, the intra-uterine phantasy is still punishable by castration, even if it is produced by the desire to reverse the separation from the mother at birth (Freud, *New Introductory Lectures* 88).

In the context of reversing the priority between repression and anxiety, and saying that anxiety produces repression, Freud acknowledges his previous exclusion of external fears: "With this new perspective, the function of anxiety to indicate danger, with which we were not unacquainted before, after all, has moved into the foreground, and the question what anxiety is made of has become less interesting."[123] Freud remarks that the role of anxiety to signal an external danger has moved into the foreground, although he assures us that this role was not alien to him before. Freud's peculiar admission that external fears were not alien to him before is perhaps an implicit admission that he has understated the role of external fears in the past, including the role he attributes to external fears in "The Uncanny."

Freud applies the idea of a reversal of a repressed wish also to the alleged uncanny feeling of the female genitals: "In this case too, then, the *unheimlich* is what was once *heimisch*, familiar; the prefix '*un*' is the token of repression" (SE 17, 245, 20–2; Freud's emphasis). For Freud, this fear is the disguised wish to return to the "former *Heim* [home]" (SE 17, 245, 13–14).[124] As proof, Freud cites the proverb "Love is homesickness." Nonetheless, the meaning and implications of the proverb are not at all clear. Freud limits its meaning to the vagina, but the proverb could refer to the state before birth, nothingness, and thus to death, or it could refer to the reunification with the mother to overcome the trauma of separation at birth.[125] However, this desire is not gender specific, so that the fear of genitals would have to apply to women as well.

In sum, neither the fear of being buried alive nor that of the vagina are very convincing examples of the uncanny, and Freud himself reveals doubts regarding the pertinence of these examples when he prepares the reader for the alleged connection between the proverb and the fear of the female genitals:

> To conclude this collection of examples [...] I will relate an instance taken from psychoanalytic experience; if it does not rest upon mere coincidence, it furnishes a beautiful [better: "the most beautiful"] confirmation of our theory of the uncanny. (SE 17, 245, 7–11)[126]

Freud is obviously eager to include this example, as the expression "most beautiful confirmation" indicates, even if it rests on a mere coincidence. It appears that Freud introduces the examples regarding womb phantasies only to consolidate his emphasis on the familiar in the uncanny.[127] Freud again exploits the pun on "Heim" (home), just as he did in the statement "the *unheimlich* is what was once *heimisch*, familiar" (SE 17, 245, 20–1, italics original).

Freud's seemingly unassailable pun that "un-" denotes the token of repression draws its power from the association of the prefix, in the reader's mind, with its function in the word "unbewußt" (unconscious) in Freud's sense, for which the statement is appropriate. "Un-" can indeed be seen as a token of repression for the cases Freud discusses, but in a manner not made explicit by Freud, if we shift the emphasis from the "familiar" (heimlich) component in the repressed to the fact that the repressed resides in a sphere shielded from the scrutiny of consciousness.

The Freudian definition of the uncanny, as the familiar appearing strange, although not at all foregrounded in Freud's essay, warrants a serious examination. Critics have deducted the concept of the domestic or "homely" as uncanny from Freud's justifiable claim that repression is one of the sources of the uncanny.[128] Nevertheless, the familiar that appears as uncanny appears only on the periphery of Freud's investigation, contrary to Freud's announcement at the beginning of the essay:

> [...] the uncanny is that class of the frightening that leads back to what is known of old and familiar. How this is possible, in what circumstances the familiar can become uncanny and frightening, I shall show in what follows. (SE 17, 220, 25–9)

Freud never deals with familiar objects that suddenly appear uncanny in his essay. His examples illustrate the familiar origin of phenomena that appear at first peculiar and strange. Freud then explains how these frightening things can be traced back to something familiar in the past. Nevertheless, in the more recent reception of the uncanny, the concept has become increasingly identified with those instances when the familiar suddenly appears frightening. Familiar phenomena can suddenly appear uncanny from a purely cognitive perspective if one of their qualities was previously overlooked, and the new quality adds a disorienting ambiguity. In the cases that are linked to repression, the uncanniness is caused by the defamiliarizing power of repression that Freud excludes in his essay.[129]

Although Freud deals mainly with the estranged or unrecognized familiar eliciting the uncanny impression, the subject matter of the strangely familiar appears on the periphery of his essay, in the topics of *déjà vu* and involuntary repetition, although they are not classified by Freud explicitly as instances of the familiar appearing uncanny:

> [...] whenever a man dreams of a place or a country and says to himself, while he is still dreaming: "this place is familiar to me, I've been here before", [we may interpret the place as being his mother's genitals or her body]. (SE 245, 16–20)

Déjà vu can take two basic forms.[130] We are either confronted with something that is in fact familiar, but we are unable to explain why it appears familiar to us.[131] This case still conforms to the strange that has a concealed familiar kernel. Alternatively, *déjà vu* can occur when we have in fact never been at a certain place before, but it appears familiar to us nevertheless. It is possible that some aspect of the strange place, possibly some hidden contiguity with a repressed familiar content, has prompted us to project familiarity onto the strange place. Alternatively, repression need not play a role at all. The false recognition could be a memory malfunction, in which we falsely process an impression as recognized when it is in fact new.[132] The disorientation caused by this malfunction would still be perceived as uncanny.

We can illuminate the uncanniness of *déjà vu* by drawing on Freud's comments regarding "fausse reconnaissance."[133] Freud gives an explanation for the connection between repression and false recognition (fausse reconnaissance) in a letter regarding his visit to the Acropolis (1936a). He traces his exclamation "So all this really *does* exist [...]" to a repressed shame about achievements formed in childhood.[134] Although the example makes it quite clear that repression acts not on the object of perception but on the observer's ability to perceive the object clearly, this aspect is not made explicit by Freud himself.[135] It is surprising that Freud's inclusion of *déjà vu* in "The 'Uncanny'" did not prompt him to focus more strongly on the observer's role. Instead, Freud focuses exclusively on the class of objects constituting the uncanny, and uncanniness is never described as repression's effect on perception. Once we focus on the observer, however, it becomes clear that the uncanny is always the effect of some disturbance of perception, the "lack of orientation" identified by Jentsch, regardless of whether the disturbance has internal origins, as in the case of repression, or external ones, such as mist, darkness or optical illusions.

In the majority of Freud's examples, we are confronted with phenomena that are erroneously perceived as strange, because repression disables recognition. In the events of *déjà vu* and fausse reconnaissance, on the other hand, re-cognition occurs, but the reason for the recognition is concealed, because the phenomena were repressed. Both cases are troubled forms of recognition, encounters with the strangely familiar, but in the first instance, the object appears first as strange and then reveals a familiar component, whereas in the second case, the object appears familiar, and then reveals a strange or unsettling component.[136]

Critics have suggested that there is something intrinsically un-canny about the home and the familiar. Let us consider the following statement by Cixous:

> Why is it that [...] the familiar become[s] so disquieting? The answer is less buried than we might suspect. The obliteration of any separation [...] all that which [...] assures satisfaction and appears to affirm the life forces [...] has another face turned toward death. (Cixous 544–5)

This observation uncovers why extreme coziness can become uncanny. If we define "coziness" as a state of mind in which the fear of outside dangers is temporarily forgotten, the outside dangers are the phenomenon that made coziness possible in the first place. Perfect and absolute familiarity is unthinkable without strangeness. The exclusion of threat is always an illusion, because the inevitability of death is only temporarily put out of mind. The familiar in a pure form never appears in reality. The division between inside and outside is only possible when an "inside" and an "outside" exist. A complete "obliteration of any separation" is impossible, because meaning requires separation. Nevertheless, if death is complete nothingness, then absence of separation is also a theoretical representation of death.[137] If repression is interpreted in this most extreme form, as an attempted exclusion that runs counter to logic, then the return of the repressed is a consequence of logic, embodied in the laws of language, rather than only an empirical process. Lacan's (1966) dictum that "in the unconscious is the whole structure of a language" thus finds expression in Cixous's reflections about Freud (Lacan, "Function and Field" 147). The uncanny feeling arising when a threat cannot be clearly identified is possibly not a conscious perception. Nevertheless, it need not have unconscious causes in the manner defined by Freud. Freud's enterprise may not only have been overzealous in disregarding the factors for the uncanny in the cognitive and perceptual realm, but the prevalence of especially sexual repression in Western culture may have and may still be creating a distortion about the factors involved in the uncanny. This exclusion accounts for some of the unresolved questions in Freud's model of the uncanny.

In the stories treated in the following chapters, the uncanny events depicted on the plot level contain the element of cognitive uncertainty, but this uncertainty is recreated also by the formal indeterminacy of the text as a whole. The indeterminacy of these texts forms the counterpart to the cognitive uncertainty we have identified as the overlooked factor in every uncanny experience. The selected stories enable the readers' interpretative activity to enter and affect the plot. The stories generate a type of textual paranoia by leaving the reader uncertain about the significance of the contiguous or similar elements that appear to be presented as clues. While in psychoanalytic readings modeled on Freud's definition of the uncanny the changing reality status in the texts only represents the madness of characters, a reading of these stories as *uncanny texts* allows us to view the madness represented *in* the text as a manifestation of the paradoxical reading experience, the madness *of* the text.

Chapter 3:
E.T.A. Hoffmann's "Der Sandmann" –
A Story of Persecution
Told by a Persecuted Narrator

> Why are some poetic works so ineffectual, even if they
> are well executed in form and detail, so that we are not
> enticed by them? It can only be that the poet did not
> really see what he is describing. [...] Can the char-
> acters of such a poet – who is not a true prophet [*poeta
> vates*] according to the old word – be anything but de-
> ceiving puppets, arduously glued together from
> unfamiliar materials![1]

A reinterpretation of Hoffmann's "Der Sandmann" (1816) is
crucial for a reevaluation of the uncanny, because both Freud
(1919h) and Jentsch (1906) use the story as a paradigm (Freud,
"The 'Uncanny'"; Jentsch). Furthermore, Freud's interpretation of
"Der Sandmann" has become an integral part of the definition of
the uncanny.[1] As stated in the Introduction and the discussion of
Freud, it is essential to reintroduce Jentsch's emphasis on the
factor of cognitive uncertainty into the uncanny.

It might be helpful to recapitulate the main events in the story,
although known to most readers. The student Nathanael has been
obsessed with the Sandman since childhood. Nathanael's nanny
tells him that the Sandman comes at night to pluck out children's
eyes. Nathanael identifies the Sandman with the lawyer Coppelius,
who collaborates with Nathanael's father on secret experiments.
The childhood obsession comes to a head when Nathanael hides
in the father's laboratory to get a glimpse of the Sandman, only to
be discovered and threatened by Coppelius. Nathanael has a
breakdown, recovers, but his father continues his association with

Coppelius and is killed in a laboratory explosion. Nathanael, now a student, suspects that Coppelius has returned as the lens-salesman Coppola. While Nathanael at first tries to convince himself that he is only paranoid, his suspicions are confirmed when he finds out that Olimpia, with whom he has fallen in love, is a life-like doll, created by Coppola and Prof. Spalanzani. He has another break-down, but again recovers and is reunited with his former fiancée, Clara. Just before he is about to get married to Clara, Coppelius reappears, and it is suggested that this drives Nathanael to madness and suicide.

Freud's exclusion of uncertainty is particularly pronounced in his interpretation of "Der Sandmann," and this exclusion becomes a dominant theme in the rest of his essay. This is very clear in Freud's discussion of Coppelius and Coppola:

> [...] the conclusion of the story makes it quite clear that Coppola the optician really *is* the lawyer Coppelius, and also, therefore, the Sand-Man. There is no question therefore, of any intellectual uncertainty here [...]. (SE 17, 230, 28–32 [emphasis in the translation only])

> Der Schluß der Erzählung macht es ja klar, daß der Optiker Coppola wirklich der Advokat Coppelius und also auch Der Sandmann ist. Eine "intellektuelle Ungewißheit" kommt hier nicht mehr in Frage [...]. (GW XII, 242)

This statement is indicative of Freud's general opinion that intellectual uncertainty is irrelevant for the uncanny. Whether or not the two men are identical is a crucial question. Although Freud is correct in finding reasons to agree with Nathanael's perspective, the text does not resolve the issue of his paranoia conclusively. While we find instances in the text that confirm that Coppola and Coppelius are both incarnations of the Sandman, we can only infer this identity, by circumstantial textual evidence, rather than finding any explicit confirmation for it anywhere in the text. Instead, the very fact that we are unsure about this issue contributes greatly to the uncanny uncertainty that disorients us as readers.[2]

Hoffmann's text embodies the Freudian concept of the uncanny as the return of the repressed. Clues in the text suggest that the phantom Sandman, the figure that may be both Coppelius and Coppola and that constitutes the uncanny on the diegetic level, is the personified return of the repressed, created by a retreat into the idyllic. The idyllic appears as an artificial exclusion of threat that leads to the unnoticed invasion by the very threat that was forcibly denied, represented by Nathanael's fiancée Clara and her brother Lothar. Finally, however, the text's ambiguities result also from extradiegetic components.[3] The text possesses a structure that creates uncertainty about the significance of its clues. The text employs its extradiegetic structure to achieve the uncanny effect. It supplies an additional layer of evidence for the conspiracy that is not visible to the characters. This body of evidence, although it supports the suspicions Nathanael rejects, is ultimately as inconclusive as the evidence Nathanael takes into consideration. The formal elements of the text thus create an uncanny reading experience.

One of the factors contributing to our unstable position as readers in "Der Sandmann" is our reliance on Nathanael as a possibly insane focalizer of the action, which leads to a contamination of the reader by Nathanael's paranoid uncertainty about the interpretation of his observations as clues to a conspiracy.[4] The first half of the story consists of an exchange of letters and the second half is told by the narrator, but the events are reported mainly from Nathanael's perspective, with very few exceptions.[5] In particular, the long letter at the beginning, in which Nathanael retells his childhood, constitutes a case in which a possibly insane narrator suspects and then rejects the possibility of being persecuted.[6] Punter mentions this scenario in a passage in which he discusses the centrality of paranoia as a primary motif in the Romantic prose: "[…] it is very difficult to know where the reader is situated in an encounter with a story of persecution told by the persecuted" (Punter, *Literature of Terror* 157). Within the context of his first letter, Nathanael as first person narrator presents us with a special case of narrative unreliability. Wayne C. Booth (1961) defined the term unreliable narrator in the following way:

> For lack of better terms, I have called a narrator *reliable* when he speaks for or acts in accordance with the norms of the work (which is to say, the implied author's norms), *unreliable* when he does not. (Booth 158–9, Booth's emphasis)

We will use "unreliable narrator" in a somewhat modified sense, because the discrepancy in "Der Sandmann" exists not in relation to the implied "norms of the work" but to the seemingly incorrect conclusions Nathanael draws from the events that we witness through him as focalizer. In "Der Sandmann," we are on unstable ground in relation to the inconclusive events in the text, not only when they are reported by the possibly insane first person narrator, but also when the allegedly objective third person narrator takes over in the second half of the story.[7]

More specifically, the uncanniness of Hoffmann's story lies in what can be called a *textual paranoia*.[8] Paranoid individuals are unable to assess the significance of their perceptions concerning a possible threat because of deficient reality testing skills. They are convinced of a conspiracy because they resolve particular ambiguities in an obsessively one-sided manner. The definition of paranoia used here is more recent than Freud's. Repressed homosexual impulses are no longer seen as the primary cause of paranoia.[9] "Der Sandmann" can be called a *paranoiac text* because we share with Nathanael an initial uncertainty about how to interpret what constitutes a meaningful clue. While deficient reality testing ability plagues Nathanael, who denies clues that he is persecuted, the reader cannot reject Nathanael's denials conclusively. The paranoid individual misinterprets ambiguous or inconclusive evidence.[10]

Furthermore, the uncertainty that can lead to paranoia is recreated not only through our identification with the character's experiences on the diegetic level but also by the more subtle elements of the text's inner organization. While we find instances in the text that seem to confirm that Coppola and Coppelius are both incarnations of the Sandman, we can only infer this identity, by circumstantial textual evidence, rather than finding any explicit confirmation anywhere in the text. The paranoid individual "reads into" occurrences and believes that their coherence signifies a conspiracy. The reader of "Der Sandmann" is confronted by ambiguities that are structurally similar to the ones confronting the protagonist. While Nathanael at times draws one-sided, obsessive conclusions, the certainty we believe to have in the world that creates the backdrop to Nathanael's world, and which we recognize as a representation of our own, is itself subjected to doubts. "Der Sandmann" raises the suspicion that reality is itself a result of interpretation and that our certainty about reality is perhaps a selective perception similar to a paranoid delusion.

The most important source of the uncanny in "Der Sandmann," is neither the doll Olimpia, nor the Sandman in his various incarnations, but the involvement of the reader in Nathanael's madness through poetic attributes that constitute the text's unity as a work of art. All literary texts motivate the reader to go beyond literal meaning, and extradiegetic elements always create a poetic dimension. In the case of uncanny texts, however, these poetic elements recreate the disorienting aspects of the uncanny experiences of an often insane, paranoid protagonist.

As we uncover buried textual evidence in Hoffmann's story, a gradual shift in our evaluation of the text's genre takes place, from realistic to fantastic, and a strange interplay begins between what we at first may perceive as madness, and a scenario that becomes increasingly plausible. The gradual revelation of clues supporting what must be supernatural events contributes greatly to the uncanniness of the text. We may, for example, at first see Nathanael as the romantic individual who has become prone to delusions because of a childhood trauma. Nevertheless, we later come to doubt the assuaging admonitions of Clara and her brother Lothar, the advocates of common sense rationality, who insist that the uncanny phenomena Nathanael reports are only figments of his imagination. Our initial insecurity about the life status of the automaton Olimpia, for example, or the unclear relationship between Coppelius and Coppola, gradually recedes.[11] Therefore, we have to revise our initial evaluation of the story as a realistic tale with a mad protagonist, and it increasingly becomes a Fantastic tale in which automata and supernatural metamorphoses like walking bushes exist. This transformation from one genre to the other is never fully completed, however, and the realistic and supernatural contexts coexist as conflicting but equally viable interpretations. This simultaneity of the two genres is an important source of the extradiegetic uncanny.

juxtaposed

In addition, the self-reflexive incorporation of the text's poetological program into its own fictional world adds another uncanny dimension. Clara's admonition that Nathanael's fears are only the product of his imagination turns out to be an accurate description of the fantastic possibilities inherent in the fictional world Hoffmann has created. Nathanael as author is given the uncanny ability to affect his own fate. The text allows for a reality in which the interpretations the characters offer for ambiguous phenomena are able to affect the reality they inhabit.

The First Encounter with the Sandman

Nathanael's home may appear peaceful at first, with the father reading from books and smoking his pipe. Nevertheless, the visits by Coppelius reveal a different side of this world. Before such visits, the father is silent. Maybe he does not let his wife know ahead of time when Coppelius is coming, because he knows she disapproves of these visits. On such evenings, the mother is sad, but she does not openly express her disapproval with the father's experiments (SmE 39; SmG 332, 22). The mother also tries to get the children to go to bed by saying: "[...] the Sandman is coming. I can tell" (SmE 29). In the German original, the statement "the Sandman is coming" ("Der Sandmann kommt") expresses several things at once. The mother could be referring to the Sandman of folklore, who helps children go to sleep, because she senses Nathanael's fatigue. She could also, however, be "reading" the father's silence as a sign that Coppelius is coming. The utterance "I can tell" would then be a concealed allusion to the feared visitor. She thus avoids both the direct confrontation with her husband, and conceals the identity of the visitor to her son. The identification of Sandman and Coppelius, which becomes such a powerful obsession for Nathanael, has its origin in his mother's avoidance of the conflict with her husband. Nathanael's obsession with the Sandman begins with his mother's ambiguous explanation.[12] Even Nathanael's challenge to the evasion leads to more dodging:

"There is no Sandman, dear," Mother replied; "when I say the Sandman is coming, it only means that you are all sleepy and can't keep your eyes open, as if someone had scattered sand in them." (SmE 39)

"Es gibt keinen Sandmann, mein liebes Kind", erwiderte die Mutter: "wenn ich sage, der Sandmann kommt, so will das nur heißen, ihr seid schläfrig und könnt die Augen nicht offen behalten, als hätte man euch Sand hineinge-streut." (SmG 332, 30–3)

The mother seems to be saying that the Sandman does not exist in reality, only in legend. Nathanael rightly suspects that his mother is hiding something, even if he believes the motive is to shield him and his sister from fear (SmE 39; SmG 332, 36–7). The mother gives an evasive answer even after the experience in the laboratory, when Nathanael finally awakens and screams: "Is the Sandman still here?" (SmE 47). His mother never asks him where the fear of the Sandman originated and thus never finds out about the nanny's cruel modification of the Sandman myth, in which the nanny explains that the Sandman comes at night to tear out the eyes of children to give them to his bird-children to eat (SmE 47, 49; SmG 336, 40–337, 2).[13]

Nathanael asks the nanny about the Sandman because he does not receive an explanation from his mother. The nanny's tale gives Nathanael's obsession with the Sandman more nourishment. It is important to note that the nanny's explanation deviates from the traditional Sandman belief in folklore. She takes the traditional belief only as her starting point and adds a cannibalistic extension all her own. The Sandman belief is the same in Germany as in other Western cultures; he is part of the inventory of childhood folklore that is given up later. He is a little fairy or dwarf who comes at night to put the children to sleep. The "sand" in the corners of the eyes in the morning is proof that he was there.[14] The nanny's explanation of the Sandman's significance, as a man who comes at night to steal children's eyes to give them to his own bird children as fodder, is a gruesome alteration.[15]

Nathanael's fear of the Sandman also originates in a coincidence. When Nathanael sees Coppelius in the father's laboratory, he expects to see Sandman. Nonetheless, he has modeled his image of the Sandman based on the most gruesome real person he has met, Coppelius. The confrontation with Coppelius in the laboratory is, from Nathanael's point of view, the materialization of an imagined figure. For Nathanael, the accuracy of the image he has created confirms the image, rather than revealing its origin. Nathanael believes the fearsome real person he has known all along is the feared imagined person. These circumstances weld the spheres of reality and imagination together and help to explain why Nathanael has difficulty in keeping these realms apart later.

Critics have interpreted the first laboratory experience as a modified primal scene and a Lacanian confrontation with the law of the father.[16] These interpretations are helpful if we see the roots of Nathanael's troubles in his difficulties with his sexuality.[17] Nonetheless, such interpretations reduce the fantastical events in the story to an allegorical representation of unconscious processes, in which the Sandman represents the return of the repressed. Instead, the laboratory scene is the first instance in which the spheres of reality and imagination become intermingled. At this early stage, this intermixture occurs only in Nathanael's mind, but it becomes a model for the unstable status of the reality in "Der Sandmann." Nathanael's imagination is endowed with the power to materially create the phantoms in the fictional world that he inhabits.

Three factors in his childhood contribute to Nathanael's later troubles. One is the secrecy between his parents, the second the nanny's horrific version of the Sandman belief, which becomes an obsession fuelled by Nathanael's artistic inclinations (demonstrated in drawing and reading), and the third is the traumatic confrontation with the feared figure of the Sandman himself, the incident in the father's laboratory, discussed below. This incident constitutes the first time in his life when prophesy and expectation, in the form of the nanny's tale and his own fantasies, are fulfilled.

The Ambiguous Depiction of Nathanael's Insanity

Two factors determine our evaluation of Nathanael's insanity. His own experiences on the one hand, and the evaluation of his experiences by his environment on the other hand. The first is exemplified by his coma-like state after the first laboratory scene, and later his frenzy on the tower. Our first close look at the childhood scenario has shown how Nathanael would be prone to such states. The other factor, third party confirmation of abnormal events, decides whether these are products of his imagination or real within the world that the characters inhabit. If the events are inexplicable and not corroborated by the world around him, he is likely to be insane, whereas if his extraordinary experiences are publicly acknowledged, and thus established as fact, it is not justified to call him insane. The degree to which Nathanael's experiences fall either into the first or the second category influences how the reader evaluates his sanity and, as we shall see later, also affects

Hoffmann's critique of the world surrounding Nathanael. The public recognition of the doll Olimpia moves the text into the fantastic genre and changes the evaluation of Coppelius's miraculous operation on Nathanael. Hidden clues foreshadowing Olimpia's true nature as automaton appear. These clues reveal how Coppola and Spalanzani conspire to deceive the public with their lifelike creation. The discussion of these clues will prepare for the examination of the possible identity of Coppelius and Coppola.

What we might label Nathanael's paranoia has its roots in a crucial event in his childhood, the moment when he discovers that his father and Coppelius are at work in the laboratory. Coppelius allegedly unscrews Nathanael's limbs, places them at different joints, and puts them back the way they were before, all without physical injury. We rely entirely on Nathanael's recollection of this scene, because he reports this incident in his first letter to Lothar. We can therefore doubt its truth in two ways. It is possible that Nathanael is so shocked to see Coppelius that his perceptions become distorted from this moment on. The episode is then part of a madness during childhood. Nathanael might also have distorted the events in his memory. In either case the event never would actually have taken place. This possibility exists because there is no outside corroboration for the accuracy of Nathanael's recollections.

Alternatively, if we believe Nathanael's report, Coppelius has supernatural surgical abilities, because unscrewing limbs is impossible without serious injury. If we decide the event actually did take place, we have to reevaluate the genre of the story. While the story presents itself up that point as grounded in the laws of everyday reality, it now becomes a fantastic tale.[18] This shift of genre is complete in the second laboratory scene, where Olimpia's artificiality is revealed. Again, there are two men experimenting in a laboratory, one of whom may be Coppelius's returned double. The product of their work, the human doll Olimpia, is not Nathanael's fantasy, but must be real, because she is presented to and witnessed by the general public.

Reader-Dependent Clues about Olimpia

There are hidden clues suggesting that Olimpia is an automaton before this is confirmed. These are also examples of Hoffmann teaching us how to become better readers. Olimpia is such a good imitation of a human being that everyone is fooled at first. Nathanael's friend, Siegmund, expresses some doubts, but does not notice she is a puppet: "Do me a favor [...] and tell me how you [...] could be smitten with that waxface, with that wooden doll?" (SmE 87); "[...] tu mir den Gefallen und sage mir, wie es dir [...] möglich war, dich in das Wachsgesicht, in die Holzpuppe da drüben zu vergaffen" (SmG 356, 9–11). Siegmund's derogatory remarks characterize someone he believes to be a living woman. He compares Olimpia to a "wooden doll" to express that she lacks grace or dances badly, but he unknowingly also expresses the truth. At this point neither Nathanael nor the reader knows she is an automaton.

A more concealed reference to Olimpia's true status appears when Nathanael leads her out to dance after she has sat down: "[...] to his amazement, Olimpia sat out every dance afterward and he did not fail to lead her out again and again" (SmE 85); "[...] zu seinem Erstaunen blieb darauf Olimpia bei jedem Tanze sitzen und er ermangelte nicht, immer wieder sie aufzuziehen" (SmG 354, 32). The word Hoffmann uses is "aufziehen," which is lost in the translation. The word means both "to pull up" – literally, by her hands, while she is sitting on the chair – and "winding up," as of a clock. Hoffmann makes sure we do not suspect immediately that Olimpia is a robot, but gives us a glimpse of what we find out later.[19]

Another reference to Olimpia's artificial status is contained in the awkward spelling of her name. Based on the classical root, the spelling should be "Olympia," but Hoffmann changes the spelling to "Olimpia."[20] Consequently, when reading the German original, the reader will feel that there is something peculiar about this woman's name from the moment she appears. It is thus regrettable that the English translations have erased this intentional misspelling and rendered the doll as "Olympia."

Finally, Olimpia's puppet status is confirmed beyond Nathanael's individual experience by outside observers. In contrast to the first laboratory scene, the Olimpia story is told in the third person.[21] We leave all uncertainty behind when Olimpia is discussed in public, in tea-circles, by lawyers, and a professor of literature, and when there is a criminal investigation, which prompts both Spalanzani and Coppola to flee.[22] The events of the first laboratory scene, especially the miraculous operation performed on Nathanael, now can be seen as actual, albeit fantastical occurrences. Once the story has crossed the genre boundary into the region of the fantastic, the likelihood increases that Coppola is indeed Coppelius in disguise.

Chapter 4:
Clues Confirming the Existence of the Sandman

Nathanael's fears are warranted by several elements of the plot. As already mentioned, his death constitutes the confirmation of the dark fate that he feels awaits him. This is true regardless of whether his fears are based on erroneous assumptions or whether we are clear about what exactly causes his death. After all, either a fantastical power is directing his fate or his death is the result of psychic derangement. Regardless of these alternatives, we have seen that some of Nathanael's fears are confirmed by third parties, indicating that Nathanael, although he has paranoid fears, may indeed be the victim of persecution. Such confirmation sometimes comes from textual signals visible only to the reader.

Diegetic Signals

There are a number of incidents on the plot level that are ambiguous, because of a similarity that could be entirely accidental or that points to some hidden connection. Freud comments on coincidences in "The 'Uncanny'" (1919h), where he cites a personal experience involving the number 62: "[…] or if we begin to notice that everything which has a number […] invariably has the same one, or at all events one which contains the same figures" (SE 17, 238, 2–5). As Freud puts it, if you are not immune to the temptation of superstition, you will attribute some secret meaning to the recurrence of the number. As discussed in the Freud chapter, incidents that conflict with the randomness of experience appear as more than only coincidences. We suspect some agency behind the unlikely regularity. The first coincidence that confirms

Nathanael's allegedly irrational fear of the Sandman is the unexpected confirmation of Coppelius in the role of the Sandman.

Coppelius is linked to Coppola also through the threat to Nathanael's eyes. This threat first appears in the nanny's tale and is repeated by Coppelius's demand: "Bring some eyes, bring some eyes!" (SmE 47) "Augen her, Augen her!" (SmG 336, 18). It is not surprising that Nathanael, given his traumatic childhood experience, will become suspicious of Coppola, because apart from reminding him of Coppelius in appearance, Coppola calls his optical instruments "nice eyes" ("Sköne Oke"). Later, Spalanzani's ominous claim that Olimpia's eyes were taken from Nathanael further emphasizes the threat to his eyes.[1] The reader is given no indication, however, that Nathanael notices the connection between the two men.

Extradiegetic Signals

The connection between Coppelius and Coppola is confirmed through details of characterization and metaphoric links. While these are extradiegetic connections, visible only to the reader, the details of characterization are part of the diegesis but overlooked by Nathanael. Nonetheless, such elements also have an extradiegetic dimension, because they are only recorded as inconsequential sense impressions for Nathanael yet are meaningful clues for the reader.

There are a number of traits shared by Coppelius and Coppola, which increases the likelihood that they are the same person. Coppelius has "two greenish cat's eyes" that "gleamed piercingly" (SmE 43).[2] Although the color of the glass salesman's eyes is not mentioned, the description of his eyes exhibits certain similarities to Coppelius: "But then Coppola stepped completely into the room and [...] his small eyes gleamed piercingly [...]" (SmE 77); "Da trat aber Coppola vollends in die Stube und sprach mit heiserem Ton, indem [...] die kleinen Augen [...] stechend hervorfunkelten" (SmG 351, 3–4). We find not only the same trait but also the same syntax, the same adverb-verb-combination ("gleamed piercingly"; "stechend hervorfunkel[te]n"). We detect a similar parallel in Nathanael's first description of Coppelius, which establishes that "[H]is crooked mouth was frequently twisted into a malicious smile" (SmE 43).[3] Coppola exhibits a "malicious smile" (SmE 79) during the sale of the telescope.[4] Nathanael does not comment on these parallels, so we cannot be sure whether he notices them consciously or whether they contribute subliminally to his suspicion that Coppelius and Coppola are the same person.

The identity between Coppelius and Coppola is also hinted at in the similarity of their voices. Although it is a hint visible to the reader, the second laboratory scene demonstrates that Nathanael overlooks this similarity. When Nathanael goes to Spalanzani's apartment to visit Olimpia, he hears voices inside: "The voices that were thus buzzing and raging confusedly were those of Spalanzani and the hideous Coppelius" (SmE 91); "Es waren Spalanzanis und des gräßlichen Coppelius Stimmen, die so durcheinander schwirr-ten und tobten" (SmG 358, 34). Although Nathanael apparently expects to find Coppelius inside, he discovers Coppola. Neverthe-less, he does not notice the mix-up, nor does the narrator mention it. For the reader, however, this misidentification shows that Nathanael's hearing may be more accurate than he himself ac-knowledges. When Nathanael approaches Spalanzani's apartment, he hears only the sound of a voice. Nathanael has relied only on his hearing during the numerous times in his childhood when the Sandman visited, and Nathanael only hears him behind closed doors. Coppelius's voice may thus have left a lasting impression on Nathanael. We would therefore expect that he could trust his ears when he hears Coppelius. Nevertheless, once he sees Coppola, he apparently forgets that he has just heard the voice of Coppelius.

The voices of Coppelius and Coppola are similar also in a shared hoarseness. When he first appears, "Coppelius [...] call[s] [...] in a hoarse, snarling voice" (SmE 45, and 47); "mit heiserer, schnarrender Stimme" (SmG 336, 1). The same hoarseness is associated with Coppola's voice three times: "[...] Coppola [asked] with his repellent, hoarse voice" (SmE 79); "frug Coppola mit seiner widerwärtigen heisern Stimme" (SmG 352, 11–13), "Coppola [...] said, hoarsely" (SmE 77); "Coppola [...] sprach [...] mit heiserem Ton" (SmG 350–1), and again: "[Coppola], [w]ith a hoarse, repellent laugh [...]" (SmE 77); "Coppola [...] mit heiserem widrigen Lachen [...]" (SmG 351, 23). From the reader's perspective, these parallels validate Nathanael's sense that Coppelius is identical to Coppola, although neither Nathanael nor the narrator ever focus on the parallels. The question of whether Nathanael is paranoid thus remains open, although the corresponding traits could be seen as confirmation that he is being persecuted.

is he a victim of paranoia or a conspiracy?

Potential Insights Contained in Instances of Disavowal

The above-discussed parallels between Coppelius and Coppola are visible only to the reader, while Nathanael is unaware of them. Let us assume that the clues we discussed have a subliminal effect on Nathanael. Together, they may prompt what is commonly understood as an intuition, an indefinite notion whose exact cause we cannot identify. Nathanael seems to be torn between acknowledging these disturbing discoveries and shying away from them.

Coppelius and Coppola exhibit an idiosyncrasy of speech that is an indication that they are doubles. To select only a prominent example for each man, let us look at the first laboratory scene:

> It seemed to me as if human faces were visible all around, but without eyes – with hideous deep, black cavities instead. "Bring some eyes, bring some eyes!" Coppelius called in hollow rumbling tones [...]. (SmE 47)

> Mir war es als würden Menschengesichter ringsumher sichtbar, aber ohne Augen – scheußliche, tiefe schwarze Höhlen statt ihrer. "Augen her, Augen her!" rief Coppelius mit dumpfer dröhnender Stimme [...]. (SmG 336, 16–18)

Coppola offers his eyeglasses with the same repetitious figure of speech to Nathanael: "beau'ful eye – beau'ful eye!" (SmE 77)[5] and later "beau'ful glass – beau'ful glass!" (SmE 79).[6] The personal mannerism of the Sandman in his different incarnations suggests his double existence. Nathanael also jumps to his death with the cry "'*Sköne Oke – Sköne Oke.*'" (SmG 362, 41).

Clara and Lothar struggle to convince Nathanael that Coppola and Coppelius are not identical. The reader can detect, however, that Nathanael has merely denied his anxious feelings. His fears are still visible in the ideas he entertains to calm himself, just after he buys the spy-glass from Coppola, albeit in the negative:

> As soon as the spectacles were gone, Nathanael grew perfectly calm and, thinking of Clara, he realized that the terrible apparition had only been a figment of his imagination, and that Coppola might be a highly honorable mechanician [sic! not "mechanic"] and optician, but could in no way be the accursed double and ghost of Coppelius. (SmE 77, 79)

> Sowie die Brillen fort waren, wurde Nathanael ganz ruhig und an Clara denkend sah er wohl ein, daß der entsetzliche Spuk nur aus seinem Innern hervorgegangen, sowie daß Coppola ein höchst ehrlicher Mechanikus und Optikus, keineswegs aber Coppelii verfluchter Doppeltgänger und Revenant sein könne. (SmG 351, 26–31)

Nathanael's denial of his earlier suspicion is not unqualified. He acknowledges that he is not sure about Coppola's identity ("might be an honorable mechanician"). However, the persuasiveness of the phrase "he realized that Coppola might be [...] highly honorable" is diminished by the tentativeness of "might be" ("keineswegs [...] sein könne"), which invalidates the assertiveness that "realized" ("sah wohl ein") implies. The forced attempt at calming himself makes the reader suspect that Nathanael suppresses an insight, namely that Coppola is indeed Coppelius's "accursed double and ghost." On the other hand, we are given no hard evidence to reject Clara's rational opinion.[7] One of the terms Nathanael uses is "*Revenant*" (ghost). The German word has

French origin and means, literally, "the one who has returned." There is no reason to assume that Coppelius has died, and his appearance at the end proves indeed that he is not dead and has returned. Hence, Nathanael, when rejecting his suspicion that Coppola could be the ghost of Coppelius, reveals his disavowed suspicion to the reader that Coppelius has indeed returned, disguised as Coppola.

Let us examine another instance in which Nathanael tries to make himself believe that Coppola has nothing to do with Coppelius:

> Anyway, it is fairly certain that the barometer vendor Guiseppe Coppola is not at all the same man as old lawyer Coppelius. I am attending lectures given by a newly arrived professor [...]. [Spalanzani] has known Coppola for many years and, besides, one can tell from his speech that he really is a Piedmontese [...].
> My mind is not completely at ease [...]. I cannot rid myself of the impression which Coppelius' [sic!][8] accursed face makes on me. (SmE 59)

> Übrigens ist es wohl gewiß, daß der Wetterglashändler Guiseppe Coppola keinesweges [sic] der alte Advokat Coppelius ist [...]. [Spalanzani] kennt den Coppola schon seit vielen Jahren und überdem hört man es auch seiner Aussprache an, daß er wirklich Piemonteser ist [...]. Ganz beruhigt bin ich nicht [...] nicht los kann ich den Eindruck werden, den Coppelius' verfluchtes Gesicht auf mich macht. (SmG 342, 4–15)

When we hear later that Coppola and Spalanzani are collaborating on the outrageous project of creating a human doll, we see why Spalanzani may not have told Nathanael the full truth about Coppola. Therefore, Nathanael's suspicion ("My mind is not completely at ease [...]") that Coppola is feigning an accent may be justified. It is possible that in his childhood, Nathanael heard Coppelius speak with an Italian accent, without yet being able to identify it. Accents can be simulated, but the sound of a voice remains the same. Coppelius and Coppola's voice would have the same sound, and the similarity is indeed indicated by the incident discussed above, when Nathanael mistakes Coppola for Coppelius.

It is remarkable that Nathanael overlooks this similarity in the tone of voice and engages instead in dubious reasoning about accents.

Is Nathanael denying the connection between the two men? The incident could be an example of what Freud calls "Verneinung" (negation):

> Thus the content of a repressed image or idea can make its way into consciousness, on condition that it is *negated*. Negation is a way of taking cognizance of what is repressed [...]. (Freud, "Negation" 235, Freud's emphasis)

> Ein verdrängter Vorstellungs- oder Gedankeninhalt kann also zum Bewußtsein vordringen, unter der Bedingung, daß er sich *verneinen* läßt. Die Verneinung ist eine Art, das Verdrängte zur Kenntnis zu nehmen [...]. (GW XIV, 12, Freud's emphasis)

Freud uses the expression "zur Kenntnis nehmen" ("to acknowledge"). The *Standard Edition* adds a footnote regarding issues of translation: "The German '*verneinen*' is here translated by 'to negate' instead of by the more usual 'to deny', in order to avoid confusion with the German '*verleugnen*', which has also in the past been rendered by 'to deny'. In this edition, 'to disavow' has in general been used for the latter German word" (Freud, "Negation" 235, Footnote 2). This explanation supports the usage of "disavowal" and "denial" as a synonym for negation. Through negation, repression is in effect not truly undone, because although the repressed is partially acknowledged intellectually, the emotional aspect remains unacknowledged. Repression is different from disavowal, because repression is a completely unconscious process (a "forgetting").[9] Negation is a common reaction to a confrontation with the uncanny. Negation may evoke the uncanny, not only because it involves a partial return of the repressed, but also because it evokes the uncanny by association.

Nathanael's denial of a possible connection between Coppelius and Coppelius is visible in his odd usage of the German word "ehrlich" (honest). The word creates a suspicion about their

105

honesty and also adds a purely textual link between the two men. In the passage quoted earlier, Nathanael reminds himself that he considers Coppola's Piedmontese accent to be genuine. He reasons that Coppola could not be the same person as Coppelius, because he would have spoken German with an accent from that Italian region. Nathanael does not remember Coppelius having had such an accent, but then he begins to question the accuracy of his memory: "Coppelius was a German, but, as I believe, not a respectable one" (SmE 59); "Coppelius war ein Deutscher, aber wie mich dünkt, kein ehrlicher" (SmG 342, 13). Nathanael uses "honest, respectable" (ehrlich) instead of "genuine" (echt) or "real" (wirklich). This can mean that Coppelius was "not truly a German after all." In addition, it expands the scope of Nathanael's doubts and raises questions about Coppelius's respectability (implying "Coppelius was a lying or deceiving German"). In this instance, Nathanael's awkward usage raises precisely the kinds of doubts for the reader that Nathanael's utterance aims to dispel.

Nathanael uses the same adjective, "ehrlich," with a different connotation, "honorable," when he buys the telescope from Coppola:

> [...] that Coppola might be a highly honorable mechanician and optician, but could in no way be the accursed double and ghost of Coppelius. (SmE 77, 79)

> [...] daß Coppola ein höchst ehrlicher Mechanikus und Optikus, keineswegs aber Coppelii verfluchter Doppeltgänger und Revenant sein könne. (SmG 351, 29–31)

In this instance, "ehrlich" can mean that Coppola is truly a mechanician and optician, or it can mean that he is an honest salesman because his prices are fair. In either case, however, we are reminded of the earlier, awkward usage of "ehrlich." Therefore, the word "genuine" (ehrlich) sets questions in motion regarding not only the honesty of Coppola as a salesman but of his earnestness as a person. Uncommon usage of the word occurs twice,

106

characterizing once Coppelius and once Coppola, and thus further connects the two men. The awkward use of "honest" consequently suggests the exact opposite of honesty, namely, that this man, if he is indeed one person, is deceptive regarding his identity. Consequently, he may indeed be involved in a conspiracy.

We are made aware that Nathanael still has doubts about the salesman Coppola when he hears him laughing on the stairs, and Nathanael asks himself whether he has paid too dear a price for the telescope.[10] He feels both tricked and ridiculed by Coppola.[11] Nevertheless, Nathanael pays a very dear price for the telescope indeed, figuratively speaking, if we consider the chain of events arising from his seeing Olimpia through the telescope. We already have some doubts about Coppola's identity, instilled by the awkward use of "ehrlich" (honest, real). When we then find out that Coppola is laughing on the stairs, our doubts may go beyond Nathanael's worry that Coppola has inflated the price of the telescope. Coppola's laughter may confirm that he is engaged in a more serious kind of deception.

Another textual detail that confirms such suspicions occurs in the sentence that ends "[not] the accursed double and ghost of Coppelius" (SmE 77, 79); "keineswegs aber Coppelii verfluchter Doppelgänger und Revenant" (SmG 351, 30–1). Nathanael could express that Coppola is not the double of Coppelius with a prepositional phrase instead of using the odd genitive: "*Coppelii*."[12] The consonant-vowel structure of "*Coppelii*" is closer to "*Coppola*" than "*Coppelius*." In this instance, the names of the two characters both end in vowels. In addition, if Coppola is indeed the double Coppelius, then the double "i" in "*Coppelii*" reproduces doubling onomatopoetically. All these hints allow us to side with Nathanael's original point of view, that there is indeed some plot in the making. On the other hand, we are never offered any "hard evidence" for such suspicions.

To some degree, Nathanael's uncertainty mirrors the reader's response to the ambiguity of the text. In addition, when Nathanael rejects his doubts, he tries to conform to the rational attitude of his bourgeois surroundings. And to the degree that we readers begin to favor the idea of an actual conspiracy, we distrust not only Nathanael's adoption of the rational mode but also the world-view of the people who represent it, Nathanael's parents, Lothar, and Clara.

Nathanael's "Dark Fate"

To complete this survey of uncanny clues for the reader, we must study elements in the final scene that have appeared earlier in the text and that make the return of the Sandman appear inevitable. They are the textual equivalent of the dark fate that Nathanael fears. The elements to be explored are shadows, giants, and the color gray. These motifs gradually materialize one after the other throughout the story. At the beginning of the final scene, they all appear together. They are incorporated into the description of the physical setting of the clock tower, and we shall see that jointly they foreshadow the return of the Sandman. This return is thus presented as something that becomes an external, physical occurrence, even if it originates in Nathanael's deranged imagination.[13]

The association of the Sandman with a primordial power confirms an image Nathanael uses in his letter at the very beginning of the story, in which he speaks of a fate that he feels is "looming over [him] like black clouds, casting shadows [...]" (SmE 37).[14] A shadow appears again at the end of the story:

> It was about the time when the four happy people were about to move to their small property. At midday they were walking through the streets of the town. They had made various purchases; the tall tower of the town hall cast its gigantic shadow over the marketplace. (SmE 99)

> Es war an der Zeit, daß die vier glücklichen Menschen nach dem Gütchen ziehen wollten. Zur Mittagsstunde gingen sie durch die Straßen der Stadt. Sie

hatten manches eingekauft, der hohe Ratsturm warf seinen Riesenschatten über den Markt. (SmG 361, 33–4)

Hoffmann introduces the looming disaster skillfully into a scene that is the equivalent of the *peripeteia* before the *catastrophe* in a play.[15] The shadow of the tower appears at first only as welcome protection from the noonday sun. Its significance becomes evident later, when the events on the tower unfold. The "gigantic" shadow also links the tower to the Sandman through the imagery of the gigantic. The reference to the shadow of the clock tower hints at the Sandman's return, but the shadow imagery also links the Sandman to the idea of the dark fate hovering over Nathanael's life.

The giant motif appears first in Coppola's struggle with Spalanzani for the possession of Olimpia: "[…] but at that moment Coppola, writhing with the strength of a giant, twisted the figure out of the professor's hands […]" (SmE 93); "[…] aber in dem Augenblick wand Coppola sich mit Riesenkraft drehend die Figur dem Professor aus den Händen […]" (SmG 358, 42; 359, 1). The gigantic appears again in the last scene. First, in the narrator's description of the vista from the tower: "[…] gazing at the fragrant woodlands behind which the blue mountains rose like a city of giants (SmE 101)"; "[…] und schauten hinein in die duftigen Waldungen, hinter denen das blaue Gebirge, wie eine Riesenstadt, sich erhob" (SmG 361, 40–2). Only a little later Clara discovers an object approaching the tower, which later turns out to be Coppelius. Coppelius standing below the tower in the marketplace is described as a giant: "Hearing the wild shouts, people assembled; towering like a giant among them was lawyer Coppelius […]" (SmE 101); "[…] unter [den Menschen] ragte riesengroß der Advokat Coppelius hervor […]" (SmG 362, 33–4). The giant Coppelius ("riesengroß") has arrived from the city of giants ("Riesenstadt") and stands under the clock tower, which casts a gigantic shadow ("Riesenschatten"). These elements thus serve the double function of connecting Coppelius and Coppola, and leading to the culmination of the "giant" motif. The Sandman seems larger-than-life, a supernatural force.

Hoffmann also associates the color gray with the Sandman. Gray at first characterizes Coppelius's clothing in the first laboratory scene: "Coppelius always went abroad in an ash-gray frock coat of an old-fashioned cut, with waistcoat and trousers to match [...]" (SmE 43); "[...] in einem altmodisch zugeschnittenen aschgrauen Rocke, ebensolcher Weste und gleichen Beinkleidern [...] (SmG 334, 42; 335, 1).[16] The word for the color gray in German (grau) is also the root of German "graulich," "grausig," the equivalent of English "gruesome." These words are frequently used to characterize Coppelius. First, in the childhood episode: "Once, that hollow, rumbling step was especially frightening to me" (SmE 39); "Einmal war mir jenes dumpfe Treten und Poltern besonders graulich" (SmG 332, 27). Nathanael uses a similar word a second time, when he discovers that Coppelius is the father's visitor: "So, when I saw this Coppelius, it became clear in my mind, to my fear and horror [...]" (SmE 45); "Als ich nun diesen Coppelius sah, ging es grausig und entsetzlich in meiner Seele auf [...]" (SmG 335, 32–3). The German words "graulich" and "grausig" are used here to characterize Coppelius, thus lending a special significance to the appearances of the color gray in the narrative. The text-specific connotation of the fear-inspiring adds a particularly threatening quality to the connection that "gray" creates between Coppelius and Coppola. The tentative quality of the connection between the two men recreates Nathanael's uncanny fear of the Sandman for the reader. It is therefore significant that the word gray, which creates the connection here, itself expresses tentativeness.

The color gray links the two men frequently, appearing in Coppelius's "bushy, gray eye-brows" (SmE 43),[17] for example, and Coppola's "long, gray lashes" (SmE 77).[18] When Coppelius walks towards the tower at the end of the story, he appears to Clara like a "gray bush."[19] Nathanael does not notice the connections we have been discussing, and this oversight allows Hoffmann to increase the discrepancy between Nathanael's limited and the reader's more enlightened perspective.

The German word "grau" fulfils a double function in underscoring the uncanniness of the Sandman because of its associations with the frightening, through "graulich" and "grausam," and the indistinctness associated with the color itself, which is a result of mixing black and white. We had mentioned in the Freud chapter that the uncanny is frequently associated with fog and darkness. The color gray thus emphasizes the role of uncertainty for the uncanny.[20] The Sandman in Hoffmann's story remains a mystery, and the color gray becomes his fitting attribute.

The motifs that connect Coppelius and Coppola, which corroborate the existence of the Sandman from the reader's point of view, reappear in the description of the gray bush approaching the tower. The mystery of its significance is never completely solved, but we are given some clues as to the identity of the bush at the end: "[Coppelius] [...] who had just come to town and had walked directly to the marketplace" (SmE 101); "[Coppelius] [...] der eben in die Stadt gekommen und gerades Weges nach dem Markt geschritten war" (SmG 362, 34–5). Although Clara calls the bush "little," it appears small only as long as it is still in the distance. Although it probably signifies the approach of Coppelius, the fact that the bush appears quaint and little at first and that Clara admires it, can be seen first in the context of plot structure. As already mentioned, the scene on the clock-tower constitutes a moment before the tragic ending that briefly raises the hope for a different outcome. Nathanael's recuperation, the planned marriage to Clara, and the shopping spree before leaving town all precede the tragic events at the end of "Der Sandmann." This optimism is sustained in Clara's amusement about the gray bush. We do not know what she sees. Perhaps she sees a shrub being blown towards them by the wind and jokingly compares this motion to majestic walking. Or she sees a man and uses the bush analogy to allude to his bushy gray hair. Clara's lighthearted attitude is still in keeping with the optimistic atmosphere, while the bush is also the initially harmless seeming indication of the impending catastrophe. The appearance of the bush marks the turning point in the action, at which the plot returns to its catastrophic course.

The bush's association with the aforementioned motif of the gigantic also appears implicitly in Clara's use of the verb "schreiten," instead of "gehen" (to walk), for the bush: "Just look at that strange little gray bush that actually seems to be walking toward us" (SmE 101); "Sieh doch den sonderbaren kleinen grauen Busch, der ordentlich auf uns los zu schreiten scheint" (SmG 362, 1–2). The German verb "schreiten" means "walking with dignity" and is appropriate for a person invested with power, such as a king or nobleman. The narrator uses the same verb when describing Coppelius's arrival. [21] In both instances, the verb's connotation suggests Coppelius's gigantic, fantastical power. The bush is connected to Coppelius's "bushy" eyebrows.[22] An additional textual parallel also suggests this connection, because Clara refers to the bush as moving "swiftly," or "directly" ("[...] der [...] ordentlich auf uns los zu schreiten scheint") towards the tower, an aspect lost in the translation.[23] At the end, the narrator describes Coppelius as having come "directly" (SmE 101)[24] to the market. The approach, in both instances, is undeviating and purposeful, and thus retroactively connects Coppelius with the bush. Therefore, the color gray, "bushiness," the verb "schreiten," and the direct quality of the approach all implicitly connect Coppelius with the mysterious bush.[25]

Coppelius's appearance in the university town, where only Coppola has appeared so far, suggests yet again that he is indeed Coppola's double. On the other hand, the narrator does not say that Coppelius has literally "returned" but states only that he has just come into town, allowing for the possibility that Coppelius has not seen Nathanael since childhood. The text only hints at the identity of the two men until the end. Although Coppelius could

112

simply be hiding behind the bush, it is also possible that he has transformed himself into a bush, in keeping with his fantastical powers. The metamorphosis turns him into a creature belonging to that pagan realm of animated nature from which the belief in the Sandman originates.[26] All these elements strengthen the reader's suspicion that Nathanael is indeed the target of a conspiracy.[27]

Chapter 5:
Nathanael's Precarious Position as a Writer

It is not clear what brings about Nathanael's attack of madness. Does he see Clara or Coppelius through the telescope? Right after Clara has pointed out the gray bush to Nathanael, the following events ensue:

> Nathanael reached automatically into his side pocket; he found Coppola's telescope, pointed it to one side – Clara was in front of the lens! – There was a convulsive jerking in his pulse and veins – pale as death, he stared at Clara [...]. (SmE 101)

> Nathanael faßte mechanisch nach der Seitentasche; er fand Coppolas Perspektiv, er schaute seitwärts – Clara stand vor dem Glase! – Da zuckte es krampfhaft in seinen Pulsen und Adern – totenbleich starrte er Clara an [...]. (SmG 362, 2–5)

This sequence of details has been the material of many interpretations. It is unclear whether Nathanael looks sideways at Clara or beyond Clara, because she is blocking his view. When Nathanael pales and looks at Clara, it is unclear whether he has already taken the telescope from his eyes, but this is likely, because he is described as having lost control of his movements.[1] Does Coppelius, the first "incarnation" of the Sandman (it is he, not Coppola, who appears in the marketplace), bring about an attack of madness through his presence alone?

The Mystery of Nathanael's Death

After his recuperation from the experience with Spalanzani and Olimpia, Nathanael is ready to marry Clara and live on a small farm in the country with her brother Lothar and his mother. He has given up his aspirations to become a poet and artist.[2] As mentioned above, the scene creates a contrast to the impending disaster:

> It was about the time when the four happy people were about to move to their small property [...] They had made various purchases [...]. "Ah!" said Clara, "why don't we go up once more and enjoy the view of the distant mountains?" (SmE 99)

> Es war an der Zeit, daß die vier glücklichen Menschen nach dem Gütchen ziehen wollten [...]. Sie hatten manches eingekauft, "Ei!" sagte Clara: "steigen wir doch noch einmal herauf und schauen in das ferne Gebirge hinein!" (SmG 361, 30–5)

The vista from the clock tower is introduced as a moment of leisure, but it also has the connotation of providing closure. Looking down once more ("noch einmal"), from above, over the university town allows Nathanael to leave behind the terrible events that have transpired. The scene has attributes of the idyll, which has been called the locus amoenus, the cozy place where horror is absent (Curtius). In the introduction, we defined coziness as the feeling of security associated with a well-protected place where all threats from the outside are forgotten. It is the exact opposite of the uncanny, but this very opposition and exclusion invokes the uncanny implicitly. Threats, although they may be temporarily put out of mind, can return at any unforeseen moment. The illusion of the perfect exclusion of threat is comparable to an "inside" without the "outside" that surrounds it.[3] This perspective offers one way to interpret the significance of the uncanny in Hoffmann's story. The Sandman represents the impossibility of excluding the threat.

References to the idyllic appear throughout the text, not only in the pipe smoking of the father at the beginning or the closing vignette. Clara withdraws into the arbor (SmE 73), for example, after Nathanael has recited his poem. The German word is "Laube" (SmG 349, 3), a secluded place in the garden, overgrown with plants, a classic location associated with coziness. A particularly comic effect is achieved by situating the duel between Lothar and Nathanael behind the same garden (SmE 73; SmG 349, 13). Clara later runs to separate the duelists through "the garden gate" (SmE 73, SmG 349, 22), which could almost be translated "the gate in the picket fence." Clara's world is thus made to represent the exclusion of threat in the coziness of idyll.

The plot also associates Clara with a desire for a life that is quaint and cozy in the very last paragraph of the story:

> People say that they saw Clara several years later [...]. Clara was still able to find that peaceful domestic happiness which suited her [...] and which Nathanael, [who was torn apart internally] [...] would never have been able to offer her. (SmE 103)

> Nach mehreren Jahren will man in einer entfernten Gegend Clara gesehen haben [...] daß Clara das ruhige häusliche Glück noch fand, [...] das der im Innern zerrissene Nathanael niemals hätte gewähren können. (SmG 363, 4–9)[4]

From the reader's point of view, this image has ironic undertones, created by the ellipsis of several years of narrated time between Nathanael's death and the idyll that immediately follows.[5] Nathanael has been the focalizer and hence the object of the reader's identification. Whether Clara indeed found happiness is fairly irrelevant for the shocked reader. In addition, the details of Clara's domestic bliss only seem to affirm the cozy world of a life on the small farm. Although the narrator states that Nathanael could not have provided this kind of life, this does not amount to a condemnation of Nathanael. The developments up to this point associate Clara with a limited consciousness. Therefore, Nathanael's inability to conform to Clara's aspirations appears as an ambiguous failure, which may even be interpreted as a sympathetic trait.

Nathanael is shown earlier as split between acknowledging the existence of the Sandman, an intuition that Clara perceives as paranoid, and agreeing with Clara that ignoring the suspicion can defuse its power. Hoffmann shows the reader how Nathanael denies his intuition, and how he comes to favor Clara's view before the final catastrophe. But he also makes the reader aware that Nathanael may have been justified in his suspicions all along. Thus, the idyll that Clara has found, which also represents the bourgeois aspirations of the time, is shown to be an illusion, threatened by the very forces it attempts to exclude.

Nathanael is presented as both artist and seeker after knowledge, whereas those around him, including Clara's brother Lothar and his friend Siegmund, his family, and Clara herself, are directed by the ideal of prospering in the material world. Clara writes:

> If our mind, strengthened by a cheerful life, is firm enough always to recognize outside hostile influences for what they are, and to pursue with calm steps the path onto which our inclinations and vocations have led us, that uncanny power will surely perish [...]. (SmE 55)

> Haben wir festen, durch das heitre Leben gestärkten, Sinn genug, um fremdes feindlichen Einwirken als solches stets zu erkennen und den Weg, in den uns Neigung und Beruf geschoben, ruhigen Schrittes zu verfolgen, so geht wohl jene unheimliche Macht unter [...]. (SmG 340, 35–9)

The remedy that Clara suggests is twofold: she believes the Sandman to be the product of Nathanael's imagination, and she recommends work as an antidote. For Clara, the Sandman is solely a "phantom of our own ego" (SmE 57).[6] Kittler, whose essay centers on this issue and takes its title from this phrase, is correct in maintaining that Clara's advice contains an etiology of madness:

> Clara's etiology of madness is supported by Hoffmann's entire oeuvre [...]. This oeuvre erects its poetology by defining the madman as the negative double of the poet. Madness also produces an inner world, but it cannot, like poetry, reflect and thus separate it from the outside world.[7]

Kittler is correct in claiming that Hoffmann establishes Nathanael as a double of the poet. Nonetheless, Hoffmann goes beyond Clara's etiology of Nathanael's madness. Her advice appears simplistic because we learn that the Sandman represents forces that are beyond the control of Nathanael, regardless of whether or not he is deranged. The ineffectiveness of Clara's advice thus also serves as an ironic critique of the naïve belief that we can banish fears by simply excluding them from thought. The tale in its entirety indeed allows for the double irony that Clara's advice, rather than describing the antidote against the Sandman, in fact accurately explains why he is so powerful. The Sandman is the phantom created by Nathanael, but once created, it cannot easily be taken back.

The poetological program that we can extract from the text implies that something belonging to the realm of the imagined can ultimately become part of material reality, as the Sandman does in the context of this story. Consequently, like Nathanael, we readers cannot turn back. The world that Hoffmann creates becomes endowed with the characteristics of madness, a world in which it becomes impossible to separate what is imagined and what is real. Nathanael is thus more than the deficient double of the poet; he becomes the poet's double within the story.

The story makes it clear that the conflict between Nathanael's parents would be repeated between himself and Clara. Clara revealingly expresses her disapproval of Nathanael's father, who allegedly only wasted money with his search for "higher wisdom":

His [Coppelius's] eerie nighttime activities [...] which the two of them carried on secretly and which could not fail to upset your mother, not only because a lot of money must have been squandered to no purpose, but also, as is always the case with researchers of that sort, your father's mind was completely filled with the illusory thirst for higher wisdom [...]. (SmE 53, 55 and 57)

Das unheimliche Treiben [des Coppelius] mit Deinem Vater zur Nachtzeit [...] womit die Mutter nicht zufrieden sein konnte, da gewiß viel Geld unnütz verschleudert und obendrein, wie es immer mit solchen Laboranten der Fall sein soll, des Vaters Gemüt ganz von dem trügerischen Drange nach hoher Weisheit erfüllt, der Familie abwendig gemacht wurde. (SmG 339, 39–340, 4)

The final lines undermine Clara's idea of a peaceful domesticity, from the reader's point of view, because the father's secret activities, the silences between the parents, and the distance between parents and children may have had a certain justification in the search for higher knowledge.

The story's implicit critique of the proponents of common sense who surround the aspiring poet Nathanael is also visible in a suggested parallelism between Clara and the automaton Olimpia. When Nathanael twice exclaims, "Wooden doll, turn"; "Holzpüppchen dreh dich" (SmG 359, 26–7; 33–4) in his frenzy on the tower, it is not only a relapse into his obsession with Olimpia but also a clue about Clara's puppet-like nature, which is expressed in earlier parts of the narrative. In Nathanael's poem, composed during his visit home, before he encounters Olimpia, Clara appears as a figure with the eyes of death: "Nathanael looks into Clara's eyes; but it is Death that looks at him amicably with Clara's eyes" (SmE 71).[8] Clara's dismissal of the poem as a "mad – senseless – insane tale [better 'fairy tale']" (SmE 73)[9] provokes Nathanael's response: "You damned lifeless automaton!" (SmE 73).[10] The exclamation "Wooden doll, turn" refers first to Olimpia in the laboratory (SmE 95),[11] then to Clara on the clock tower (SmE 101).

While Clara's name is associated with clarity and perhaps enlightenment rationality, she is characterized also as a mirror that is empty before anything is reflected in it. One of Clara's admirers, whom the narrator ridicules as "babbling" about her beauty, compares her eyes to a work of art:

One of them [...] a real fantasist, compared Clara's eyes in the most peculiar fashion to a Ruisdael lake, in which were reflected the pure azure of the cloudless sky, the tract of forest and flowers, and the whole variegated and merry life of the opulent landscape. (SmE 65)

Einer von ihnen, ein wirklicher Fantast, verglich aber höchstseltsamer Weise Claras Augen mit einem See von Ruisdael, in dem sich des wolkenlosen Himmels reines Azur, Wald- und Blumenflur, der reichen Landschaft ganzes buntes, heitres Leben spiegelt. (SmG 345, 8–12)

This portrayal of Clara is ironic by virtue of exaggeration. The comparison with the lake painted by Ruisdael alone might still be convincing as a genuine compliment, but the extensive details of the comparison undermine its purpose. It is hardly conceivable how "forest and flowers, and the whole variegated and merry life of the opulent landscape" reflected in a lake could look like a pair of eyes. Apart from satirizing the poeticism of the amateur Romantic, the lake image also implicitly relates Clara to Olimpia. While the lake, used to represent Clara's eyes, reflects the surrounding landscape, Olimpia's eyes reflect Nathanael's animating gaze. The extensive projection of the painting onto Clara's eyes, undertaken by the "fantasist," is comparable to Nathanael's passionate projection of life onto Clara. Olimpia's de facto lifelessness as automaton questions the authenticity of the idyllic vista developed by the Biedermeier "fantasist" and by extension Clara's rationality.

Clara's reflective quality is emphasized by one of Nathanael's emphatic compliments addressed to Olimpia:

> "Oh, you splendid divine woman! – You ray of light from the unattainable promised land of love – you profound spirit in which my entire being is reflected," and more of similar purport. (SmE 85)

> "O du herrliche, himmlische Frau! – du Strahl aus dem verheißenen Jenseits der Liebe – du tiefes Gemüt, in dem sich mein ganzes Sein spiegelt" und noch mehr dergleichen [...]. (SmG 355, 4–6)

The passage contains direct references to the reflective quality of Clara's eyes, as well as a concealed reference to the light emanating from Clara's eyes. Hoffmann's irony of Nathanael's aspirations towards poetry is visible not only in the comment "more of similar purport," but also in the association between love and death, which was favored by the early German Romantic poets (Bronfen).

Clara is uncommunicative like Olimpia. While Clara, like Olimpia, is uncommunicative, the author seems to portray her in a consistently flattering tone. The narrator ironically mentions her aversion to long speeches, seemingly praising her habit of getting straight to the point, and we are told that anything else would not have been in accord with "her taciturn character" (SmE 65); "Claras schweigsame[r] Natur" (SmG 345, 26–8). Although Clara's letter is articulate, Clara is perhaps more comfortable writing than speaking. Clara's willingness or ability to communicate with Nathanael appears in an ambiguous light. A parallel is visible between her "taciturn character" and Olimpia's reserved manner. Olimpia's vocabulary consists almost exclusively of the word "Oh" ("Ach").[12] Although Clara appears uncommunicative by choice, and Olimpia's reserve is the result of her technical lack of speaking ability, Olimpia shares Clara's taciturn character.[13] This parallel creates a metaphoric link between the absence of a soul in the automaton Olimpia and Clara's lack of understanding for Nathanael's poetic aspirations.

Clara's enlightenment rationality is metonymically related to Olimpia's lifelessness:

> Clara had [...] a very bright mind capable of subtle distinctions [...] and that subtle, ironic smile [...]. Many people, therefore, called Clara cold, unfeeling, prosaic [...]. (SmE 65)

> Clara hatte [...] einen gar hellen scharf sichtenden Verstand [...] und jenes feine ironische Lächeln [...]. Clara wurde deshalb von vielen für kalt, gefühllos, prosaisch gescholten [...]. (SmG 345, 25–32)

Despite the contrast between Clara's highly developed consciousness, she shares the coldness and lack of feeling with Olimpia.[14] By creating such parallels between Olimpia and Clara, Hoffmann expands his critique of the bourgeoisie, characterizing it as lifeless and puppet-like.

Perhaps Nathanael raves when looking at Clara through the telescope because he feels surrounded by a world which, in its sterility and denial of the fantastical, is removed from reality. Maybe he can see Clara's lifelessness now because it has been revealed to him through Olimpia. Coppola's telescope, which previously "animated" the puppet, now works in reverse and removes the illusion, teaching Nathanael to detect the lifelessness in the world that surrounds him. The telescope now gives him such clarity of vision that he can no longer overlook Clara's puppet-like nature. Nonetheless, the Sandman is not Nathanael's only antagonist. Nathanael is boxed in by the obvious enemy Coppelius/Coppola on the one side, and by the double-female figure Clara/Olimpia on the other side, with whom he cannot communicate. Both Clara and Olimpia appear cold and distant.

The Implicit Poetological Program

The uncanny effect of "Der Sandmann" relies on factors that are specific to literature. In Hoffmann's story, the fantastical elements that become physical realities are products of Nathanael's imagination. If the reality of the characters was governed throughout by the laws that we presuppose for the material world, Nathanael's inability to distinguish between the productions of his imagination and external reality would lead us to diagnose him as mad. Hoffmann creates a fictional world, however, in which Nathanael's imagination is capable of producing real monsters. In that world, Nathanael unwillingly becomes the author of his own fate.

Nathanael's poem, or rather the summary of it given by the narrator, draws together the three themes that we discussed above, shadows, giants, and the color gray. The poem is uncanny because it foreshadows Nathanael's death and features many elements that appear in the last scene. The images have their source within Nathanael, but at the point of their recurrence in the final scene, they have materialized and become part of his external surroundings.[15] The poem is never quoted, but summarized by the narrator instead:

Coppelius appears and touches Clara's lovely eyes, these jump into Nathanael's chest like burning sparks of fire [...]. Coppelius seizes him and throws him into a blazing circle of fire [...]. The tumult is like that of a

123

hurricane furiously whipping up the foaming waves of the sea, which in their raging struggle rear up like dark, white-haired giants. (SmE 71)

Endlich [...] erscheint der entsetzliche Coppelius und berührt Claras holde Augen; die springen in Nathanaels Brust wie blutige Funken sengend und brennend, Coppelius faßt ihn und wirft ihn in einen flammenden Feuerkreis [...]. Es ist ein Tosen, als wenn der Orkan grimmig hineinpeitscht in die schäumenden Meereswellen, die sich wie schwarze, weißhäuptige Riesen emporbäumen in wütendem Kampfe. (SmG 347, 30–8)

The poem, written before the second laboratory scene and before Coppelius's return, constitutes an inadvertent prediction of subsequent events. The eyes jumping out at Nathanael prefigure the scene in Spalanzani's laboratory. Coppelius here appears in Coppola's role, and Clara is cast in the role of Olimpia.[16] The approach of Coppelius, which is compared to a force of nature in the final scene (mountains, walking bush), is represented here as a storm on water, in which the waves are compared to giants. This comparison precedes the imagery of the gigantic discussed above. "Circle of fire" is the phrase Nathanael obsessively repeats just before his death.

Finally, the narrator himself explicitly inserts the idea that the poem has the power to predict the future:

[...] [Nathanael] had no distinct idea to what purpose Clara was to be kindled, and where it was actually to lead if she *were* frightened by the gruesome images predicting a terrible fate destructive of their love. (SmE 71, emphasis Freud)

[...] wiewohl [Nathanael] nicht deutlich dachte, wozu denn Clara entzündet, und wozu es denn nun eigentlich führen solle, sie mit den grauenvollen Bildern zu ängstigen, die ein entsetzliches, ihre Liebe zerstörendes Geschick weissagten. (SmG 348, 15–19)[17]

The verb "predict" (weissagen) indicates not only that the poem paints a terrible image of the future, but the verb also literally means, "to foretell." Nathanael's own literary production becomes a blueprint for his later experiences. The metaphorical framework traced earlier, which gives credibility to a conspiracy by the Sandman, extends into Nathanael's own textual productions. Nevertheless, his situation as author of his own fate is a precarious one. The influence of mind on matter is conceivable only in the realm of fiction. Only in a fantastic tale can the literary productions of a character join forces with some external demonic power, or even become the cause of such external events.

The connection between the limitations of Nathanael as poet[18] and his inability to distinguish between the productions of his imagination and reality can be carried further.[19] The adherence to stereotypes is observable in his writing, in the exaggeration of both terror and sentimental idyll. These are equivalent to a negation of terror associated with Clara that leads to the conversion of the idyllic Sandman of childhood to the phantom Sandman in Hoffmann's story. We have seen above how the denial of conflict began in Nathanael's childhood with the silence of his parents. Clearly, such conclusions are extensions of psychoanalytic notions that Freud himself did not apply in his comments on "Der Sandmann."

One reason why Nathanael's textual productions unleash the uncanny may lie in his limitations as a poet. Hoffmann implicitly questions the quality of Nathanael's poem itself, because it is never itself quoted, and Clara is not much impressed by the finished product.[20] We have already commented on earlier instances where Hoffmann identifies the exclusion of the uncanny as a source for the uncanny itself. We can observe clichés of the type associated with such exclusion in Nathanael's first letter:

> [...] daily and hourly I remember you all, and in my sweet dreams the genial figure of my lovely Clara goes by, smiling at me with her bright eyes as graciously as she did when I lived among you in person. (SmE 37)

> [...] täglich und stündlich gedenke ich Eurer aller und in süßen Träumen geht meines holden Clärchens freundliche Gestalt vorüber und lächelt mich mit ihren hellen Augen so anmutig an, wie sie wohl pflegte, wenn ich zu Euch hineintrat. (SmG 331, 5–9)

Hoffmann suggests that there may be a connection between Nathanael's idealization of Clara, which betrays a penchant for exaggeration and the idyllic, and the prophetic effects of his poem. The dramatic scenario Nathanael develops in the poem appears as drama for drama's sake because the events seem entirely unconnected.[21] Although the poem constitutes an attempt by Nathanael to come to terms with the threat he perceives, it heaps the elements together without creating any connections. Hoffmann has already suggested that Nathanael is limited as a reader. He has revealed Nathanael's inability to uncover the clues in his childhood, although he himself lays them down in his letter, or to perceive the possible connection between Coppelius and Coppola. Hoffmann suggests that Nathanael is the author of his fate because he does not have full control over his writing. Like his reading of reality, it follows stereotypes and does not draw the full conclusions from his observations.

Hoffmann also suggests that writing more generally has an essentially uncanny potential. In the case of Nathanael, this uncanny potential becomes ungovernable and develops a dynamic beyond the writer's control. When reading the poem to himself, before reading it to Clara, he suddenly believes someone else is speaking: "[…] he was seized by fear and terror and shouted out: 'Whose awful voice is that?'" (SmE 71); "[…] da faßte ihn Grausen und wildes Entsetzen und er schrie auf: 'Wessen grauenvolle Stimme ist das?'" (SmG 348, 14–15). When Nathanael does not recognize himself as author, we get a glimpse of the process that makes him lose control of his imagination. We have traced this deficiency to the childhood trauma of being coincidentally confronted in material reality by what he believed to be only a product of his imagination.

As mentioned above, the Sandman in Hoffmann's story becomes more than a personification of Nathanael's wild imagination. The text hints at the possibility that the Sandman indeed exists as an external, demonic force, which may be responsible for

Nathanael's death. Insofar as the subliminal clues in the text corroborate Nathanael's fears, our ability to simply distance ourselves from the protagonist's alleged madness is reduced. Even the text's implicit explanation of the uncanny's origin in sentimentality and idyll does not obliterate its uncanny effect. The Sandman's existence depends on our interpretation, and thus involves us in the production of the uncanny.

The uncanny is unleashed not only by clichés characterizing inferior writing, or a latent tendency inherent in our interpretation of the text. Hoffmann expresses the belief that texts release powers beyond the writer's control in a passage in which Nathanael comments on the relationship between imagination and external reality:

> He [Nathanael] went so far as to assert that it was foolish for artists and scientists to believe they were creating things of their own free will; for the inspiration that alone makes creativity possible does not come from within a person but is the effect of some higher principle lying outside ourselves. (SmE 67)

> Er ging soweit zu behaupten, daß es töricht sei, wenn man glaube, in Kunst und Wissenschaft nach selbsttätiger Willkür zu schaffen, denn die Begeisterung, in der man nur zu schaffen fähig sei, komme nicht aus dem eignen Innern, sondern sei das Einwirken irgend eines außer uns selbst liegenden höheren Prinzips. (SmG 346, 14–19)

Although Nathanael expresses his personal beliefs, the central idea can be applied to the text itself. Nathanael mentions explicitly a "higher power" when he aims to describe the unpredictable element in both scientific and artistic productions. According to Nathanael, some outside force influences such productions. A principle that lies outside us is also beyond our control.[22] If this force influences writing in general, it affects not only Nathanael but also Hoffmann. Nathanael's poem is a metanarrative, uncanny because it is not only caused by the Sandman's influence over him, but also possibly, by virtue of the prophetic power bestowed upon it by Hoffmann, the cause of the Sandman himself. The metaphoric signals associated with the Sandman, which at first only have the extradiegetic function of corroborating the Sandman's existence for the reader, are endowed with the power of making the Sandman materialize on the diegetic level. This process, which takes place in the interaction between reader and text, parallels the prophetic power of Nathanael's poem for his own future, a process that takes place in the interaction between the poem and the frame narrative on the diegetic level. In the end, the Sandman is indeed the phantom of Nathanael's ego. If Clara is correct, and the Sandman ceases to exist if Nathanael stops believing in him, then the opposite is also true. The Sandman continues to exist as long as Nathanael cannot rid himself from his belief. And in the uncanny world that he inhabits, his thoughts become realities.

The narrator addresses the uncanny reality status of all representations in this frequently quoted passage:

> Perhaps, like a good portraitist, I shall succeed in depicting many a figure so well that you will find it a good likeness, without knowing the original – that you will in fact feel as if you had already seen the person quite often with your own eyes. Perhaps, reader, you will then believe that nothing is stranger and droller ["toller" = wild, out of control] than real life, and that, after all, the poet can only conceive this life as a dark reflection in a frosted mirror. (SmE 63)

> Vielleicht gelingt es mir, manche Gestalt, wie ein guter Porträtmaler, so aufzufassen, daß du es ähnlich findest, ohne das Original zu kennen, ja daß es dir ist, als hättest du die Person recht oft schon mit leibhaftigen Augen gesehen. Vielleicht wirst Du, o mein Leser! dann glauben, daß nichts wunderlicher und toller sei, als das wirkliche Leben und daß dieses der Dichter doch nur, wie in eines matt geschliffnen Spiegels dunklem Widerschein, auffassen könne. (SmG 344, 21–9)

Orlowsky (1988) comments that this comparison of writing with a darkened, ground down mirror constitutes a paradox:

> Hoffmann knew very well from his acquaintance with glassmaking that a mirror is ruined through polishing [to a matte finish]; as a dull mirror it loses its properties as medium for reflection.[23]

Orlowsky, whose study gathers a stunning amount of supplementary information, is inaccurate regarding this issue. Had Orlowsky consulted an encyclopedia of Hoffmann's time about glassmaking, she would have found that a mirror is always ground during the production process:

> The molding of a mirror is performed on very thick, copper plates [...] on which the mass is first flattened with the help of a metal roll, and, when it has cooled off in the cooling oven, is ground down, polished and then covered with foil.[23]

A mirror that is ground down does not fully lose its reflective capabilities. Thus, the image of the darkened mirror first expresses Hoffmann's distrust of the accuracy of literary representation.[24] Hoffmann expresses self-doubt in the metafictional aside, quoted above, as to whether literature can represent reality adequately, and throughout the story he also upsets the reader's ability to find a stable footing in relation to the events in the story. Thus, perception and the reproduction of reality, regardless of whether they occur in the realm of art or science, are assigned crucial importance in constituting reality itself. In addition, Hoffmann emphasizes this point by making the seemingly most reliable of the five senses, vision, the center of a metaphoric field in which the determination of reality by the inner world is exposed. Hoffmann makes fiction a measure of the degree to which we constantly construct and reconstruct reality.

It is remarkable that Freud argues directly against the interpretation suggested here yet uses a figure of speech to illustrate the lack of uncertainty in "Der Sandmann" that emphasizes the instability of vision:

But this uncertainty [whether he is taking us into the real world or into a purely fantastic one of his own creation] disappears in the course of Hoffmann's story, and we perceive that he intends to make us, too, look through the demon optician's spectacles or spy-glass [...]. (SE 17, 230, 23–7)

Aber im Verlaufe der Hoffmannschen Erzählung schwindet dieser Zweifel [ob er uns in die reale Welt oder in eine ihm beliebige phantastische Welt einführen wird], wir merken, daß der Dichter uns selbst durch die Brille oder das Perspektiv des dämonischen Optikers schauen lassen will [...]. (GW XII, 242)

It is not clear how Freud uses the comparison of looking through the demonic spyglass. Considering that Freud believes the story unequivocally asserts the identity of Coppelius and Coppola, he seems to be using "demon optician's spectacles" as a metaphor for a textual world that allows for the existence of the fantastical. Freud concludes that once we know the text belongs to the fantastic genre, our doubts about the reality-status of events no longer contribute to the uncanny effect. The choice is not solely between two options, however. We are not just certain or uncertain whether the text is depicting fantastic events, such as Coppelius unscrewing Nathanael's limbs without killing him. Instead, we cannot determine whether events are imagined only by a mad protagonist, whose perspective we share, or whether they are viewed by Hoffmann as really happening within the framework of the story. As mentioned in the Freud chapter, Freud's exclusion of uncertainty is not only a misreading of Hoffmann but serves as an argument against Jentsch, to emphasize the familiar component of the uncanny. Instead, "Der Sandmann" is another example for Jentsch's claim that the uncanny arises from intellectual uncertainty.[25]

From the reader's perspective, the text constitutes a paranoid framework in its metaphoric connections. The "Sandman" functions indeed like Coppola's telescope, in that it plays a demonic trick on the reader. Contrary to Freud's claim that uncertainty plays no part, the reader is subjected to the same uncertainty that affects Nathanael. We continually check the data provided by our senses for connections. In cases where the discovery of the connection is coupled with indications that the connection was supposed to have remained hidden, we suspect an agency or motive. The correction of a thus established "delusional system"[26] involves both an evaluation of the probability of misreading, and definite proof or disproof for our assumptions. Literary texts of the type examined here are not subject to the laws of probability, and can intentionally withdraw the basis for such proof. They consequently destabilize the parameters which govern the activity of "reading into" the text and can thus have an uncanny effect.

Nathanael's paranoia contaminates the reader because possible proof for a persecution remain elusive enough to be unsettling but justified enough, through "circumstantial" textual evidence, to materialize within the metaphorical framework. If, as pointed out in the introduction, the aesthetic experience is understood as the reader's activity necessary to uncover those aspects that turn the text into a work of art, "Der Sandmann" proves to be a highly suitable example for defining the uncanny as a poetical phenomenon.

The Uncanny Effect Caused by Literary Elements

The uncanny in "Der Sandmann" is caused by an ambiguity that gives rise to conflicting but equally valid interpretations. In this story, our activity as readers corroborates the persecutory delusion of the main character. The effect of "Der Sandmann" thus relies on a poetical uncanny. Coppelius and Coppola, if we view them as one person, may be some type of demon, possibly an incarnation of the devil. Nathanael's father and Spalanzani would then both be Faust figures who have made a pact with the devil. Such an assumption, based on the notion that the story indeed asserts some fantastical presence, would explain how Coppelius could reappear as Coppola, how he could create a human doll, and how he could cause Nathanael's suicide. Nevertheless, this explanation is never fully substantiated by any explicit statement in the text. Alternatively, we can follow Freud and read the Sandman as an incarnation of Nathanael's repressed sexual drive.

Freud's interpretation allegedly answers the following question: "[…] why does the Sand-Man always appear as a disturber of love?" (Freud, "The 'Uncanny'" 231). The Sandman does not always appear only when Nathanael comes in contact with women, although there are three such occasions. Coppelius's visits in Nathanael's childhood, while sparking conflict between his parents, do not yet disturb Nathanael's love interest. Furthermore, if Coppola is an incarnation of the Sandman, his sale of the telescope acts as a stimulant for Nathanael's infatuation with Olimpia, not as a disturbance. And why does Coppola not interfere in Nathanael's dance with Olimpia? He destroys Olimpia not to slight Nathanael, but in a fight with Spalanzani. Coppelius's intervention at the end, if we link it to Nathanael's suicide, separates Nathanael from Clara only as a secondary consequence of killing him (Freud, "The 'Uncanny'" 231).[27] In contrast, we have suggested that the significance of the Sandman is a personification of the uncanny itself, which arises out of the indeterminacy of interpretation, in accordance with the "principle lying beyond our reach" mentioned in the metafictional passage discussed above.

This explanation increases the reader's affiliation with Nathanael. He does not appear as crazy as the people around him think. Nevertheless, his limitations as a writer show him bound to cliché. Cliché and paranoia are both processes that block certain aspects of reality from view. The exclusion of threat in cliché by blocking out fresh experiences, for example, and the obsession with persecution in paranoia are both instances of selective perception. Hoffmann's text, in a self-reflexive mode, uncovers the process of selective perception as "bad reading" of both paranoia, in Nathanael's inability to distinguish imagined from real threats, and of the idyllic, in Clara's and the family's repression of the uncanny.

Nathanael remains a limited reader when he rejects the conspiracy he first suspects. Hoffmann asks us to go on to see what he himself sees, beyond Nathanael and beyond paranoia. We now understand how the demonic is excluded from the world that Clara represents. This interpretation confirms Freud's definition of the uncanny as a result of repression. Nonetheless, we have discovered elements of repression beyond the purely sexual, such as the unresolved conflicts between the parents and the role of the nanny in Nathanael's childhood, and the overall nonresponsiveness to Nathanael's trauma by both mother and father.[28]

Freud disregards the open nature of the text and reduces it to a representation of an Oedipal scenario. What is lost in all such attempts is the indeterminate quality of the text. The repressed in "Der Sandmann" is not only Nathanael's feminine attitude towards his father. The notion of the repressed also includes sources of the uncanny such as the Faustian pursuit of scientific knowledge or the bourgeois exclusion of the demonic. In the unmasking of the philistine idyll, we discover how repression means an exclusion of threat, so that the return of the repressed constitutes a potentially dangerous situation.

Furthermore, the uncanny in "Der Sandmann" is a textual phenomenon. Even when the uncanny is caused by the return of the repressed, it returns in altered form, unrecognizable, and causing disorientation. The text mimics this disorientation by asking the reader to remove the disguises that the repressed has undergone. Uncanniness is caused by intellectual uncertainty, produced by both diegetic and extradiegetic elements in the text. The uncanniness of the text as a whole has to do with a particular kind of ambiguity, resulting from paradox. While we can explain the Sandman as a phantasm created entirely by Nathanael's deranged imagination, the Sandman's existence is also substantiated as an externally valid fact. Although both possibilities cannot both be true in real life, Hoffmann makes them both appear plausible in his story. The contradictory alternatives are substantiated by extradiegetic elements, such as hidden allusions, irony, and metaphoric links. These poetic elements contribute to the mysterious impression of the text, yet simultaneously this mysteriousness is closely related to the text's property as a literary work of art. Far from simply presenting a case study to show how sexual repression causes the uncanny, Hoffmann instead demonstrates his skill as an artist by recreating the alluring effect of the uncanny through imitation and performance.

Chapter 6:
Ludwig Tieck's "Der blonde Eckbert" –
The Uncanniness of Indifferent Fate

[...] for me, as you well know, the *locus classicus* of a
theory of forgetting [...] is "Der blonde Eckbert."

Walter Benjamin, in a letter to
Theodor W. Adorno, May 5, 1940[1]

Ludwig Tieck is considered one of the major contributors to Early
German Romanticism, together with Wackenroder, Novalis,
Friedrich Schlegel and his brother August Wilhelm von Schlegel.
"Der blonde Eckbert" (1797) is customarily included in the canon
of great German short stories (Hofmannsthal). It was translated
into English in 1827 by Carlyle, 30 years after it was published
(Tieck, "The Fair-Haired Eckbert"). The story marks an important
contribution to the uncanny as an aesthetic device. As outlined in
the introduction, the uncanny is understood here in the original
German sense of the word "unheimlich," meaning eerie, strange,
weird. It is caused by uncertainty that is perceived as threatening,
independent of possible causes in the individual's past. The disorienting aspect of the uncanny is not accounted for by the
classical Freudian interpretation. Certain literary texts derive their
uncanny effect not only from depicting uncanny events but
through a structure that disorients the reader. These texts create an
uncanny impression through their poetic elements.

Let us recall the central events in Tieck's story. Walther, Eckbert's friend, stays with Eckbert and his wife Bertha one night.
Eckbert, eager to deepen his friendship with Walther, asks Bertha
to tell them the story of her youth. She recounts how she, when
very young, leaves her home and spends many years with an old

woman in the forest. When Bertha comes of age she runs away from the old woman, taking her talking bird and jewelry, leaving only her dog behind. The bird torments Bertha with its song, reminding her of her betrayal, and, in an act of non-conscious volition, she kills the bird. Soon afterwards, Bertha meets Eckbert and marries him. After Bertha has ended her story, Walther reveals that he has known her secret all along by reminding Bertha of the dog's name. Bertha's health quickly deteriorates. Eckbert, now distrustful of Walther, goes on a hunting expedition, and, meeting him coincidentally, shoots him with a crossbow, in an act reminiscent of Bertha's absentminded killing of the bird. When Eckbert returns to the castle, Bertha has died. After some years, Eckbert befriends Hugo, but starts to distrust him, after having divulged his secret of having killed Walther. Finally, in a hallucinatory incident, Eckbert recognizes Hugo as "none other than" Walther. Horrified, Eckbert escapes into the woods, only to encounter the old woman. She tells him that she was both Walther and Hugo. She also reveals that Bertha was Eckbert's sister. When Eckbert asks why he has always sensed this, she tells him that he once heard his father mention a sister by a different woman. Eckbert goes insane and dies.

Tieck's "Der blonde Eckbert" contains a number of incidents to which we can apply Freud's concept of the uncanny, particularly where Tieck represents the process that Freud defines as denial.[1] Both protagonists deny their guilt on several occasions, and then act upon the denied impulses in dream-like states. It is possible to interpret the phantom as the return of the repressed personified. As discussed in the Freud chapter, Freud mentions in passing that repression alienates the repressed impulse from the mind.[2] Nevertheless, he does not comment on the fact that the alienation makes the impulse unrecognizable and causes disorientation. We shall demonstrate first that uncertainty and disorientation play a role in the uncanny incidents portrayed in Tieck's story. Second, the text also generates an indeterminacy that creates an uncanny reading experience. Readers can interpret the same events as hallucinations of mad protagonists, or as events that they accept as objectively happening on the diegetic level. Third, the poetical uncanny is often aided by subliminal layers of meaning that are only visible to the reader.

The sources of the uncanny to be discussed in the story are the mixing of genres through the literary fairy tale, the unreliable narrator, the uncanniness of death itself, the issue of guilt, and the possibility of interpreting the phantom not only as a personification of the return of the repressed, but also as a manifestation of the reader's response on the plot level.[3]

The Mixing of Genres

The uncanny reading experience in "Der blonde Eckbert" stems first from the unstable genre of the literary fairy tale, or "Kunstmärchen," which obscures the reality status of events.[4] This genre combines the marvelous elements of the classic fairy tale and medieval romance with the psychological realism of the novella. Tieck creates one of the first literary fairy tales in German literature following the poetological proposals expressed by Schlegel, discussed briefly in the introduction. Fairy tale elements infiltrate a world that we first take to be a plausible representation of reality. This makes it impossible to determine the reality status of the fantastical phenomena. Are the characters encountering the marvelous as in fairy tales, where we expect talking animals and magical transformations to be part of the fictional world? Alternatively, do we read the story as a novella and believe the same laws that govern our reality govern the world of the characters? In the latter case, their encounters with the fantastical are hallucinations. Or are hallucinations transformed from mental into real phenomena in the world of this story? Second, the text's uncanniness results from the reader's dependence upon unreliable narrators.[5] Bertha narrates the

137

story in the first person, and we cannot determine whether she is deluded during her stay in the woods.[6] The third person narrator tells the rest of the narrative, which relates Eckbert's experiences. Eckbert dies a madman and it is unclear when his madness begins. The four brief narrator commentaries at different points in the story do nothing to remove the ambiguity resulting from the diminished reliability of the characters. Overall, the reader's knowledge of the crucial events in the story depends on characters who are possibly deluded. Third, the mysterious deaths of Bertha and Eckbert are uncanny in themselves. While both characters show symptoms of madness, it is unclear how much these afflictions contribute to their deaths. Alternatively, the being that haunts both Eckbert and Bertha might cause their deaths.

Another source of uncertainty for the reader is the issue of guilt. Eckbert and Bertha commit acts that they later regret. In the end we find out that fate has implicated them, unknowingly, in the crime of incest. While extenuating circumstances mitigate the gravity of the earlier crimes, the incest is presented as an unalterable fact. The reader is left uncertain whether the phantom is to be seen as an agent of justice or whether it carries out a personal revenge for what it may view as a violation of its realm.

The complicated issue of guilt, along with the question of incest and narcissism, has been the primary focus of the majority of interpretations, but not with a focus on the uncanny in Tieck's story as an aesthetic strategy (Fickert; Gellinek; Finney). Certain critics have attempted psychoanalytic explanations, such as Finney, who claims that the incest is borne out by the narcissism of both characters.[7] This type of interpretation does not account for the fact that any attraction between the characters, if it exists, is excluded from the narrative. The marriage is portrayed, instead, as one of convenience. The incest appears as a curse cast by blind fate, which condemns the characters and exacts an absurdly violent punishment. Tatar ascribes guilt to Eckbert, because he allegedly "has been harboring premonitions of incest but has kept such thoughts both to himself and from himself."[8] As we shall see below, we can detect denial or disavowal in Eckbert, but Tieck abstains from any explicit condemnation of Eckbert.[9]

Critics have interpreted the story with no more than passing reference to Freud's discussion of the uncanny. Barry uses "uncanny" as a descriptive term, not as a tool for analysis:

> [...] the tales [...] all return to the marvelous, uncanny and the sense of being unreal or negated in one's existence and the role of fantasy in its positive and negative forms in the lives of the protagonists. (Barry)

J.M.Q. Davies refers to Freud's theory of the uncanny indirectly: "[...] [the old woman] might also be seen as a manifestation of what Wright terms the 'return of the repressed.'"[10] Davies does not make the connection between this observation and Freud's definition of the uncanny as the return of the repressed, and he does not go beyond proposing that future critics explore this topic. He suggests only that the story would help uncover the strengths and weaknesses of Freud's essay. Nevertheless, he draws a parallel to Hoffmann's "Der Sandmann" and describes the plot in terms of an oedipal constellation, in which Walther and Bertha manifest Eckbert's "father and displaced mother *imagos*:"[11]

> Both [stories] start by recapitulating childhood events, in both, the protagonist is pursued by a demonic figure who appears in different guises, and in both he is driven to distraction [...]. (Davies 185)

One might add that in both stories the uncertain reality status of the phantom is a primary cause of the poetical uncanny.[12] While Freud's uncanny can be applied to the story, the uncanny effect is not limited to the return of repressed. Swales already captures this narrative ambiguity, although he only briefly summarizes Freud's essay at the end of his article.[13]

As mentioned in the introduction, the critical controversy surrounding the uncanny has been dominated by psychoanalytic literary criticism in general and by Freud's 1919 essay in particular

(Freud, "The 'Uncanny'"). Freud locates the origin of the uncanny in the return of the repressed, or in events seeming to confirm a superstition that we thought we had overcome.[14] The return of the repressed comes into play in "The Fair-Haired Eckbert" because Eckbert and Bertha feel they are guilty and disavow their feelings of guilt. Disavowal, or "negation," is a partial return of the repressed, because the repressed enters the mind in an intellectual form, while the emotional aspect remains unacknowledged.[15] When Bertha kills the bird, and when Eckbert kills Walther, Freud's definition offers a viable explanation for the consequences of disavowal. The phantom's naming of the dog or the transformations of the phantom itself can also be interpreted as manifestations of the return of the repressed. Freud's theory of the uncanny can thus be applied to the story, but the theory neither accounts for the intellectual uncertainty accompanying the return of the repressed, nor does Freud's theory explain all aspects of the story's uncanniness.

The uncanny in "Der blonde Eckbert" is both psychological and textual. The story exhibits a peculiar relation between the text itself and the experiences of the characters. The extradiegetic level of the text and the world that the characters inhabit appear to be interrelated.[16] The phantom that drives Bertha and Eckbert to insanity is not only a symptom of their unconscious but becomes the representation of the fluctuating reality levels arising out of the interaction between reader and text. Beyond its myriad transformations on the diegetic level, the phantom becomes the incarnation of the poetical uncanny.

Fairy Tale Elements in "Der blonde Eckbert"

The movement between novelistic features and fairy tale elements affects the interpretation of the fantastical events in this story. Tieck uses a great number of elements from the fairy tale and some elements of Medieval romance. Apart from these implied references to the distant past, the opening, "In a district of the Harz, dwelt a Knight [...]" (EckE 18),[17] emulates many fairy tales, even if "once upon a time" is omitted. The opening also invokes the fairy tale with the couple's childlessness:

> His wife loved solitude as much as he; both seemed [...] [to love each other with all their hearts], only now and then, they would lament that Heaven had not blessed their marriage with children. (EckE 18)

> Sein Weib liebte die Einsamkeit eben so sehr, und beide schienen sich von Herzen zu lieben, nur klagten sie gewöhnlich darüber, daß der Himmel ihre Ehe mit keinen Kindern segnen wolle. (EckG 126, 9–12)

Childlessness at the beginning of fairy tales is a common indication of future hardships. The classical model for a story of this type is that of the prodigal son. Sometimes, the parents make some pact with the supernatural, but a price is exacted, as in "Tom Thumb" (Daumesdick), from the collection of Grimm's fairy tales:

> There was a poor farmer who sat at his fireplace every evening, and his wife sat and spun. So he said: how sad it is that we have no children!

> Es war ein armer Bauersmann, der saß abends beim Herd und schürte das Feuer, und die Frau saß und spann. Da sprach er, wie ists so traurig, daß wir keine Kinder haben! (Grimm, "Von dem Machandelbaum" 260, my translation)

"Sleeping Beauty" follows the same plot structure: "There was once upon a time a King and Queen, who were so sorry that they had no children, so sorry that it was beyond expression."[18] A third example for this kind of opening is found in "Of the Almond Tree" (Von dem Machandelbaum), another fairy tale in Low German:

> It is now all very long past, about two thousand years, when there was a rich man, who had a beautiful, pious wife, and they loved each other very much, but they had no children, but they wished very much for children, and the

woman therefore prayed day and night, but they didn't have any and didn't have any.

Dat is nu all lang heer, wol twe dusend Johr, do wöör dar ein ryk Mann, de hadd ene schöne frame Fru, un se hadden sik beyde sehr leef, hadden awert kene Kinner, se wünschden sik awerst sehr welke, un de Fru bebdd'd so veel dorüm Dag und Nacht, man se kregen keen un kregen keen. (Grimm, "Von dem Machandelbaum" 260, my translation)

In this and the preceding example, the child has to endure a multitude of adventures before the parents appreciate the wished-for child. Although the parents in the folk fairy tale have their wish fulfilled at last, the childlessness bodes ill for the near future. The magic spell is revoked only after the child has endured certain adventures. In Tieck's story, Bertha's fate is similar to that of the wished-for child in the fairy tales mentioned above. She is clumsy at first, and then proves her worth while living in the woods.[19] Nonetheless, her fate denies her the fairy tale ending of being welcomed by her parents. When she returns home, her caretakers are already dead.

The setting and time of "Der blonde Eckbert" draws not only on the folk fairy tale but also on Knightly Romance, fulfilling another of Schlegel's demands for mixed genres. The story begins in one of the places that is traditionally associated with Medieval Romance, the "Harz" mountains. According to legend, the famed "Barbarossa" resides there.[20] Although the first paragraph places the story in the time of knights, the sentences that immediately follow are untypical of Medieval Romance because of the type of information revealed and the attention to small details:

He was about forty years of age, scarcely of middle stature, and short light-coloured locks lay close and sleek round his pale and sunken countenance. He led a very quiet and solitary life, had never interfered in the feuds of his neighbors. (EckE 18)

Er war ohngefähr vierzig Jahre alt, kaum von mittlerer Größe, und kurze, hellblonde Haare lagen schlicht und dicht an seinem blassen eingefallenen

Gesichte. Er lebte sehr ruhig für sich und war niemals in die Fehden seiner Nachbarn verwickelt [...]. (EckG 126, 4–6)

Eckbert neither has the physical stature of the knightly hero, nor does he conform to the stereotype of the underestimated dwarf of the fairy tale, who later performs impressive deeds. He is not tall and his hair is "simple," suggesting a lack of virility, because it is contrary to the full hair in the description of heroic knights.[21] Eckbert's lack of involvement in feuds underscores his solitary lifestyle.

The blurring of genre boundaries was apparently Tieck's intention. An earlier version of the story was more strongly rooted in the Middle Ages, as demonstrated by Manfred Frank's commentary on one of the differences between an earlier handwritten draft and the published version:

> The character called Hugo in the final version (Ph₁) was called Hugo von Wolfsberg in the earlier version (E), which is proof of Tieck's intention to move the story out of the milieu of knights and into an undefined present. ("Tiecks Redaktion der Erstfassung" 1254–5, my translation)

Tieck inserts fairy tale elements, but their context undercuts fairy tale conventions in two ways. First, Tieck inserts a number of such elements as explicit quotations, which runs counter to the straightforward narrative style of the fairy tale. Apart from the aforementioned childlessness of the couple, Bertha has daydreams that constitute such a quotation:

> Often I would sit in a corner, and fill my little heart with dreams, how I would help [my parents], [...] and then spirits came hovering up, and showed me buried treasures, or gave me little pebbles which changed into precious stones [...]. (EckE 20–1)

> Oft saß ich dann im Winkel und füllte meine Vorstellungen damit an, wie ich [meinen Eltern] helfen wollte, [...] dann sah ich Geister herauf schweben, die mir unterirdische Schätze entdeckten, oder mir kleine Kiesel gaben, die sich in Edelsteine verwandelten [...]. (EckG 128, 9–16)[22]

Another self-referential element appears later in Bertha's story, during her stay in the woods at the old woman's house. Bertha takes the books she reads as a point of departure for her dreams (EckE 29; EckG 135, 12–14). These elements thus also appear like quotations from folk fairy tales and turn Bertha's tale into a self-conscious fairy tale. Bertha's account is a story within "The Fair-Haired Eckbert" and thus transforms the rest of the story into a frame narrative. This runs counter to the straightforward narrative structure of the traditional fairy tale, a technique indicative of the literary fairy tale in general.

Second, Tieck inserts fairy tale elements but uses them in an ambiguous fashion. On the one hand, Bertha's description of her life with her foster parents resembles that of many fairy tales. She has the role of the impractical child who burdens the family. As mentioned above, such children run away from home after over-hearing that they are unwanted. They later often perform some unexpected act of bravery (Grimm, "Hänsel und Gretel"). On the other hand, Tieck makes ambiguous use of the role of the impractical child. He turns Bertha into an outsider, impervious to the practical demands of society, a role more typical of protag-onists in the literary fairy tale. Returning briefly to the description of Eckbert in the first paragraph, these elements not only constitute deviations from the fairy tale convention, but also have a possible psychological significance. Eckbert's emaciated face could express the burdens of his past, both known (Bertha's stealing of the pearls) and yet unknown to him (the incestual marriage).[23] His "pale" and "sunken" face even foreshadows his death. Tieck thus departs from the conventions of the folk fairy tale from the very beginning and attaches the uncanniness of death to Eckbert's character.

Bertha's tendency to daydream is an element that introduces ambiguity into the narrative. As mentioned above, dreamy characters appear in fairy tales as the seemingly least practical of several children, only to prove later that they are the most capable. We find the same type of character in the Romantic novel of development, but with a different function.[24] There, such protagonists are artists who are not successful in the mercantile world of their present, but prove to be in touch with their inner lives and a spiritual dimension existing beyond the visible world. They are, however, also threatened individuals who do not find the happiness granted to their fairy tale counterparts. Bertha's daydreams characterize her as an individual with a Romantic subjectivity:

> [...] in short, the strangest fancies occupied me, and when I had to rise and help with anything, my inexpertness was still greater, as my head was giddy with these motley visions. (EckE 21)

> [...] kurz, die wunderbarsten Phantasien beschäftigten mich, und wenn ich nun aufstehn mußte, um irgend etwas zu helfen [...] so zeigte ich mich noch viel ungeschickter, weil mir der Kopf von allen den seltsamen Vorstellungen schwindelte. (EckG 128, 16–20)

The dreaminess in Bertha's youth is similar to that of Heinrich in Novalis's *Heinrich von Ofterdingen* (1802) or Anselmus in Hoffmann's "The Golden Pot" (1814). It characterizes her as endowed with imagination, and thus casts her as the Romantic outsider. The ambiguous status of certain fictional elements, between folk- and literary fairy tale, extends beyond aspects of Bertha's character to the fantastical elements that confront Bertha.

The Uncanny Caused by the Repressed at the Moment of its Return

The talking bird that Bertha encounters at the old woman's house is a manifestation of the marvelous. We can read it as another fairy tale element, but this phenomenon is also an example of the marvelous that possesses mysterious and uncanny qualities. The talking bird can indicate Bertha's special sensibility or madness.[25] Bertha's delusion of the talking bird is also a partial hallucination. She hears a bird song, translates these sounds into human language, but is unaware of her own translating activity or unable to control the association with human language, so that she perceives the bird as talking to her.[26] The process also involves a "referential delusion," because Bertha imagines that the bird is speaking directly to her.[27] The talking bird in Bertha's account is a fantastical, surreal episode, which contributes to moving her tale further away from the conventions of the folk fairy tale.

The old woman's bird enters the story as a mystery. The bird's capacity to speak is not introduced as a simple fact, which would be customary in a folk fairy tale. Instead, we do not know at first who or what is singing:

> On reaching the bottom of the hill, I heard the strangest song, which seemed to come from the hut, and it sounded as if it was coming from a bird. It sang thus [...]. (EckE 26)

> Als wir vom Hügel hinunter gingen, hörte ich einen wunderbaren Gesang, der aus der Hütte zu kommen schien, wie von einem Vogel, es sang also [...]. (EckG 121, 17–19)[28]

The gradual revelation of the bird's qualities is an example of the uncanny on the diegetic level. We re-experience Bertha's uncertainty through identification. Bertha is sure neither who is singing nor where the sound is coming from. The impersonal construction "it sang," instead of "he sang" ("bird" is masculine in German, "der Vogel") creates doubt about who is singing. Furthermore, the attribute "as if coming from a bird" does not explicitly identify the bird as the singer. "As if" could mean that Bertha hears something that only resembles a bird song, someone singing in a human language, for instance, with a sound reminiscent of a bird's song. Alternatively, the singer could be an invisible spirit that inhabits a bird:

> My curiosity was wonderfully on the stretch; without waiting for the old woman's orders, I stept [sic] into the hut. It was already dusk [...] in a glittering cage, hanging by the window, was a bird, and this in fact proved to be the singer. (EckE 26)

Meine Neugier war außerordentlich gespannt; ohne daß ich auf den Befehl der Alten wartete, trat ich mit[ten] in die Hüte. Die Dämmerung war schon eingebrochen, [...] in einem glänzenden Käfig hing ein Vogel am Fenster, und er war es wirklich, der die Worte sang. (EckG 132, 34–6)

It is important that Bertha explicitly mentions her curiosity. In fairy tales, we expect talking animals as part of the conventions of the genre. The confrontation with the sound in this semirealistic context creates an uncanny impression, because of the uncertainty generated by the fantastical attributes of the bird.

The sequence of events is also important. Only after Bertha has stepped into the hut, her catching sight of the bird removes her uncertainty about the sounds. Up to this point, the reader shares her uncertainty. In this passage, we also encounter the ambiguity of fantastical occurrences typical of the literary fairy tale. The marvelous event has an uncertain reality status, being either the product of Bertha's imagination or an occurrence that contradicts the laws of reality. The marvelous here is much more frightening than in a fairy tale because it is integrated into a realistic context.

The folk fairy tale element of the talking animal is a recurring technique in German Romantic literary fairy tales. In another example, E.T.A. Hoffmann's novel "The Golden Pot" (1814), uncertainty is again generated by withholding the origin of human language. We observe the same sequence of events as in "Der blonde Eckbert." Anselmus hears words first, then he identifies the animal as the speaker:

Between – in-between – between branches, in between budding blossoms, we swing, we sling, we twist – little sister – little sister, sling yourself in the glimmer, swiftly, swiftly upward – downward [...]

Zwischen durch – zwischenein – zwischen Zweigen, zwischen schwellenden Blüten, schwingen, schlängeln, schlingen wir uns – Schwesterlein – Schwesterlein, schwinge dich im Schimmer – schnell, schnell herauf – herab [...][29]

The delayed verification in Hoffmann accentuates the fact that we are confronted with an occurrence that is unheard of in everyday reality.

It is this uncertainty and surprise, and the insistence on witnessing what now suddenly appears as fantastical and extraordinary, that redefines Bertha's story as part of a literary fairy tale, and makes the talking bird uncanny. In the case of "The Fair-Haired Eckbert," the observer is Bertha alone, without witnesses. When the bird confronts Eckbert in the last scene, he too is alone. The reliability of a character is always in question in fictional encounters with a phantom.[30] There are some psychological clues that explain why Bertha might be projecting human language onto innocuous animal sounds. Her projections might be the cause of deep-seated emotions, or she might be suffering from the referential delusion that the bird is talking directly to her.[31] Bertha may have developed the proclivity for such delusions when she was younger.

Bertha's tendencies toward escapist fantasies in her childhood and her wanderings through the forest predispose her to the delusions she suffers later. Bertha wanders through the forest for three days and two nights, without food and with little sleep. There are hints that Bertha is already on the verge of experiencing delusions during the last night of her journey, before she meets the old woman:

> [...] in the darkness I heard the strangest noises; sometimes I took them to proceed from wild beasts, sometimes from wind moaning through the rocks, sometimes from unknown birds. (EckE 23)

> [...] in der Nacht hörte ich die seltsamsten Töne, bald hielt ich es für wilde Tiere, bald für den Wind, der durch die Felsen klagte, bald für fremde Vögel. (EckG 130, 14–16)

This situation forms an early parallel to the encounter with the talking bird. In both instances, Bertha hears strange sounds and is unsure about their origin, and again we are left uncertain about the degree to which the sound is coming from a being endowed with some kind of consciousness. The sound of the wind appears

148

uncanny because the verb "moaning" animates it. The scene shows Bertha on the verge of having hallucinations and makes it more likely that she will hallucinate later. We realize Bertha is already sensitized to bird sounds and may be projecting her emotions onto them. From this point onward, while she experiences complete and life-threatening helplessness, Bertha is more likely to believe that random events in her environment have a special meaning and are directed specifically at her.

Whereas the delusion of the talking bird at first appears as a result of Bertha's deliriousness after days of wandering, the significance of the bird's imagined linguistic ability changes after her years of living with the old woman: "[...] the bird replied to all my questions with his rhyme [...]" (EckE 30).[32] This detail plays an ambiguous role as both fairy tale element and uncanny phenomenon. In a folk fairy tale, we can accept a wise bird that has an answer to every question. If we view Bertha as delusional, however, this exchange of questions and answers means that the bird has become an externalized part of Bertha's psyche. It is possible that the bird fulfills the function of supplying her with an imaginary companion.

The words of the song also change in relation to the person listening. The song first describes Bertha's decision to stay with the old woman. In the stanza appearing at the end of Bertha's narrative, the bird laments having been abducted. Interpreted as a projection, the stanza expresses Bertha's bad conscience for having stolen the bird from the old woman. In the final appearance, when Eckbert hears the bird, it reclaims its life that was taken away by Bertha. Here, it expresses Eckbert's bad conscience of having attempted to kill Walther. In each instance, we can interpret the bird sounds as a projection of the listener's feelings.[33]

Tieck creates a consistent narrative structure to support the sense that Bertha is mad. She exhibits a proclivity towards derangement even before her meeting the old woman. We already noted her childhood conflict with the world of commerce when we discussed the role of the outsider in the literary fairy tale (above on p. 145). Bertha describes her impracticality as the root of her problems with her foster parents:[34]

> [...] and in truth [indeed] I was extremely inexpert and helpless; I let things fall, I neither learnt to sew or to spin [...]. (EckE 20)

> [...] und wirklich war ich äußerst ungeschickt und unbeholfen, ich ließ alles aus den Händen fallen, ich lernte weder nähen noch spinnen [...]. (EckG 128, 5–8)

The impractical children in folk fairy tales are often the ones blessed by the fates and are given a chance to redeem themselves in a situation that challenges their ability to be charitable or courageous. Moreover, while staying with the old woman, Bertha proves that she is capable of practical work. The old woman says that her house, since Bertha belonged to it, "was managed far more perfectly" (EckE 30).[35] Bertha's story differs from that of a folk fairy tale, however, because although she learns domestic skills in captivity, these do not secure a happy end for her. Instead, they signal her growing independence, which will lead to a conflict with the old woman and brings about her escape from the woods. In addition, her handiness in the later part of the episode creates a contrast to her continuing madness, indicated by the second appearance of the song. This contrast obscures the reality status of the bird song. Is Bertha not deranged after all?

If we consider Bertha's troubles before her encounter with the old woman and the talking bird, her becoming delusional appears plausible indeed. She flees the house of her foster parents because she is physically threatened there:

> My father in particular was always very cross to me; he scolded me for being such a burden to the house; indeed he often used me [treated me] rather cruelly [...] he set upon me with furious threats, and as these made no improvement, he one day gave me a most cruel chastisement, and added that the same should be repeated day after day [...]. (EckE 21)

Mein Vater war immer sehr ergrimmt auf mich, daß ich eine so ganz unnütze Last des Hauswesens sei, er behandelte mich daher oft ziemlich grausam [...] er setzte mir mit Drohungen unbeschreiblich zu, da diese aber doch nichts fruchteten, züchtigte er mich auf die grausamste Art und fügte hinzu, daß diese Strafe mit jedem Tage wiederkehren sollte [...]. (EckG 128, 21–32)

This incident and the threat of more physical abuse from her caretaker, who, we find out at the end, is not her father, prompts her flight. The home Bertha finds in the woods is a place of refuge. Although the old woman takes her in, Bertha does not stay with her out of her own free will. Instead, she is stranded with her as if on an island, surrounded by the hostile woods she has traversed. Her situation at the house of her foster parents is similar to that of the unwanted children in "Hänsel und Gretel," another famous Grimm fairy tale (Grimm, "Hänsel und Gretel"). The solitude in the woods is as much a reprieve from her situation at home as it is its replication.[36] Once we view the stay in the woods in this context, we understand the theme of loneliness in the song "Waldeinsamkeit," as an expression of Bertha's sorrow.

While the old woman may appear at first as Bertha's savior, she exhibits peculiar and, as we shall see, uncanny attributes from the beginning.[37] The danger she represents is not clearly visible, but it can be sensed in certain disquieting details of her appearance. The old woman evokes the stereotypical witch because of her age and her cane. Rather than introducing her into the plot as a stock character, Tieck endows her with particular features that make her uncanny. At her very first appearance, the old woman is characterized as inscrutable because of her black clothing and the black hood that covers a large part of her face.[38] Nevertheless, when Bertha later catches a glimpse of her face, she encounters another obstacle obscuring the old woman's features: "[...] at every step she twisted her face so oddly, that at first I was like to laugh" (EckE 25).[39] The nervous twitching does not seem to be associated only with her limp:

> Looking at her so, many qualms and fears came over me; for her face was in perpetual motion; and, besides, her head shook from old age, so that, for my life, I could not understand what sort of countenance she had. (EckE 27)

> Indem ich sie so betrachtete, überlief mich mancher Schauer, denn ihr Gesicht war in einer ewigen Bewegung, indem sie dazu wie vor Alter mit dem Kopfe schüttelte, so daß ich durchaus nicht wissen konnte, wie ihr eigentliches Aussehen beschaffen war. (EckG 133, 4–8)

The quivering in her face has a distinctly maniacal quality, and the text explicitly expresses that Bertha is frightened ("Schauer" means literally "shudder"). Furthermore, the uncanniness of the twitching is analogous to the uncontrolled movement during an epileptic fit, which is one of the phenomena included by Freud in his essay on the uncanny (Freud, "The 'Uncanny'" 243). Finally, the motility of the old woman's features foreshadows the phantom's transformations into different beings.[40] All of these aspects emphasize the uncertainty associated with the phantom, and the story's development demonstrates how this feature, carried to an extreme, becomes threatening and thus uncanny.

Bertha's stay in the woods has an ambiguous status in the narrative. This is especially important in the context of previous interpretations, according to which the song is an expression of Romantic longing, and Bertha is seen as entering a forest paradise (Finney 247; Schulz; Gellinek). The text of the bird song itself is puzzling, and the song has had a somewhat odd history of reception. It was separated from its context within the story and attained the status of a folk song praising the unadulterated beauties of nature.[41] Nevertheless, the song can be interpreted as an expression of melancholy or even unhappiness experienced in the "solitude" of the forest:

> Alone in wood so gay [Forest solitude]
> 'Tis good to stay,
> Morrow like to-day,
> For ever and aye:
> O, I do love to stay,
> Alone in wood so gay. (EckE 26)

Waldeinsamkeit
Die mich erfreut,
So morgen wie heut
In ewger Zeit,
O wie mich freut
Waldeinsamkeit. (EckG 132, 20–5)

The title and first line of the poem "Waldeinsamkeit" was translated by Carlyle as "Alone in Wood so Gay." A literal translation
of the term is "Forest Solitude," however, which reduces these
affirmative connotations. The cheerful interpretation reflected in
the Carlyle translation is itself indicative of the development of the
poem "Waldeinsamkeit" into a central tenet of German Romanticism. More than a hundred years later, "Waldeinsamkeit" returns
as a song by Max Reger, during the late 19th Century Romantic
Revival in the "Kunstlied," in which the uncanny elements of
Tieck's story are now entirely absent.[42] A German literary history
quotes the Tieck poem as a direct expression of German Romantic
ideology: "These lines give poetic expression to the longing for a
new paradise and a golden age, a longing that arose from the
utopian ideas of peace current at the time."[43] The work is made to
attest to a Romantic myth of authenticity, while the text's inherent
ambiguities are overlooked. The separation of "Waldeinsamkeit"
from the context in which it appears may have led critical
commentators to interpret the Bertha episode as an Eden analogy
instead of recognizing its ambiguity.[44]

If we accept the view that the bird song is indeed Bertha or
Eckbert's projection, the song in its very first appearance expresses
Bertha's lament about her ordeal. For Bertha, the solitude in the
woods means being cut off from the outside world. The lines
"Morrow like to-day / For ever and aye" (EckE 26),[45] rather than
expressing an adoration for nature, refer to six years of forced exile
that Bertha endures in the woods as the old woman's captive.[46]
Plot development further indicates that this "loneliness in the
forest" is not a refuge from civilization but a site of frightening

imprisonment.[47] Once Bertha realizes she is being held captive, she escapes.

The formal attributes of the poem "Waldeinsamkeit" further promote the uncanny effect. Bertha says of the first stanza that it was "continually repeated" (EckE 26). Repetition is also a trait of the stanza itself, because the first and the last lines of the song are identical. A repetition of the stanza results in an immediate clash of identical lines: "[...] / Forest solitude. // Forest solitude/[...]." We get the impression that the bird may have language, but not consciousness; it appears programmed like an automaton. The repetition creates the effect of a dead music box; it gives the song a compulsive quality. We can see the repetitions in the song as a type of prison reflex. The bird prefigures Bertha's incarceration in the realm of the old woman, which prompts a retracing of one's own steps like a caged animal. The repetition of this single word thus adds an obsessive quality to the delusion of the talking bird, and has an uncanny effect through the contrast between the folk song refrain and the cruel reality expressed in the word "Waldein-samkeit." Unwanted repetition is one of the phenomena discussed in "The 'Uncanny'" (Freud, "The 'Uncanny'" 237). The concept becomes central in the definition of the death instinct later in *Beyond the Pleasure Principle* (1920g). The desire to return to an earlier state proves "the conservative nature of the drives" (Freud, "Beyond"). Nevertheless, apart from Freud's explanation, every instance of repetition compulsion arouses the suspicion of some hidden force governing the process and is uncanny solely because of the uncertainty about the force's origin.[48]

When we abandon the idealized reading of the bird song, we find additional factors that make the song uncanny. Upon closer examination, the music attributed to the song has an eerie quality. Bertha describes the sounds she hears before she sees the bird: "[...] and to describe the sound, it was as if you heard forest-horns and shalms sounded together from a far distance" (EckE 26); "[...] so war es fast, als wenn Waldhorn und Schalmeien ganz in der

Ferne durcheinander spielten" (EckG 132, 26–9). French horns and shalms (or "shawms") are stock instruments of German folklore, and they could appear at first as an attempt to heighten the bucolic atmosphere of the scene. French horns in particular are associated with the pleasure of hunting. But the verb "durcheinander spielen" can mean not only "sound[ing] together" but also "playing in disharmony, in a mixed up fashion." The nasal sounds of the shawm commingled with the French horns produce a dissonance, which metaphorically represents the awkwardness with which any uncanny phenomenon first comes to the attention of the observer. Furthermore, we need to remind ourselves that this music is presumably not the accompaniment to the bird's singing but the timbre of the bird's voice, heard indistinctly from afar. The odd and uneven quality of this sound adds to the mysterious and frightening quality of the song.

The poem "Waldeinsamkeit" has a simple folk song structure, but its "near" or "imperfect" rhymes introduce another source of ambiguity. Tieck and his contemporaries, Wackenroder, Novalis, Brentano and Eichendorff, all made use of the meter- and rhyme structure of the folk song in their poetry.[49] While imperfect rhymes are forgivable, because they are attributable to the nonartistic aspirations of the folk tradition, they reinforce the disharmony described above. In the song, the sound "-eit" from "Waldeinsamkeit" in lines 1 and 6, and "Zeit" in line 4, clashes with the sound "-eut" in "erfreut" line 2, "heut" in line 3 and "freut" in line 5.[50] These imperfect rhymes onomatopoetically mimic the sound of the intermingled wind instruments. They increase the awkward atmosphere and again heighten the song's uncanniness.[51]

If Bertha's experience of the bird song is a referential delusion, there is a striking similarity to the Schreber case. Freud describes the lines produced by Schreber's "miracled" talking birds ("gewunderte Vögel") as entirely arbitrary:

They cannot understand the meaning of the words they speak, but they are by nature susceptible to similarity of sounds, though the similarity need not necessarily be a complete one. Thus, it is immaterial to them whether one says:

"Santiago" *or* "Karthago",

"Chinesentum" *or* "Jesum Christum",

"Abendrot" *or* "Atemnot",

"Ariman" *or* "Ackermann" etc. [...]⁵²

The words that Schreber's mind produces when projecting words onto bird sounds possess a volatility we can observe in other literary examples, such as in the talking snakes that Anselmus encounters in Hoffmann's "Golden Pot."⁵³ If we attempt to reconstruct the mental processes leading to the delusion, the rhymes could result from an uncontrolled mental activity that strings words with similar sounds together, through a process akin to free association. Thus, a primordial rhyme-making activity could be a common trait of the imagined songs that individuals create when they project thoughts onto neutral sense data like bird sounds. The examples support the hypothesis that the talking bird is a symptom of Bertha's madness.

Let us now turn to the question of Bertha's mysterious death, which is an important source of uncertainty for the reader. We have already found justifications for her escape from the old woman's realm, but the uncanny impression of Bertha's death on the reader has several other sources. The cause of her death is shrouded in mystery. If we view Bertha as a victim of traumatic events in her past, her death may be the result of succumbing to a nervous ailment, which originates in the delusions we have already traced. We have examined the bird song and the events preceding it as indications of psychotic derangement. Bertha's past may therefore be the breeding ground for an overpowering anxiety that destroys her at the moment when this past is revived. If we assume that Walther possesses supernatural powers, Bertha's death may be the enforcement of the threat announced by the old woman:

156

"[…] but none ever prospers when he leaves the straight path; punishment will overtake him, though it may be late." (EckE 30)

"[…] aber nie gedeiht es, wenn man von der rechten Bahn abweicht, die Strafe folgt nach, wenn auch noch so spät." (EckG 135, 36–136, 1)

The phantom's power is itself uncanny, however, because Bertha's punishment appears unjustified and entirely disproportional in relation to her transgressions. The phantom appears as an inscrutable force, and has an uncanny effect on the reader, because of this combination of threat and inscrutability. As we shall see below, we can also interpret the phantom as the manifestation of a pagan force of nature that is indiscriminately hostile to human beings.[54]

Strohmian

The revelation of the dog's name marks an important turning point in the story. Bertha dies soon afterwards, and her death appears to be a direct consequence of a few words, seemingly spoken innocently by Walther:

"Many thanks, noble lady; I can well figure you beside your singing bird, and how you fed poor little *Strohmian*." (EckE 35, emphasis Tieck)

"Edle Frau, ich danke Euch, ich kann mir Euch recht vorstellen, mit dem seltsamen Vogel, und wie Ihr den kleinen *Strohmian* füttert." (EckG 140, 22–4, emphasis Tieck)

It is possible to apply Freud's notion of the uncanny to the incidents surrounding the end of Bertha's stay with the old woman and Walther's revelation. Nevertheless, Freud's definition does not account for everything that is uncanny in the text.

Walther's revelation of the dog's name can be understood as a pre-psychoanalytic representation of the return of the repressed. If we understand repression as an overdetermined instance of oblivion, Tieck embodies this insight in the representation of how Bertha forgets the dog's name:

> I am surprised that I have never since been able to recall the dog's name, a very odd one, often as I then pronounced it. (EckE 28)
>
> Ich habe mich immer nicht wieder auf den seltsamen Namen des Hundes besinnen können, sooft ich ihn auch damals nannte. (EckG 134, 21–3)

Considering that Bertha spends six years with the old woman, it appears unlikely that Bertha would forget the dog's name. The name thus comes to represent the repressed guilt about killing the bird, abandoning the dog, and stealing the pearls. The English translation of "habe mich immer nicht wieder" as "never since been able" is not a completely accurate rendition of the odd German antithesis "immer nicht wieder," which translates literally as "always not again," instead of "never again" (niemals wieder) or "never" (nie). The syntax mirrors the process of repression and its return. Instead of expressing failed recollection for a continuous period, it expresses how the recollection of the dog's name becomes impossible each time the incidents arise in the mind. "Immer wieder" means "repeatedly," mirroring the individual instances where the repressed tries to gain access to consciousness. Furthermore, the two words "always" (immer) and "again" (wieder) emphasize the pressing insistence of the memory.[55] We can apply Freud's definition of the uncanny to this passage and view Walther's revelation as a pre-psychoanalytic representation of the return of the repressed. Nevertheless, the element of uncertainty is contained in the text in the old woman's transformation into Walther. Tieck thus creates an equivalent on the plot level for the fact that we do not recognize the repressed as something familiar when it returns. Nevertheless, we found in the Freud chapter that Freud excludes precisely this uncertainty in his description of the uncanny. Furthermore, the psychoanalytic explanation, even if we append the aspect of disorientation, does not account for the uncanny impression of the text as a whole, as we will show in more detail below.

Walther's naming of the dog suggests the phantom's knowledge of the past.[56] Kenneth Northcott has correctly identified this point as crucial for evaluating the role of the supernatural in the story.[57] At this moment, the world of Bertha's childhood has an effect on the frame narrative of Eckbert's marriage with Bertha.[58] With the ending in mind, the phantom is established here as a supernatural reality on the plot level, apart from its possible significance as a projection of Bertha or Eckbert. Nevertheless, Northcott goes too far when claiming that all doubts about Walther's supernatural abilities disappear at this point. This assumption is similar to Freud's claim that the end of Hoffmann's "Der Sandmann" removes all doubts about the identity of Coppelius and Coppola (Freud, "The 'Uncanny'" 230, 28–30). Although Walther may have a secret alliance with the old woman, naming the dog does not reveal his identity. The source of his knowledge remains a mystery and is thus uncanny for his reason alone.

One possible hypothesis about Bertha's death is to assume that she dies of bad conscience about her evil deeds, with the phantom being a manifestation of her guilt. Nevertheless, Bertha's deception of the old woman, the theft of the pearls, her abandonment of the dog and the killing of the bird can appear justified or at least ambiguous.[59] We shall find that Bertha lacks a valid reason for developing a bad conscience. If the forest episode were an Eden analogy, the phantom would play the role of the serpent. The phantom's warnings themselves against "leaving the straight path" (EckE 30) plant the seeds for Bertha's eventual discovery of the opportunity for theft:

> At last it struck me that her pearls and jewels might perhaps be something precious. Ere long, this thought grew clearer to me. But the straight path, and leaving it? What could she mean by this? (EckE 30)

> [...] und am Ende fiel mir ein, daß ihre Perlen und Edelsteine wohl etwas Kostbares sein könnten. Dieser Gedanke wurde mir bald noch deutlicher.

Aber was konnte sie mit der rechten Bahn meinen? Ganz konnte ich den Sinn ihrer Worte noch immer nicht fassen. (EckG 136, 6–11)

Bertha does not understand the concept of "leaving the straight path," because she has never contemplated evil.[60] Although Bertha herself comments that "it is the misery of man that he arrives at understanding through the loss of innocence" (EckE 30),[61] the story does not exactly replicate a biblical fall from grace. Gellinek and Tatar are prime examples of critics who fail to see the obstacles to a moral evaluation of the characters (Gellinek; Tatar). Here, the paradise is also a prison, and the master of this sphere is a phantom, who appears in the guise of the archetypal witch of the folk fairy tale.[62] Bertha's escape appears justified in the light of *Hänsel and Gretel*, who shove the witch into an oven. The phantom can hardly function as a representative of moral or even divine authority, because it deceives Bertha and later Eckbert about its identity and seeks revenge.[63] The moral ambiguity of the phantom contributes to its uncanny effect.

The reasons for Bertha's death remain unclear. Her bad conscience may play a role, but her guilt is relative, as we have seen. We have read Bertha's story as a gradual descent into madness, prompted by our investigation of the significance of the talking bird. The signals in the text on which to base an evaluation of both Bertha's and later Eckbert's sanity are thus equally ambiguous as in the case of Nathanael in Hoffmann's "Der Sandmann." The formal attributes of the bird song point to its ambiguous status between a harmless Romantic nature poem and a manifestation of the poetical uncanny caused by ambiguity. Although we can read the talking bird as a symptom of mental derangement, it is also a supernatural phenomenon. The literary fairy tale allows for both possibilities at once. The world of phantoms is not simply a symbolic representation of psychological phenomena, and an exclusively Freudian interpretation of the phantom does not explain its uncanny effect.

Chapter 7:
Paranoiac Structures of Perception in "Eckbert"

In Tieck's story, the poetical uncanny can be traced in the transient existence of the phantom. Rather than understanding the phantom only as one factor determining the reader's uncertainty, its metamorphoses prefigure all the transformations in the story, such as the doubling of Eckbert and Bertha. The phantom thus becomes the governing principle of the text, and finally represents the reader's interpretative activity, on the level that the characters inhabit. Such a projection of extradiegetic elements onto the diegetic level is possible, because the reader takes part in endowing the phantom with its uncanny qualities. Considering, therefore, that the phantom might well be responsible for the deaths of both protagonists, the text becomes uncanny because it implicates the reader in the phantom's violent acts.

Similarities between Eckbert and Bertha

An important manifestation of the uncanny in "The Fair-Haired Eckbert," apart from the phantom and the beings associated with its realm, is the problematic individuality of the two central characters. It is possible to interpret Eckbert and Bertha as one person. Consequently, they form the counterpart to the manifold incarnations of phantom. The two characters are united through their names, they share an urge to tell secrets, and both have uncontrollable aggressive impulses. Other parallels lie in such external aspects as the landscapes they traverse or the details of their encounter with the phantom. Not only Bertha but also Eckbert suffers from persecutory delusions. These connections are overdetermined. They not only foreshadow the incest between brother and sister but also bind the two central characters closely together, threatening to break down the very concept of the individual.[1] This uncertainty about boundaries not only pervades the reading experience, but Tieck also creates – in the figure of the phantom itself – a representative of this uncertainty in the world that the characters inhabit.

The two central characters are united through the similarity of their names. The letters "bert" appear in both "bert-ha" and "eck-bert." While a family relationship would normally be visible in the last, not the first name, the similarity in name is a metaphor for the hidden family relation, which is revealed only at the end of the story. The effect of the shared syllable is similar to the uncanny effect that arises when, as Freud writes, long held beliefs or superstitions seem suddenly confirmed (Freud, "The 'Uncanny'" 249). Alternatively, the uncanniness of coincidences can also be explained by considering that coincidences are threatening because they conflict with the randomness we come to expect from experience. The similarity of names violates the laws of probability. While chance in a fictional universe is frequently overstepped to come to the aid of the protagonist,[2] the coincidence of similar first names in "Der blonde Eckbert" foreshadows a transgression of which the perpetrators are unaware. If the uncanny is understood as a threat that is invisible or lurking, then the shared syllable is uncanny, because it is evidence of a fictional universe that conspires against Eckbert and Bertha.

The desire to reveal secrets is an impulse shared by both protagonists. It originates with Eckbert but manifests itself in Bertha. Before Bertha tells her story, the omniscient narrator comments on the impulse to reveal secrets in the first of four short narrator comments.[3] The narrator uses the word for "human being" ("Mensch" in German, which can refer to men and women). In the context of the story, the reader initially attributes the impulse to reveal secrets to Eckbert because we have read a full paragraph, immediately preceding this passage, about the evolving friendship between the two Eckbert and Walther:

> There are hours in which a man feels grieved that he should have a secret from his friend, which, till then, he may have kept with niggard anxiety; some irresistible desire lays hold of our [the] heart to open itself wholly, to disclose its inmost recesses to our [the] friend, that so he may become our friend still more. (EckE 19)

> Es gibt Stunden, in denen es den Menschen ängstigt, wenn er vor seinem Freunde ein Geheimnis haben soll, was er bis dahin oft mit vieler Sorgfalt verborgen hat, die Seele fühlt dann einen unwiderstehlichen Trieb, sich ganz mitzuteilen, dem Freunde auch das Innerste aufzuschließen, damit er um so mehr unser Freund werde. (EckG 126, 31–2; 127, 1–4)

Thus, when we hear that Walther is sitting at the fire with Eckbert and his wife, we expect Eckbert or Walther to reveal something about himself. Nevertheless, Eckbert encourages his wife to reveal her story, instead of talking about himself:

> "Now you must let my wife tell you the history of her youth, it is curious enough, and you should know it." (EckE 20)

> "Freund, Ihr solltet euch einmal von meiner Frau die Geschichte ihrer Jugend erzählen lassen, die seltsam genug ist." (EckG 127, 24–6)

At this point, it is still possible that Bertha's story will reveal some secret of Eckbert's. Bertha's narrative, however, yields only the relatively insignificant fact that Eckbert might have profited from the pearls Bertha has stolen. The main thrust of Bertha's narrative is to reveal her own secret. Because of the length of Bertha's narrative, it appears that not only Eckbert but also she herself is driven by the impulse to reveal a secret. At the end of Bertha's narrative, about halfway through the story, when we have heard about her transgressions, we are likely to identify the confessional impulse with Bertha. This gradual shift ties the impulse to reveal secrets to both protagonists and thus also creates a link between them.[4]

163

The second connection between the characters is their tendency to disavow aggressive impulses. Both Eckbert and Bertha commit crimes for which we can identify unconscious origins. The narrative exposes how they disavow their impulses and how these manifest themselves nevertheless.[5] Tieck takes much care to explore how persecution mania unfolds in Eckbert, and how he ends up shooting at Walther with his crossbow. At the same time, the narrative dissociates intention from action on the textual level. The entire process governing denial is depicted in its individual stages, starting with Eckbert's aggression that grows into a murderous impulse:

> It seemed as if he should be gay and light of heart, were that one thing [better: "being"] but removed. (EckE 37)

> Es schien ihm, als würde ihm froh und leicht sein, wenn nur dieses einzige Wesen aus seinem Wege gerückt werden könnte. (EckG 142, 9–14)

The passive voice in "be removed" indicates Eckbert's dissociation from his aggression from the onset. Eckbert's hunting expedition constitutes the next attempt to deny the impulse: "He took his [cross]bow, to dissipate these thoughts; and went to hunt" (EckE 37).[6] The hunt culminates in an act that seems to be independent of volition:

> All at once he saw an object moving in the distance; it was Walther gathering moss from the trunks of trees. Scarce knowing what he did, he bent his bow [...] he took aim; Walther looked round, and gave a threatening gesture, but the arrow was already flying, and he sank transfixed by it. (EckE 38)

> Plötzlich sah er sich etwas in der Ferne bewegen, es war Walther, der Moos von den Bäumen sammelte; ohne zu wissen was er tat, legte er an, Walther sah sich um, und drohte mit einer stummen Gebärde, aber indem flog der Bolzen ab, und Walther stürzte nieder. (EckG 142, 19–24)

The text dissociates agent from act in three ways. One is to leave out the firing of the arrow and to show only the effect. The attack itself takes place in a "blank space" of narration.[7] The "blank space" thus re-enacts on the textual level Eckbert's wished-for blotting out of the deed from consciousness. The second dissociation between action and deed consists in the use of the crossbow. Instead of a bow and arrow, where a physical effort is required, a crossbow allows for a delay between preparation and firing. Eckbert winds the crossbow up at the beginning of his hunt. When he fires it, he only has to pull the trigger. The crossbow is metaphorically equivalent to Eckbert's aggressions building before he goes hunting. They are stored in his unconscious, ready to be released inadvertently whenever an occasion presents itself. The crossbow represents Eckbert's psyche. The third separation between agent and deed consists in Eckbert's physical withdrawal after the deed: "Eckbert felt relieved and calmed, yet a certain horror drove him home to his castle" (EckE 37).[8] This retreat is consistent with the repression of motives that marks the entire hunting episode and pertains here to the feared outcome of the deed. The expression "certain horror" (better "shudder" – "Schauder") suggests that Eckbert does not fully grasp the implications of his actions.

A consequence of this withdrawal is that we are unsure whether Walther has been merely injured or actually killed. All we hear is that Walther collapses.[9] Undoubtedly, Walther reappears at the end of the story. His return dramatizes the return of the repressed. Walther returns as a symptom of the vengeful impulse that Eckbert has repressed. Eckbert cannot approach Walther after he has shot at him because he needs to repress the possible outcome of his deed.

When we compare this passage to Bertha's killing of the bird, we notice the similarity, even in diction. Again the impulse to kill seems to be dormant and then manifests itself suddenly:

When I rose, the aspect of the bird distressed me greatly; he looked at me continually, and his presence did me ill [...]. The more I looked at him, the more he pained and frightened me; at last I opened the cage, put it in my hand, and grasped his neck, [sic] I squeezed my fingers hard together, he looked at me, I slackened them; but he was dead [better: but he had already died]. (EckE 34–5)

Als ich aufstand, war mir der Anblick des Vogels ordentlich zuwider, er sah immer nach mir hin, und seine Gegenwart ängstigte mich [...] Je mehr ich ihn betrachtete, je bänger machte er mich; ich öffnete endlich den Käfig, steckte die Hand hinein und faßte seinen Hals, herzhaft drückte ich die Finger zusammen, er sah mich bittend an, ich ließ los, aber er war schon gestorben. (EckG 139, 30–140, 2)

In both instances the motivation to kill stems from the desire to eradicate the past. In addition, in this passage, like the arrow flying as if by itself, Bertha's fingers reach into the cage as if they were not at her command. In both instances, the victim casts a glance at the attacker, which temporarily halts the impulse to kill, but this reversal also comes too late: the deed has already been carried out. And in both cases, the deed does not yield the desired result. Just as Walther reappears in the figure of Hugo, the bird returns in the final scene, and it too functions as a representation of the return of the repressed. Although this confirms Freud's thesis that the uncanny has its origin in the return of the repressed, we will see below that this interpretation is not the only explanation for the uncanniness of the supernatural phenomena in this text.

Bertha's escape from the house of her foster parents and from the domicile of the old woman is described in similar terms. These passages are further representations of how an impulse is disavowed but returns in the form of an action performed in a dreamlike state. When Bertha leaves her foster parents, she describes her escape: "At the dawn of the day I arose, and scarcely knowing what I did, I unfastened the door of our little hut" (EckE 22); "Als der Tag graute, stand ich auf und eröffnete, fast ohne daß ich es wußte, die Tür unserer kleinen Hütte" (EckG 129, 5–6). She has not contemplated an escape before, only despaired. She does not consciously plan an escape, perhaps because she is unable to accept the disobedience to her foster parents that it entails. Bertha's escape from the old woman's domicile is portrayed in a similar fashion:

I had a sort of fear on taking leave of her, for I felt as if I should not see her anymore [...] it was almost as if my purpose had already stood before me, without myself being conscious of it. (EckE 30)

Ich nahm mit einer gewissen Bangigkeit von ihr Abschied, es war mir, als würde ich sie nicht wieder sehn. Ich sah ihr lange nach, und wußte selbst nicht, warum ich so beängstigt war, es war fast, als wenn mein Vorhaben schon vor mir stände, ohne dessen deutlich mir bewußt zu sein. (EckG 136, 33–137, 2)

Bertha's struggle between loyalty and desire for freedom is portrayed as a disavowal of the old woman's prohibition. Her desire for freedom nevertheless manifests itself in her actions, which occur seemingly without her conscious participation.

Although we recognize unconscious processes in the passages discussed above, a differentiation between Tieck's implicit and Freud's explicit notion is called for. Furthermore, Bertha's dreamlike state, in which disavowed impulses resurface as actions performed without volition, need to be distinguished from the faculty seen as a source of intuition by Schlegel:

Philosophers probably have a greater degree of ingenious unconsciousness [...] than poets. (Schlegel, "Athenäums-Fragment 299", Translation MF)

An genialischem Unbewußtsein können die Philosophen [...] den Dichtern den Rang streitig machen. (Schlegel, "Athenäums-Fragment 299")

While Schlegel talks about an unnamed source of inspiration, Tieck dramatizes the machinations of guilt. Although the manifestations of this inspiration may become visible in works of art, Bertha and Eckbert's violence follows the psychology of guilt. Their violent actions are themselves a source of the uncanny for the characters because the driving forces behind their actions are invisible to them. They are also uncanny for the reader through identification with the characters. In addition, the process of repression and its return are here "embodied in fiction," but Tieck neither "states these laws" nor needs to be "fully aware" of them (Freud, *Jensens "Gradiva"* 92).

An important feature connecting Eckbert and Bertha is their tendency to suffer from persecutory delusions.[10] After Bertha has finished her story, we are informed of Eckbert's regrets and are given a first glimpse of his persecution mania. This happens even before we hear about Bertha's illness. Eckbert gets suspicious about Walther's knowledge of the dog's name:

> It now occurred to his mind that Walther had not taken leave of him so cordially as might have been expected after such a mark of trust: the soul once set upon suspicion finds in every trifle something to confirm it. (EckE 36)

> Es fiel ihm ein, daß Walther nicht so herzlich von ihm Abschied genommen hatte, als es nach einer solchen Vertraulichkeit wohl natürlich gewesen wäre. Wenn die Seele erst einmal zum Argwohn gespannt ist, so trifft sie auch in allen Kleinigkeiten Bestätigungen an. (EckG 140, 34–141, 1)

The second sentence here constitutes the third of four narrator comments.[11] The narrator explicitly states how suspicion can grow into paranoia. We find out later that Walther's actions justify Eckbert's mistrust. For example, Walther lets Bertha tell her story without revealing to either one of his listeners that he is an incarnation of the old woman. Nevertheless, Eckbert does not know this at the time his suspicions begin. The question whether Eckbert is paranoid thus depends not only on whether he bases his suspicion on correct assumptions, but on the objective existence of a conspiracy.

Eckbert's Paranoia

The narrator isolates the urge to reveal secrets as a possible cause of persecution mania. Walther, to whom Eckbert wants to reveal a secret, has not requested this knowledge. Whenever one person forces a secret onto another, the person having divulged the secret may wonder afterwards whether the listener is indeed trustworthy.

Although the death of both protagonists appears morally unjustified, the urge to reveal secrets and the resulting paranoia may offer at least a partial explanation.

Regardless of whether Eckbert mortally wounds Walther with his arrow, Eckbert firmly believes he has killed Walther. The narrator, in his intervention, makes it clear that Eckbert reveals his secret to Hugo because he is driven by the same urge to deepen his friendship that compelled him to urge his wife to tell her secret.[12] Eckbert is unaware that Hugo is a new incarnation of Walther. The narrator further explores how the urge to reveal a secret leads to growing suspicion:

> But it seemed to be his doom that, in the very hour of confidence, he should always find materials for suspicion. Scarcely had they entered the public hall, when, in the glitter of the many lights, Hugo's looks had ceased to satisfy him [there was something about Hugo's appearance he did not like]. He thought he noticed a malicious smile; he remarked [better: noticed] that Hugo did not speak to him as usual, that he talked with the rest, and seemed to pay no heed to him. (EckE 40)

> Es schien aber seine Verdammnis zu sein, gerade in der Stunde des Vertrauens Argwohn zu schöpfen, denn kaum waren sie in den Saal getreten, als ihm beim Schein der vielen Lichter die Mienen seines Freundes nicht gefielen. Er glaubte ein hämisches Lächeln zu bemerken, es fiel ihm auf, daß er nur wenig mit ihm spreche, daß er mit den Anwesenden viel rede, und seiner gar nicht zu achten scheine. (EckG 144, 3–9)

The introductory narrator comment is similar to the one regarding Eckbert's relations with Walther (quoted above on p. 163), but the word "doom" (Verdammnis) introduces a new dimension, that of a fatal flaw. The incident is described in great detail. Eckbert's perception becomes increasingly selective. He believes he notices "a malicious smile." Does Hugo's smile in fact have a gloating quality? Perhaps it does, and Eckbert is close enough to detect it. In that case, the expression "he thought he noticed" signals that the maliciousness was hard to notice, but that Eckbert noticed it nevertheless.[13] On the other hand, it can mean that Eckbert projects maliciousness onto an entirely harmless smile. The fact that "Hugo did not speak to him as [much as] usual, and seemed to pay no heed him" (EckE 40) is natural behavior at a festivity with a large number of people, which Eckbert may be misinterpreting as hostility. Eckbert's suspiciousness leads him to interpret ambiguous impressions so that they support the persecution as a fact.[14] Ambiguous impressions here have an uncanny effect on Eckbert. Such textual ambiguities contribute to the uncanny effect on the reader.

Eckbert becomes even more suspicious when Hugo talks to an old knight, who has often asked about his riches and therefore reminds Eckbert of the wealth acquired through Bertha. The mere fact that Hugo and the old knight are talking and gesturing towards him gives Eckbert the impression that he has been betrayed. We do not know, however, what Hugo and the old knight are in fact talking about, and there is no indication that the two men are deriding Eckbert. Seen in the context of the commentary about Eckbert's increased suspicion, it is likely that Eckbert is reading into his observations and assuming that Hugo is receiving some unfavorable information about him.

This scene comes to a climax when Eckbert sees Hugo transform himself into Walther. If we take Eckbert's point of view at face value, this is a supernatural occurrence. If we see him slipping towards psychosis, then this moment marks the transition from misinterpretation to madness:

> As he continued gazing, on a sudden [sic] he discerned the countenance of Walther, all his features, all the form so well known to him; he gazed, and looked [he continued to look at him], and felt convinced [better: "was convinced"] that it was none but Walther who was talking to the knight. His horror cannot be described; in a state of frenzy he rushed out of the hall [...]. (EckE 40)

> Indem er noch immer hinstarrte, sah er plötzlich Walthers Gesicht, alle seine Mienen, die ganze ihm so wohl bekannte Gestalt, er sah noch immer hin und war überzeugt, daß Niemand als *Walther* mit dem Alten spreche. – Sein

Entsetzen war unbeschreiblich; außer sich stürzte er hinaus [...]. (EckG 144, 17–21, emphasis Tieck)

The expression "was convinced" creates uncertainty about the reality status of the event.[15] We can explain the suspicions against Hugo as a repetition of the earlier conflict of Eckert with Walther. Eckbert sees Hugo as Walther because Hugo reminds him of Walther. The issues of trust and revealing secrets are brought to the fore again in this new friendship, when Eckbert tells Hugo of his attack on Walther. When Eckbert sees Hugo as Walther we can thus firstly interpret it as a visual delusion caused by repressed guilt.

Hugo, as phantom, conceals his identity from Eckbert. This deception is indeed part of the phantom's conspiracy. Therefore, Eckbert's mistrust of Hugo is justified, even if he misinterprets this particular incident, although this too is uncertain. Rather than being a delusion, Eckbert might be getting a glimpse of the phantom's ability to change shapes.

Seen this way, we need to revise our evaluation of Eckbert's guilt. Above, we interpreted the passage as the narrator's implicit accusation of Eckbert. The narrator seemed intent on showing how Eckbert's guilt-ridden conscience alters his perceptions. Once we interpret Eckbert's observations not as delusions but as observations of fictional supernatural events, we perceive him as the relatively weak victim of persecution, notwithstanding his partial guilt, by an opponent many times more powerful than he. This overturns our original impression of the narrator's implied condemnation, and we have reason to call this narrator unreliable.[16] The ambiguity of the implied narrator commentary constitutes an important aspect of the poetical uncanny in this story. The unreliable narrator is an inherent auxiliary factor of the poetical or textual uncanny because it adds to the disorientation of the reader.

In exploring the parallel between Eckbert and Bertha, we find that both characters have a tendency to feel persecuted. In each case, the reader finds it difficult to determine whether or not this suspiciousness constitutes paranoia. We observed Eckbert's progression from bad conscience to confession to exaggerated suspicion, resulting in a persecutory delusion that turns out not only to be justified, but that loses some of its indicting qualities in the process. Bertha's case is similar. We have little information about the development of her possible paranoia after Walther has reminded her of the dog's name. Her death occurs while the action is focused on Eckbert's maniacal hunting expedition. We already found some evidence for Bertha's predisposition for madness in the talking bird. While she only attributes her deteriorating health to her inability to sleep, we can speculate that the primary cause of her death is her feeling of guilt.

On the other hand, if we assume that the supernatural exists in the world of "The Fair-Haired Eckbert," and the laws governing ordinary reality are invalidated, we can view Bertha's death as a punishment carried out by the phantom. Nevertheless, upon closer examination, her death seems as unjustified as Eckbert's. As mentioned above, the bird reappears in the last scene, leading us to question whether the bird's death was ordinary. If the phantom can revive the bird at any time, it cannot truly be killed. Bertha's theft of the pearls appears equally inconsequential, because the bird insures a never-ending supply of pearls. If Bertha's actions have no lasting consequences, is her guilt the same? How are we to judge her ill intentions against an all-powerful phantom? Bertha also has no knowledge of the incestuous nature of her marriage to Eckbert. Does Bertha's incest constitute a crime regardless of intent, only because of extraneous circumstances of which she is unaware? While guilt is established legally regardless of the ignorance of the offender, intent and knowledge of the law change our moral evaluation. Most importantly, however, Tieck creates a universe in which guilt is decided independently of moral choices and the law is enforced long after the offense. In Tieck's story, this threat invisibly hovers over Eckbert and Bertha's lives at all times, which makes it uncanny from the reader's point of view.

Landscapes and Mindscapes

Another shared element between the two central characters is the landscape in which Bertha and Eckbert encounter the phantom. Cragged rocks and the waterfall in both instances seem to indicate that the characters get lost in the same forest. Before Bertha meets the old woman, the landscape she traverses becomes increasingly threatening:

> [...] the crags grew more and more frightful; I had many a time to glide along by the very edge of dreadful abysses; by degrees my foot-path became fainter, and at last all traces of it vanished from beneath me [...].
> [...]
> Instead of the hoped-for mill, I came upon a water-fall [...]. (EckE 23, 24)

> Die Felsen wurden immer furchtbarer, ich mußte oft dicht an schwindlichten Abgründen vorbeigehn, und endlich hörte sogar der Weg unter meinen Füßen auf.
> [...]
> Statt der gehofften *[sic]* Mühle stieß ich auf einen Wasserfall [...]. (EckG 130, 6–9; 131, 12)

When Eckbert meets the old woman, the rocks become threatening and confusing as they did during Bertha's journey, and the encounter with the phantom occurs again near a waterfall:

> Having hastened on some days at the quickest pace of his horse, he, on a sudden [sic], found himself entangled in a labyrinth of rocks, from which he could discover no outlet. At length he met an old peasant, who took him by a path leading past a waterfall [...]. (EckE 41)

> Als er im stärksten Trabe seines Pferdes einige Tage so fort geeilt war, sah er sich plötzlich in einem Gewinde von Felsen verirrt, in denen sich nirgend ein Ausweg entdecken ließ [...]. Endlich traf er auf einen alten Bauer, der ihm einen Pfad, an einem Wasserfall vorüber, zeigte [...]. (EckG 144, 37– 145, 4)

If we pursue the psychoanalytic interpretation we can say that both protagonists are drawn into this landscape because they are running away from something. The further they advance, the more threatening the landscape becomes. The rocky landscape is thus first a metaphor for the course of their lives, which – seen as routes of escape – lead into self-entanglement and confusion. The waterfall, which is close to the place where the phantom resides in the woods, serves as an image for the uncontrollable events that culminate in their deaths. The mountain and forest landscape is thus also a metaphor for the jagged inner world of madness. This parallel between Eckbert and Bertha also foreshadows the hidden incestuous connection between the two central characters.

As an alternative to the psychoanalytic interpretation, we can view the landscape as the manifestation of the same uncanny hostility represented by the phantom. In terms of the aforementioned mixing of genres, the hostile landscape is indicative of the literary fairy tale. While the forest represents danger in the folk fairy tale, the characters traditionally surmount these dangers, and couples live happily ever after. In contrast, the landscape in Tieck's story represents the doom that awaits the protagonists.[17]

Eckbert's encounter with the phantom, seen as an outcome of a persecutory delusion, presents the same difficulties we have discussed above concerning Bertha. The complications arise because it is unclear whether this meeting is a supernatural event, albeit real in the world of the characters, or a hallucination of a mentally deranged character. In Eckbert's case, we have already traced clues pointing to his gradual descent into madness, such as the narrator's comments and his suspiciousness towards Hugo, which appears as a plausible reaction to the guilt of having presumably killed Walther. We find more evidence for the assumption that Eckbert is hallucinating in the frequent repetition of the antithetical syntactic structure "none other than x." This structure appears first in Eckbert's aforementioned thoughts when he sees Hugo transformed into Walther: "none but Walther" (EckE 40).[18] It appears again when he meets the old peasant by the waterfall: "it was none but Walther" (EckE 41).[19] The same syntactical structure appears in the locution of the phantom, when it finally reveals its transformations: "None other than I" (EckE 42).[20] The parallel syntax suggests not only that Eckbert supplies the text for the phantom but also that the entire incident is hallucinated.

Furthermore, the phrase "none but Walther" is itself uncanny. Let us consider that these utterances are real within the world of the text, spoken by a being with the power to take on different shapes. The correct translation of the phrases into English would be "no one (other) but Walther" and "no one but I." Rather than making a straightforward assertion, the phantom uses antithesis here, denying the contrary ("I am not Hugo; I am not the peasant") and asserting its identity ("I am only Walther"). The use of antithesis sometimes brings both parts of the construction into focus, so that the portion that is denied suddenly appears as a part of the meaning. If we look at both portions independently, the phantom also identifies itself as "no one, nobody." It thus identifies itself accurately as the thing that it is, a being made of nothing. Nevertheless, when the phantom says it has one true identity, "I am none other than Walther," it simultaneously makes a false claim about its identity. The phantom has, after all, appeared in four different incarnations (old woman, Walther, Hugo, peasant). Tieck thus heightens the phantom's uncanniness through the extradiegetic implications of one of its utterances.[21]

The encounter with the talking bird completes our survey of parallels between Eckbert and Bertha. We found indications that Eckbert imagines the final meeting with the phantom because of the antithetical syntax in the phantom's speech. We also discussed how Bertha's encounter with the bird changes from an element of the folk fairy tale to an inconclusive phenomenon, situated somewhere between a symptom of delusion and fantastical occurrence. We mentioned how differences in the words of the song seem to correspond directly to the situations of the person listening. In its second appearance, the song seems to reflect Bertha's bad conscience for having abducted the bird:

Alone in wood so gay,
Ah, far away!
But thou wilt say
Some other day,
'Twere best to stay
Alone in wood so gay. (EckE 34)

Waldeinsamkeit
Die mich erfreut,
So morgen wie heut
In ewger Zeit,
O wie mich freut
Waldeinsamkeit. (EckG 132, 20–5)

In all these instances, the characters seem unknowingly to project their own language onto the external world and then experience these projections as if they were independent external occurrences. The verses of the talking bird in its meeting with Eckbert also reflect his situation, which has a double significance. The last verse of the bird song supports the hypothesis that Eckbert is delusional, but in doing so, this verse also creates another link between Eckbert and Bertha.

In its last appearance, the bird song signals the climax of Eckbert's crisis, showing that he is now experiencing the same psychotic delusions from which Bertha suffered. Simultaneously, the song expresses the phantom's triumphant announcement that it has survived Bertha and Eckbert's attacks:

Loneliness in the Forest
Once more I stay;
None dare me slay,
No envy lives here
I am pleased again by the
Loneliness in the Forest. (EckE 41)

Waldeinsamkeit
Mich wieder freut
Mir geschieht kein Leid,
Hier wohnt kein Neid

176

Von neuem mich freut
Waldeinsamkeit. (EckG 145, 18–23)

The song also marks the most explicit conversion of an element of the folk fairy tale into a fantastical event. In Bertha's case the bird song signals the beginning of some form of derangement, but she is not disturbed by her experience. The talking bird in Bertha's story is harmless if the reader views it in the context of a folk fairy tale. Bertha in fact presents her troubled past in the form of a fairy tale, thus reducing the shocking impact of the events, not only on the reader, but also on her listeners in the frame narrative, Eckbert and Walther.[22] Alternatively, we can opt for a realistic interpretation and say that Bertha does not perceive the bird song as abnormal only because she is completely mad or completely bewitched by the phantom.[23]

Regardless of how we interpret Bertha's acceptance of the talking bird, Walther's appearance means the intrusion of the forest-world into her adult life, and this incident constitutes the true parallel to Eckbert's meeting with the phantom at the end:

> The sense, the consciousness of Eckbert had departed; it [the talking bird] was a riddle that he could not solve, whether he was dreaming now, or had before dreamed of a wife and friend. The marvelous was mingled with the common; the world around him seemed enchanted, and he himself was incapable of thought or recollection. (EckE 41)[24]

> Jetzt war es um das Bewußtsein, um die Sinne Eckberts geschehen. Er konnte sich nicht aus dem Rätsel heraus finden, ob er jetzt träume, oder ehemals von einem Weibe Bertha geträumt habe; das Wunderbare vermischte sich mit dem Gewöhnlichsten, die Welt um ihn her war verzaubert, und er keines Gedankens, keiner Erinnerung mächtig. (EckG 145, 20–9)

The text explicitly tells us that Eckbert is not sure whether he is dreaming now or was dreaming before.[25] Eckbert's doubts about his state of mind also are no different from the reader's disorientation about the significance of this scene. When the narrator states that the world around Eckbert "seemed enchanted" ("war verzaubert"), it might appear at first as a rendition of Eckbert's impression of having an experience comparable to the enchantment of the folk fairy tale. On the other hand, at this stage in the story, the enchantment may well have become a literal, objective reality, brought about by the phantom's transformation of reality through magic.

The third appearance of the talking bird marks the culmination of that disorientation. The marvelous of the folk fairy tale has become indistinguishable from the everyday world in that Eckbert believed he was living. The reader is equally unable to determine the reality status of the depicted events and is thus confronted with the uncanny like Eckbert, who is unsure whether or not he is imagining this entire scene.

The text blurs the boundaries between Eckbert and Bertha in several ways. We already mentioned the parallels that foreshadow the incestuous link between them. At the same time, however, Tieck expresses an idea even more terrifying than incest. Does Eckbert somehow become a phantom himself after Bertha's death? We noted that the description of his features at the beginning foreshadows this possibility. Does he become a kind of hybrid being that now incorporates Bertha and her past within himself? Such an explanation is also within the possibility of the romantic tradition. Even when we see Eckbert and Bertha together, during the fireside meeting with Walther, we cannot help but note that their motivations appear shared. Are they really two separate beings?[26] When Eckbert goes hunting while his wife is ill, is he carrying out the revenge against Walther in her place? Maybe Eckbert really is somehow Bertha and takes over her role after she dies. Tieck would then be telling a story about the unstable boundaries of individuality. Such an interpretation is justified if we view all the parallels between Eckbert and Bertha in conjunction: the shared base morpheme "bert" in the name, the desire to reveal secrets, the paranoid delusions in both characters, finding the same area in the forest, and the trait of committing crimes in a kind of preconscious daze.

The phantom, in its various metamorphoses, is able to change its gender. It appears as an old woman, as Philipp Walter, Hugo, and the old peasant who gives directions. The phantom thus mirrors the double gender of the figure Eckbert/Bertha.[27] The phantom correspondingly takes on a female form when confronting Bertha, and male forms when coming in contact with Eckbert. The effect of these transformations is heightened for the reader because they are moved out of the acceptable and "safe" context of the folk fairy tale. They are, first of all, a plausible explanation for the insanity to which Eckbert, and presumably Bertha, succumb in the end. Secondly, however, the transformations of the phantom, the eerie landscape of the woods, and the strange song of the bird all become expressions of the tormented inner lives of Eckbert and Bertha.

Paradoxical Ambiguity in "Eckbert"

While we were able to apply certain aspects of Freud's conception of the uncanny to Tieck's "The Fair-Haired Eckbert," we found that we could do justice to the uncanniness of the text as a whole only if we went beyond Freud and understood the uncanny as an uncertainty perceived as threatening. We suggested that Tieck's story prefigures psychoanalysis when it shows how impulses, if unacknowledged, can lead to crimes, and that these crimes come to haunt the perpetrators. "Der blonde Eckbert" demonstrates Tieck's intuitive understanding of some of the mechanisms that Freud systematically described one hundred years later.[28] As mentioned above, we can view the phantom as the personification of the return of the repressed. Bertha's repressed memory of the name of the dog or Eckbert's denial of killing Walther are deeds that come to haunt the perpetrators in the figure of the phantom. In the final scene, the phantom reminds Eckbert of a moment in his childhood when his father mentioned a sister, born by another woman. Eckbert's experience is caused by the revival of a childhood impression, and the uncanny revival is personified by the phantom. Although Eckbert wonders why he has always sensed these secrets, he has forgotten them, not because of any guilt, but because they had no significance for him. Although the family secret has resided in Eckbert's unconscious, it is problematic to speak of repression and its return. Independent of its applicability to the Freudian approach, it does not fully account for the uncanny impression of the phantom or of the text as a whole. The ambiguities surrounding the phantom produce uncanny effects that have nothing to do with the characters' or the reader's repressed childhood fears, but arise out of uncertainties occurring at the moment in which the uncanniness is felt.

The decisive conspiracy against Eckbert and Bertha lies in their fate, which has brought brother and sister together as husband and wife. The theme of incest has created much critical debate about the couple's guilt. Tatar states that "there must be a reason why they are singled out for persecution."[29] She speaks of adultery on the part of Eckbert and Bertha's father and builds an argument based on the common theme of the literary uncanny in which the "sins of the fathers" come to haunt their children.[30] Nonetheless, we learn only that the father gave Bertha away because she was born of another woman. It is possible that Bertha's mother was the father's first wife, who died in childbed, which was not uncommon in Tieck's time.[31] Eckbert's father may have remarried after her death. Bertha, the child from the first marriage, would then have been a reminder of the previous marriage, both for the grieving husband and for the second wife. The father would thus have given Bertha, Eckbert's half-sister, away to foster parents. The incest is then the result not of intentional wrongdoing but of unfortunate circumstances.[32]

The uncanny aspect of this story, on the plot level, lies ultimately in the helplessness of the protagonists against the phantom, which seems not an agent of justice but the personification of an inscrutable and unjust fate. The sin of incest is committed entirely without foreknowledge and intention. The ending, therefore, is problematic for critics and readers alike. The psychological explanation that accounts for the transformations of the phantom as a symptom of disavowed bad conscience does not explain the ending. This inadequacy notwithstanding, the text's uncanniness is caused in part by the very fact that the narrator disorients the reader by suggesting the psychological explanation throughout. The phantom's last words again point in the direction of guilt:

> "Are you bringing me my bird, my pearls, my dog? [...] See how injustice punishes itself! No one but I was Walther, was Hugo." (EckE 42)

> "Bringst du mir meinen Vogel? Meine Perlen? Meinen Hund? [...] Siehe, das Unrecht bestraft sich selbst: Niemand als ich war dein Freund Walther, dein Hugo." (EckG 145, 31–5)

The phantom is referring to the "injustices" committed by Bertha. First, the question arises why the phantom makes Eckbert responsible for Bertha's transgressions. Second, the incest constitutes a crime that has much more significance than the theft of the pearls or Bertha's other acts. It is unclear why the phantom emphasizes these relatively minor transgressions. Third, as already mentioned, the phantom asks about the bird, which we already heard singing a moment earlier. There is no need for Eckbert to bring the bird back. Furthermore, if Walther was an incarnation of the phantom, and the phantom is still alive, then Eckbert has not truly killed Walther. The phantom is not an agent of justice, but a personification of blind fate.[33] Seen in this light, Eckbert and Bertha's deaths appear entirely devoid of meaning.

The difficulty of solving the question of quilt contributes to the uncanny effect of "The Fair-Haired Eckbert" because the possible explanations for this problem are contradictory and disorienting. The narrator's commentaries, discussed above, are an unreliable guide for the reader because they imply the guilt of the characters. The unreliable narrator thus contributes to the uncanny reading experience. The text's uncanniness is finally located also in the inscrutable justice that the phantom enforces, as personification of the dark fate governing Bertha and Eckbert's life. The phantom's significance in the story thus conforms to our expanded definition of the uncanny.

The phantom appears uncanny to the reader not only through identification with the characters. On this level, it is possible to interpret the phantom as a materialization of their inner lives. Extradiegetic aspects enhance the uncanniness of the phantom. The phantom's power over the fate of the characters is not derived exclusively from plot elements, but also from poetical aspects of the text.

The supernatural events in the text cause an uncanny disorientation, for they can be interpreted either as the hallucinations of the character or as events contradicting the laws that we believe govern reality. The uncanniness of this ambiguity not only renders the reading experience of the text uncanny, but it also affects the world that the characters inhabit. The process can be compared to a type of feedback resulting from the interaction between reader and text, in which the style of representation becomes an aspect that the reader adds to the represented world. Bertha renders the episode from her childhood in the style of a fairy tale. A distance is thus generated towards the events in the past. These events are both unreal like the events in a fairy tale, and indicative of mental derangement during childhood and youth. Therefore, the fairy tale also provides Bertha with a personal means to distance herself from this unpleasant past. When this fictional past is brought into conflict with the reality of adulthood through the appearance of Walther, the reader is suddenly unable to isolate Bertha's fiction from her reality. This is the first stage of what Tieck calls the marvelous mingling with the common in the last sentence of the story. The uncanny ambiguity with which the reader was confronted in evaluating Bertha's time with the old woman now invades the fictional level of an alleged everyday reality, that of

Bertha's life with her husband. The reader's inability to assess the reality status of events in the fairy tale is now transferred onto the fictional realistic world, represented by Bertha's untold dilemma of deciphering Walther's connection to the old woman.

Similarly, Eckbert's insanity is not simply caused by the appearance of the witch or phantom but by the phantom's indeterminate textual status. The phantom receives its power to transform itself only through the ambiguous properties of the text, called "The Fair-Haired Eckbert" in which it appears. The text's reality is comparable to the counterlogical loop of a Moebius strip. The supernatural world of the fairy tale and the realistic setting of Eckbert's everyday life are two sides of the same fictional reality that form a loop, but the two sides trade places at an invisible intersection.[34] We find that what we thought were supernatural occurrences are the outcome of hallucinations and projections. When the marvelous of the fairy tale invades everyday reality, it becomes threatening. Nevertheless, the switching point of the Moebius strip is hidden. The events remain suspended between alternate explanations.[35] The phantom thus comes to represent the indeterminacy that has developed in the reader's interaction with the text.[36]

The metamorphosis of the phantom reiterates the central theme we have been discussing throughout, that of blurred boundaries. The central feature of the tale itself is its ethereal and elusive quality. First, the name Walther is a homonym of Waldherr, which can be broken up into to the two German words "forest" (Wald) and "master" (Herr).[37] The name thus underscores the significance of the phantom as a primordial force of nature or a pagan warlord, which is uncanny because it is inscrutable and threatening.[38] No critic has commented on the strange reversal of Philipp Walther's surname and first name. Although he is introduced as "Philipp Walther," he is referred to throughout the rest of the story as "Walther." This also leads the reader (and most critics) to refer to him as Walther, as if this were his first name. If he is indeed the only close friend of the couple, then why do they not call him "Philipp," or, if he is an acquaintance, "Herr Walther?" The use of the surname as a first name is an oddity, but it is concealed by the fact that Walther indeed serves both functions in German.

The awkward use of last name as first name also indicates confusion regarding familiarity and formal distance. Regardless of whether Walther himself asked to be addressed by his last name, or whether the couple chose to do so, the use of what sounds like a first name but is in fact a surname creates the illusion of false familiarity. The former amounts to a deception, the latter to self-deception. We can explain the self-deception as another symptom of repression if we choose to interpret the story from a psycho-analytic perspective. Alternatively, we can view the deception in the light of the fact that Walther is the incarnation of a being that conceals its true identity. Finally, the use of the "Walther" as if it were a first name constitutes a foreshadowing signal to the reader, because it performs the equivalent of Walther's deception on the textual level. The reader soon forgets that Walther is a surname. The true identity of this being is withheld, just as its first name, Phillip, disappears from view. Although the word refers to the same being in each instance, the text confuses the reader about the role of the signifier Walther. The ambiguous use of the word thus mimics the phantom's uncanny ability to transform itself.

The uncanny effect of "Der blonde Eckbert" thus has several origins. First, the text contains an intuitive portrayal of the process that Freud later defined as the return of the repressed. Second, the return of the repressed possesses – as a phenomenon – the property of causing uncanny sensations. It is here represented as a process in the lives of the characters, during which instincts are at first disavowed and later return as impulsive behavior. Third, this process has a figurative counterpart in the bird and the phantom, who are both immortal and who return despite efforts to kill them.[39] Fourth, the justice that the phantom enforces is uncanny

184

because it appears entirely arbitrary. The narrator commentaries only add to the reader's disorientation about the issue of guilt. Finally, the phantom and the bird are not only symbols of a psychic process but also material realities within the world of the text. In addition, the alternative interpretations of the phantom, from the reader's point of view, as a return of the repressed and actual phantom, has an uncanny effect caused by indeterminacy. The phantom thus becomes a materialization of the textual indeterminacy experienced by the reader, within the world that the characters inhabit. Its deadly power is uncanny not only because its rationale remains entirely elusive and inscrutable, but because it receives its powers only through the act of reading. In its most extreme formulation, "Der blonde Eckbert" is uncanny because the reader contributes to the death of the characters.

As we have pointed out in the introduction, there are uncanny experiences other than the ones Freud discusses. Rather than being caused by the return of the repressed, they are caused by the fear of hidden danger. "Der blonde Eckbert" evokes a feeling of apprehension caused by indistinct phenomena, denoted by the German adjective "unheimlich." The uncanny effect is similar to the kind of paradox we experience in response to optical illusions, like the following one:[40]

The effect of this text, caused by the genre fluctuation between fairy tale and realism, is uncanny in this latter sense. The metamorphoses of the phantom are an embodiment on the plot level of the transformations of the marvelous. This marvelous is no longer the benevolent power common to the fairy tale. Instead, it becomes indeterminate and hybrid, fluctuating between both a reflection of the inner lives of deranged characters and an external incarnation of a life-threatening, uncontrollable force. The fluctuating reference points about genre disorient the reader and contribute to the process of making the reading experience uncanny. Finally, the text is uncanny not only because of the confrontation with an all-powerful and unjust fate but also because of a distinctly poetical uncanny that feeds back into the world the characters inhabit.

Chapter 8: Conclusion

The poetical uncanny is produced by a combination of fantastical subject matter and poetical details of the text that call attention to themselves, such as verbal ambiguity, irony, or subliminal meaning established by metaphors. Moreover, the Romantics developed literary programs that called for the incorporation of lyrical elements into prose, which resulted in texts that exhibit a high degree of lyrical density. Consequently, we do greater justice to these texts when we focus on the formal aspects that contribute to the uncanny effect. Instances of paradoxical ambiguity disorient the reader in regard to the reality status of events. The reader's uncertainty is similar to the effects produced by optical illusions, such as M.C. Escher's tessellations, and mathematical paradoxes such as the Moebius strip. The same extradiegetic aspects that cause the uncanny reading experience are those qualities that constitute the text as literature. Consequently, this expansion of the Freudian uncanny helps to identify those textual qualities that constitute literary texts as a work of art.

The uncanny in literature is a nodal point of conflicting decoding options for the reader. An important source for the uncanny lies in the structure of the text itself, which is set up so as to make it impossible for the reader to find one governing concept connecting the various and often conflicting clues contained in the formal elements. The uncanny in Romantic prose fiction not only anticipates Freud's discovery of the unconscious but also expresses a specifically Romantic epistemological crisis. The Romantics lost the firm belief in the reality that had been established by both empiricism and idealism before Kant. The poetical uncanny inverts our familiar conceptual model and expresses an early skepticism about the formulation of objective scientific notions, doubts that erupted fully in Modernism.[1] The Romantics realized that it was impossible to regain the innocence that had been lost through the Enlightenment.[2] The uncanny structure of the narrative expresses a skepticism about the foundations of representation in literature and an uncertainty about what is knowable.

The importance of the imagination for the uncanny explains why indeterminacy in Romantic texts not only replicates the disorienting cognitive component of the uncanny in real life, but why these texts can make us conscious of the role of the imagination in the construction of reality in general. Romantic texts frequently move imperceptibly from the realistic context of the novella to a fictional world in which the fantastical is given physical existence. The switch is often initiated by a surprising event that constitutes a rupture in the fabric of reality.[3] The unfamiliar and mysterious aspects of the texts we discussed can never be completely replaced by an explanation, which integrates the unfamiliar into a familiar context. The uncanny in these texts contaminates the reader beyond the boundaries of the text, and it is different from the "hesitation" Todorov (1970) declares as the distinctive feature of his "fantastic."

Freud's model has no place for the uncanniness of silence, darkness, solitude and death, so that these topics expose the limits of his explanation most noticeably. These phenomena contain the crucial element of uncertainty in particularly threatening fashion, and Freud seemingly gives them a certain degree of space in his essay, while never acknowledging their importance. Passages in Freud's later writings indicate an awareness of the need to incorporate the importance of external dangers ("Realgefahren") into his system. He attempts to dissolve what is threatening in the uncanny. His exclusively psychoanalytic explanation for the uncanny is not only symptomatic for his continuing struggle to establish psychoanalysis in the scientific community. More specifically, it seems directed against Jentsch and psychology, which represent for Freud an exclusive focus on external and cognitive aspects. Freud's rejection of uncertainty appears as a polemical overstatement of his point of view. His general approach to the uncanny is similar to the one he applied before to dreams, jokes, and the psychopathology of everyday life. He aims to turn the uncanny into yet another piece of evidence for the existence of the unconscious and thus into proof for the originality of his theory.[4]

In both of the texts we discussed, unreliable narrators further destabilize the reader's position. Madness and sanity, reality and fiction can imperceptibly trade places. We are made unsure whether an impression reported by the narrator is to be accepted as actually happening within the context of the story, or whether it is a product of the narrator's imagination. In Hoffmann's "Der Sandmann," Nathanael's account may be affected by his psychosis. This uncertainty is supported by the text's extradiegetic elements. The clues we considered make Nathanael's persecution by the Sandman more likely on the plot level, and lead to a contamination of the reader with Nathanael's paranoia. We noted similar examples of inconclusive textual evidence in Bertha's tale, in which her encounter with the bird can be interpreted either as a fairy tale event or as a psychotic episode. Paranoia again plays a special role in the scenes in which Eckbert feels persecuted by Hugo. In both texts, unreliable narrators destabilize the reader's evaluation of the reality status of events and increase the text's uncanniness.

The selected stories generate what can be termed a *textual paranoia*. The stories contain characters that feel in some way haunted by supernatural forces: Nathanael in "Der Sandmann" is unsure whether Coppelius has returned in the guise of Coppola, and Eckbert in Tieck's story is haunted by Walther. As readers, we are contaminated by the paranoia of the characters because of the uncertain reality status of events in the text. More importantly, however, the text takes advantage of the structural similarity between our activity of "reading into" what we perceive as clues in the text and the characters' tendency to selectively "read into" their experiences. As we engage in the act of interpretation, we are confronted by a similar uncertainty about the regularities that we perceive. Are the coincidences accidental or do they indicate some plan?

It is possible, for example, to locate the uncanniness of Hoffmann's "Der Sandmann" in its textual paranoia. This does not mean that the text forces upon the reader the obsessive conviction of a paranoid individual that his or her interpretation is the only correct one. Nevertheless, the text represents its reality in a selective fashion and guides the interpretative activity of the reader. We are contaminated by the character's paranoia, because we cannot resort to the confirmation that is available in the real world to assess the validity of our observations.[5]

The term *textual paranoia* is inspired by Punter's famous study *The Literature of Terror* (1980), in which he identifies persecution as a primary motif of Romantic prose.[6] Punter spends only one paragraph on the topic, but mentions the important issue of perspective: "[...] it is very difficult to know where the reader is situated in an encounter with a story of persecution told by the persecuted."[7] *Textual paranoia* lets the reader re-experience the intellectual uncertainty that characterizes the onset of paranoia.[8] While paranoia may be characterized by certainty about a conspiracy, the paranoid individual still has to interpret whether a particular occurrence constitutes renewed confirmation for the existence of the persecution. The paranoid individual may form his or her delusion of persecution on the basis of a string of coincidences. The justification for calling the person deluded must rest on more than detected obsessive impulses or delusions of grandeur; the reader must possess objective confirmation that the coincidences are either truly coincidental or that they are the result of selective perception. Nonetheless, as described in the discussion of Freud's essay, true coincidences are uncanny because they mean a deviation from the randomness we come to expect from experience. Our perception of unusual regularities, and our uncertainty about whether they indicate some hidden agency or plan, are essential perceptual abilities.

The paranoid individual fails to assess probability correctly and integrates his or her skewed speculations into a delusional system. Nevertheless, texts like the ones we have reviewed replicate the difficulty of assessing the significance of perceived coherences because we are made aware on two levels simultaneously of the relativity of interpretation. First, the fictional world allows for the existence of fantastic phenomena that we ordinarily dismiss as impossible. The German Romantics often accomplish this first by moving from a realistic context to a fantastic one. The author's exploitation of our "willing suspension of disbelief" alerts us to the epistemological foundations we depend on to evaluate the "reality status" of an event.[9] Second, the formal elements that we resort to as additional evidence are equally inconclusive. Our reading experience is uncanny, not only because we identify with the characters when they respond to some fantastical event, but also because we are confronted with inconclusive formal evidence. The uncanny in literature recreates the character's paranoia on the level of the reader's aesthetic response. *Textual paranoia* makes us aware of the degree to which reality itself is the product of interpretation, and it expresses the epistemological crisis of the Romantic age, which we outlined in our discussions of Kant and Schlegel.

The texts we have considered ultimately alert us to the uncanniness of literature itself. Every piece of literature is in some sense uncanny because it is populated by un-dead figures. The characters in fiction blur the boundary between the animate and the inanimate because they are animated by our imagination.[10] The uncanny in real life is caused both by the indeterminacy of the phenomenon and by the observer's active participation in the process of perception. Neurological research into the connection between eye and brain has shown that perception is always constructed in the brain with the aid of elements stored in memory, even if this is a nonconscious process.[11] Optical illusions demonstrate that perception is a product of the observer's interpretative activity and thus possesses the disorienting cognitive component of the uncanny.

The parallels between the texts we have examined confirm the hypothesis suggested at the onset, that the uncanny text exists as an independent genre, in which the poetical uncanny is the defining element. The persistence of this genre could be demonstrated by incorporating later examples from fantastic short fiction, such as E.A. Poe's "The Fall of the House of Usher," (1844) Henry James's "The Turn of the Screw" (1898), and Kafka's "Metamorphosis" (1916), into a continuation of this study.

Our reading of these texts sensitizes us to the multiplicity of interpretations that the works generate. Our attention to extra-diegetic aspects leads us to apply an interpretative perspective that is more frequently applied to poetry:

> A poem is more than the sum of its interpretations [...]. An interpretation is an approximation of a poem, it teaches primarily to read carefully, similar to the way a viewer of a painting must first learn to see what is "there."[12]

Insofar as interpretation aims at developing explanations for the mysteries in the literary work of art, it is also forced to express the unfamiliar it encounters in familiar terms. Our investigation of the uncanny thus confronts us with the paradox of interpretation. The attempt at analyzing the ambiguities in the text reduces the unfamiliar and thus runs the risk of repressing its uncanny effect.[13]

The exclusion of the role of uncertainty in the uncanny in criticism is perhaps symptomatic of a larger problem involving the acceptance and incorporation of the Freudian paradigm into our culture. The tenacity of Freud's definition has its origin perhaps in our fascination with the hidden unconscious origins of the uncanny, both in our personal and political history. Also, there is a natural human need for dispensing with ambiguity by resolving it. Nevertheless, the reduction of the uncanny to a symptom of the repressed is not even primarily a consequence of Freud's interpretation but a result of a broader cultural preoccupation, especially with sexual repression. While we have indeed learned to detect the importance of hidden unconscious forces, and have been prompted to see the repressed internal origins of some seemingly external fears, we have perhaps lost sight of a more general epistemological uncertainty responsible for the uncanny that originated in the Romantic age and that is still with us.

Although we can only speculate about Freud's possible motives for excluding the importance of uncertainty for the uncanny, the difference between Freud's approach and the one we have pursued is perhaps indicative of a fundamental clash between the "exact" or "natural" sciences and the humanities. The humanities have, by virtue of their subject matter, a greater capacity for suggesting answers rather than claiming complete solutions. The study of the uncanny leads not only into the inner mystery of individual works but also reminds us that interpretation must remain aware of its limitations. If we adopt this perspective, we will view the literary work of art as a process that is re-initiated with every new reading.

Notes

Chapter 1: Introduction

1   Sigmund Freud, "The 'Uncanny'," trans. and ed. James Strachey, *The Standard Edition of the Complete Psychological Works*, vol. 17 (London: Hogarth Press/Institute of Psychoanalysis, 1953–1974).

2   The influence of Freud's uncanny is documented in one of the most recent critiques of the essay: "[...] the text that has most strikingly influenced critics working at the intersection of narratology and psycho-analysis is 'The Uncanny' ('Das Unheimliche')." Robin Lydenberg, "Freud's Uncanny Narratives," *Publications of the Modern Language Association* 112.5 (1997): 1073.

3   "Eavesdropping, automata, mystery stories are the very stuff of Gothic and of the uncanny [...]" David Punter, "Shape and Shadow: On Poetry and the Uncanny," *A Companion to the Gothic*, ed. David Punter, Blackwell Companions to Literature and Culture (Oxford: Blackwell, 2000) 198.

4   Prince defines the poetic function in the following manner: "When the communicative act is centered on the message for its own sake, [...] it (mainly) has a poetic function." Gerald Prince, *A Dictionary of Narratology* (Lincoln: University of Nebraska Press, 1987) 73.

5   E.T.A. Hoffmann, "Der Sandmann," *Fantasie und Nachtstücke*, ed. Walter Müller Seidel (Darmstadt: Wissenschaftliche Buchgesellschaft, 1971), Ludwig Tieck, "Der blonde Eckbert," *Phantasus*, ed. Manfred Frank, vol. 6 (Frankfurt am Main: Deutscher Klassiker Verlag, 1985).

6   "Stark ist der Wunsch des Menschen nach der intellectuellen Herrschaft über die Umwelt. Intellectuelle Sicherheit gewährt psychische Zuflucht im Kampfe ums Dasein." Ernst Jentsch, "Zur Psychologie des Unheim-lichen," *Psychiatrisch-Neurologische Wochenschrift* 22, 23 (1906): 205.

7   Jentsch speaks of a "lack of orientation" on the part of the observer ("Mangel an Orienti[e]rung"). Jentsch, "Zur Psychologie des Unheimli-chen," 195, my translation.

8   In a footnote Freud added to *The Interpretation of Dreams* in 1909, after he had completed his study of Jensen's *Gradiva,* Freud states: "In reply to my enquiry, the author [Jensen] confirmed the fact that he had no knowledge of my theory of dreams [...] this writer's creation is evidence in favour of the correctness of my analysis of dreams." Sigmund Freud, *The Interpre-tation of Dreams*, trans. and ed. James Strachey, *The Standard Edition of the*

Complete Psychological Works, vol. 4/5 (London: Hogarth Press/Institute of Psychoanalysis, 1953–1974) 97.

9   Gay traces this struggle from writings in 1895 to the last papers: "In his *Outline of Psychoanalysis*, the final summing up which he wrote in London during the last year of his life [...] Freud claimed flatly that the stress on the unconscious in psychoanalysis enabled it 'to take its place as a natural science like any other'." Peter Gay, *Freud: A Life For Our Time* (New York and London: Norton, 1998) 79.

10   The uncanny is also linked to curiosity and the Promethean struggle for knowledge. Cp. Meltzer, who discusses the uncanny, albeit in reference to Oedipus, not Prometheus, in connection with "[...] a transgression of the law for the sake of curiosity and an act therefore to be punished [...]" Françoise Meltzer, "The Uncanny Rendered Canny: Freud's Blind Spot in Reading Hoffmann's 'Sandman'," *Introducing Psychoanalytic Theory*, ed. Sander L. Gilman (New York: Brunner/Mazel, 1982) 222.

11   Cixous and Rubin, but especially Meltzer, emphasize the importance of Jentsch's emphasis on uncertainty. Meltzer's article formed the starting point for this study. Hélène Cixous, "Fiction and its Phantoms: A Reading of Freud's 'Das Unheimliche'," *New Literary History* 7.3 (1976), Meltzer, "The Uncanny Rendered Canny," Bernard Rubin, "Freud and Hoffmann: 'The Sandmann'," *Introducing Psychoanalytic Theory*, ed. Sander L. Gilman (New York: Brunner/Mazel, 1982).

12   Wright, in her survey of previous articles on the uncanny, already demonstrates this tendency to criticize Freud's disregard for literature, but suggests alternatives only from within the psychoanalytic paradigm. On the one hand, in her comments on Hoffmann's "Sandman," she expresses the agreed upon criticism of Freud: "What is interesting is precisely the inadequacy of his [Freud's] interpretation." Elisabeth Wright, *Psychoanalytic Criticism: Theory in Practice*, New Accents (London and New York: Methuen, 1984) 143. – Nevertheless, she accuses Freud of not applying his own theories rigorously enough and again equates the uncanny with the "return of the repressed": "Any adequate psychoanalytic reading would thus have to account not only for the return of the repressed in the form of the Sandman [...] but also in the form of Clara (and Olimpia) as objects of desire [...]" Wright, *Psychoanalytic Criticism*, 148.

13   "[...] [der Schriftsteller] braucht diese Gesetze [denen die Betätigung des Unbewußten folgen muß] nicht auszusprechen, nicht einmal sie klar zu erkennen, sie sind infolge der Duldung seiner Intelligenz in seinen Schöpfungen verkörpert enthalten" (GW IX, 121). Sigmund Freud, *Delusions and*

Dreams in W. Jensen's "Gradiva," trans. and ed. James Strachey, *The Standard Edition of the Complete Psychological Works*, vol. 9 (London: Hogarth Press/Institute of Psychoanalysis, 1953–1974) 92.

14   Cp. Punter's statement quoted in the epigraph to the chapter, Punter, "On Poetry and the Uncanny," 194.

15   Terry Castle, *The Female Thermometer: Eighteenth-Century Culture and the Invention of the Uncanny* (Oxford: Oxford University Press, 1995) 10. – Castle's thesis indeed is based on the model according to which the sleep of reason produces monsters, derived from Goya's engraving "El sueño de la razón produce monstruos," from *Los Caprichos* (1799).

16   "[…] besagt das nichts über ein zeitloses Wesen der Unvernunft, die der Kleinfamilie die Primärsozialisation überläßt." Friedrich Kittler, "'Das Phantom unseres Ichs' und die Literaturpsychologie: E.T.A. Hoffmann—Freud—Lacan," *Urszenen*, ed. Horst Turk Friedrich Kittler (Frankfurt am Main: Suhrkamp, 1977) 161.

17   Jacob Grimm and Wilhelm Grimm, "unheimlich," *Deutsches Wörterbuch. Elfter Band. III. Abteilung. Un-Uzvogel*, ed. Karl Euling, vol. 11 (Leipzig: S. Hirzel, 1936) 1057. – The entry is cited in the beginning of the detailed treatment of the etymology in the Freud chapter.

18   Joachim Heinrich Campe, "unheimlich," *Wörterbuch der Deutschen Sprache*, vol. 5 (Braunschweig: Schulbuchhandlung, 1807–1811). – See citation of the entry in the Freud chapter.

19   Critics also occasionally commit grammatical errors when they use the German word in their English sentences. They capitalize the adjective "unheimlich," creating the nonexisting noun "Das Unheimlich."

20   Most critics briefly recount Freud's argument before they employ the term: "For Freud the *Un* – this sign of negation which makes the *heimisch* into something strange – represents an act of censorship which turns into the weird and uncanny what is in fact too familiar, too close to home: a repressed primal experience." Peter Brooks, "Virtue and Terror: *The Monk*," *ELH* 40 (1973): 257. – A recent study on the Gothic employs the Uncanny in this now-established manner, only adding that "the uncanny is […] uncanny in itself." Julian Wolfreys, *Victorian Hauntings. Spectrality, Gothic, the Uncanny and Literature* (Houndmills, Basingstoke, Hampshire, New York: Palgrave, 2002) 15.

21   Even the most recent study on the Uncanny, despite its scope and admirable detail, falls victim to what I call the etymological fallacy, and in fact asserts its adherence to the "English" Freud: "It is with an English 'uncanny' and with an English Freud (as much as a German or a French

197

Freud) that we are concerned in the present study." Nicholas Royle, *The Uncanny* (New York: Routledge, 2003) 13. Subsequently, however, the German Freud, and, more importantly, the German word "unheimlich," is not incorporated into the discussion, although it would benefit the argument, which resembles the one presented here in emphasizing the "resistant strangeness of literature to psychoanalytic [...] accountability" Royle, *The Uncanny*, 15.

22   Although Freud uses "heimlich" in its prevalent meaning (secretively), he never discusses the importance of secrecy for the uncanny, which is another symptom of his repression of the role of threat in the uncanny.

23   Freud's tendency to overstate the origins of the uncanny in the repressed familiarity of childhood and superstitions is an understandable impulse to reduce the threatening element of the uncanny through explanation.

24   The genitive of the nouns is quoted out of context: "[...] zwei Vorstellungskreisen angehört, [...] dem des Vertrauten, Behaglichen und dem des Versteckten, Verborgengehaltenen [...]" (GW XII, 235).

25   Lydenberg, "Uncanny Narratives," 1073. – Lydenberg shows how narrative paradoxically invades Freud's essay, because he attempts to exclude it.

26   "In einem Spiel mit Worten setzt Freud das Unheimliche dem Heimlichen und das Heimliche dem Heim gleich; er bestimmt die Kindheit also als Stätte einer ursprünglichen [...] Unheimlichkeit." Kittler, "Das Phantom unseres Ichs," 149, my translation.

27   Kittler is also sensitive to the influence of the historic conditions in which psychoanalysis evolved. See Kittler, "Das Phantom unseres Ichs," 160–1. – Nevertheless, Kittler does not look beyond the psychoanalytic paradigm to investigate the uncanny.

28   Heinrich von Kleist, "[Letter dated March 22, 1801]," *Sämtliche Werke*, eds Roland Reuß and Peter Staengle, vol. 4 part 1, Brandenburger Ausgabe (Stroemfeld/Roter Stern, 1988) 506, line 9 – line 11, Kleist's emphasis, my translation.

29   Friedrich Schlegel was the Romantic theorist in the group, while August Wilhelm, less prominent as a theorist, collaborated with Tieck on the famous Schlegel/Tieck translation of Shakespeare.

30   Schlegel's definition also reflects, among other things, the Romantic emphasis on the union of thought and feeling. – Friedrich von Schlegel, "Athenäums-Fragment 116," *Charakteristiken und Kritiken I, 1796–1801*, ed. Ernst Behler, vol. 2 (München, Paderborn, Wien, Zürich: Ferdinand Schöningh, 1967) 182, my translation.

31 The introduction to the Tieck chapter will focus on the importance of the mixing of genres for the poetical uncanny, which not only leads to a mixing of poetry with prose but entails a change in the role of the "marvelous" and "fantastical."

32 The drawing appears in Ludwig Wittgenstein, *Philosophical Investigations*, trans. G.E.M. Anscombe (London, New York: Macmillan, 1953) 194. It is referenced there as having been taken from Joseph Jastrow, *Fact and Fable in Psychology* (Boston: Houghton Mifflin, 1900).

33 The "extradiegetic" dimension is another way to refer to what DeMan calls the text's "literariness": Paul de Man, *The Resistance to Theory* (Minneapolis: University of Minneapolis Press, 1986) 9. Quoted following Lydenberg, "Uncanny Narratives," 1072.

34 See the entry for "diegetic" in David Bordwell and Kristin Thompson, *Film Art: An Introduction* (New York: McGraw-Hill, 1993).

35 The separation of the two realms is clearer in film, because in literature, the reader creates both the diegetic and the extradiegetic levels by transforming the words on the page.

36 From Poe's commentary on "The Raven," Edgar Allan Poe, "The Philosophy of Composition," *Selected Writings* (Harmondsworth: Penguin Books, 1979) 482.

37 Poe refers to this dimension when he demands that the literary work should have "some amount of suggestiveness – some under-current, however indefinite, of meaning." Poe, "Philosophy of Composition," 491.

38 Although some novels also employ poetic coherence to convey subliminal meaning, the evolution of the uncanny text is linked to the rise of the modern short story.

39 The Fantastic is defined following Todorov. A detailed discussion follows on p. 32 below.

40 Tzvetan Todorov, *The Fantastic: A Structural Approach to a Literary Genre*, trans. Richard Howard (Ithaca, NY: Cornell University Press, 1973) 41. – M.H. Abrams points out that the Romantics dissociate the supernatural from theological meaning and that their "general tendency was [...] to naturalize the supernatural and to humanize the divine." M. H. Abrams, *Natural Supernaturalism: Tradition and Revolution in Romantic Literature* (New York: Norton, 1971) 68.

41 This observation is identical to Freud's and is the reason why Freud gives fairy tales as examples for the appearance of the circumstances that would appear uncanny in real life but do not have that effect in fiction. (SE 17, 250, 3–10). We will show that this is a contestable opinion.

42   The two choices recall Freud's discussion of Hoffmann's "Der Sandmann," discussed in the subsequent section, when Freud reads the first laboratory scene either as a "first delirium of the panic stricken boy" (SE 17, 228, 19) or "a succession of events which are to be regarded in the story as being real" (SE 17, 228, 20–1). Freud overlooks that this ambiguity remains unresolved in Hoffmann, and this uncertainty is reinforced by the uncanniness of the text as a whole.

43   The full-length reading of Freud's essay forms a chapter in the author's dissertation: Marc Falkenberg, "The Poetical Uncanny: A Study of Early Modern Fantastic Fiction," Ph.D. Diss, University of Chicago, 2000.

44   Whereas we can already discover uncanny elements in texts from antiquity or in passages of Shakespeare plays, it appears that entire texts become uncanny only after Early German Romanticism.

Chapter 2: Freud's "Uncanny" Re-evaluated

1   Jentsch does not use the term "intellectual uncertainty," which Freud uses to paraphrase the key point of Jentsch's argument (SE 17, 221, 7).

2   Freud, "The 'Uncanny'." – See Abbreviations, page 13. – The essay has never been subjected to a critique as extensive as the one undertaken here.

3   Cixous, "Fiction and its Phantoms," 526. – Cixous writes that we can treat Freud's text as a "strange theoretical novel," indeed as an uncanny text, if we consider that Freud emphasizes the familiar to a point where the mechanism attributed to coziness sets in: "Insistence of the familiar gives rise to what is uncanny, in the long run." Cixous, "Fiction and its Phantoms," 542. – Although not fully developed by Cixous, this idea will guide our discussion of "coziness."

4   Cixous, "Fiction and its Phantoms," 542. – This statement nevertheless reveals a problem we will discuss below, a problem which originates in Freud's essay, the failure to distinguish clearly between the uncanny and the unconscious.

5   "Unheimlich, adj. u. adv. [...] 1) Keine so behagliche angenehme Empfindung habend und erweckend, als die ist, wenn man in seiner *Heimath* sich wohl befindet, [...] 2) Ein unheimlicher Ort, wo es nicht richtig, nicht sicher ist." Campe, "unheimlich."

6   For "ungeheuer," the Grimm entry reads: "*ungeheuer* [...] something lacking the protection, safety, security, and the familiar comfort of house

and home, while 'geheuer' expresses what makes us especially conscious of these qualities. Thus, a warm room is called 'gehür.'" "[…] bezeichnet u.[ngeheuer], was schutz, sicherheit und trauliches behagen von haus und heim vermissen läszt; dagegen geheuer, was diese so recht zum bewusztsein bringt, z. b. so ist ein warme stuobe gehür." Jacob Grimm and Wilhelm Grimm, "ungeheuer," *Deutsches Wörterbuch*, ed. Karl Euling, vol. 11 (Leipzig: Hirzel, 1936) 693, Grimm's lowercase nouns, my translation.

7   See the Grimm dictionary: "4) That meaning [of 'unheimlich'] that corresponds to 'ungeheuer' ['monstrous, ghastly;' see the previous footnote] is well known in the 16th and 17th centuries […] but was suppressed by the enlightenment, until it was revived by the end of the 18th century; then it becomes ubiquitous." – "die […] *ungeheuer* 5 […] entsprechende bed[eutung] ist im 16. u. 17. jh. wohlbekannt, im 18. jh. […] zwar erwähnt, doch von der aufklärung zurückgedrängt, bis das ende des 18jhs. sie wieder hervorzieht; dann wird sie allgemein." Grimm and Grimm, "unheimlich," 1058, Grimm's lowercase nouns, my translation.

8   "Only since the end of the 18th Century with closer reference to emotional life, terrible, gruesome; causing shudder, anxiety, terror, fear, worry, unease, etc. […]" – "erst seit dem ende des 18. jhs. mit engerer beziehung auf das gefühlsleben schrecklich, grauenvoll; schauder, angst, entsetzen, furcht, beklemmung, unbehagen, […] u.ä. verursachend […]" Grimm and Grimm, "unheimlich," 1057, Grimm's lowercase nouns, my translation.

9   See the definition of "unheimlich" in the current edition of the Duden: "[…] ein unbestimmtes Gefühl der Angst, des Grauens hervorrufend […]" "unheimlich," *Duden: Das große Wörterbuch der deutschen Sprache in acht Bänden*, ed. Wissenschaftlicher Rat und die Mitarbeiter der Dudenredaktion unter der Leitung von Günther Drosdowski, 2nd edn, vol. 7: Sil–Urh (Mannheim, Leipzig, Wien, Zürich: Dudenverlag, 1993).

10   "[…] im Dunkeln wurde [es] ihm u[nheimlich]." "unheimlich," 3569.

11   Sigmund Freud, *Inhibitions, Symptoms and Anxiety*, trans. and ed. James Strachey, *The Standard Edition of the Complete Psychological Works*, vol. 20 (London: Hogarth Press/Institute of Psychoanalysis, 1953–1974) 96. – As mentioned above, any attempt to explain the uncanny is naturally subjected to the more general limitations of all scientific explanations.

12   The following example for the uncanny caused by impaired perception may be relatively common: A person walking down a country road and seeing a deserted car might take the headrest for the head of a person sitting in it.

13 The "little gray bush" becomes the kernel of the uncanny at the end of Hoffmann's "Der Sandmann." Mist also appears as an example in one of the dictionary entries cited by Freud: "the unheimlich mist called hill fog" (SE 17, 224, 25) ["Haarrauch" GW 12, 235, literally "hair smoke"].

14 I avoid the term "intellectual uncertainty" that Freud uses to characterize Jentsch's point about the uncanny, as I explain in more detail later, because the intellect is not always fully involved in cognitive processes, a distinction that is already implicitly contained in the examples presented by Jentsch.

15 In recent colloquial German, "unheimlich," similar to the colloquial use of "uncanny" in English, has taken on the meaning "extraordinary" or "incredible." This shade of meaning supports our claim, namely, that the uncanny feeling is due to something for which we lack an explanation (the meaning "incredible" was not in use when Freud discussed the term in 1919).

16 Freud, "Inhibitions, Symptoms and Anxiety," 164–5, Freud's emphasis. (GW XIV, 197–8). – See also the similar passage distinguishing between "fright," "fear" and "anxiety" ("Schreck, Furcht, Angst") in Sigmund Freud, *Beyond the Pleasure Principle,* trans. and ed. James Strachey, *The Standard Edition of the Complete Psychological Works*, vol. 18 (London: Hogarth Press/Institute of Psychoanalysis, 1953–1974) 12.

17 GW = Gesammelte Werke. Roman numerals indicate volume numbers, Arabic numerals indicate page and, if given, line numbers. See "Abbreviations" p. 13.

18 *Random House Webster's College Dictionary* (New York: Random House, 1991). – The OED adds: "uncomfortably strange or unfamiliar." *The Oxford English Dictionary*, 2nd edn (Oxford: Clarendon Press, 1989). – Roget's Thesaurus, under "uncanny," redirects us to *"weird"*: "Of a mysteriously strange and usually frightening nature: eerie, uncanny, unearthly. *Informal:* spooky." *Roget's II. The New Thesaurus*, 3rd edn (Boston: Hougthon Mifflin, 1996).

19 Jentsch mentions admiration that can have traces of the uncanny: "A slight nuance of the uncanny effect is occasionally even present in the case of true admiration. Its cause is the lack of an explanation for the foundations of the respective accomplishment, which is why there is usually no uncanny effect on a person familiar with the respective area of expertise." Jentsch, "Zur Psychologie des Unheimlichen," 197, my translation. – "Eine leise Nüance unheimlichen Effects kommt aber auch bei der echten Bewunderung dann und wann zum Vorschein und erklärt

sich psychologisch aus der Rathlosigkeit rücksichtlich des Zustande-kommens der Entstehungsbedingungen für die betreffende Leistung, weshalb sie auch beim speciellen Kenner des betreffenden Gebiets zu fehlen pflegt."

20   See the dictionary entries quoted in footnotes 5 and 7 in this chapter.

21   "Let me also add that my investigation was actually begun by collecting a number of individual cases, and was only later confirmed by an examination of linguistic usage" (SE 17, 220, 29–31). – Freud might be trying to prove even more conclusively than Jentsch that the German language "seems to have produced a rather fortunate creation" in the creation of the word.

22   This method had an established reputation within the humanistic discourse of the time. It also informs Freud's famous essay (1910e): Sigmund Freud, "The Antithetical Meaning of Primal Words," trans. and ed. James Strachey, *The Standard Edition of the Complete Psychological Works*, vol. 11 (London: Hogarth Press/Institute of Psychoanalysis, 1953–1974). – It is visible in Heidegger's writings as well as, and subsequently, in deconstruction.

23   "[…] certain traces of sensing psychic uncertainty develop, especially in cases when either the ignorance is very apparent or when the subjective perception wavers greatly." Jentsch, "Zur Psychologie des Unheimlichen," 196, my translation.

24   The translation of "heimlich" (cozy) "homely" could also be questioned, because "homey" or "homelike" would have been more accurate, to avoid the connotation "simple, unattractive" in "homely."

25   The meaning "cozy" is still in use today in Southern German dialects.

26   It is possible that Freud himself overlooked the importance of investigating the relationship between the two meanings.

27   Expressed in "[t]he German word 'unheimlich' is obviously the opposite of […] what is familiar; […] what is 'uncanny' is frightening precisely because it is *not* known and familiar" (SE 17, 220, 33–7, Freud's emphasis).

28   In the translation, a footnote rendering "unheimlich" with the neologism "un-cozy" would have retained the emphasis on the observer's experience and the aspect of threat.

29   Grimm explains that "ávåsa" translates literally as "bad cow." Jacob Grimm and Wilhelm Grimm, "un-," *Deutsches Wörterbuch. Elfter Band. III. Abteilung. Un-Uzvogel*, ed. Karl Euling, vol. 11 (Leipzig: S. Hirzel, 1936 [1854–1971]) 10.

30 An extensive study of the phenomenon was undertaken by a German linguist: Barbara Lenz, *un-Affigierung: unrealisierbare Argumente, unausweichliche Fragen, nicht unplausible Antworten*, Studien zur deutschen Grammatik, 50, ed. et al. Werner Abraham (Tübingen: Gunter Narr, 1995).

31 Although such formations have completely disappeared from English, words such as "the untime" (still existing in the German phrase "zur Unzeit kommen") survived until the 15th Century (see the English adjective "untimely"). There were a number of Old English nouns that constitute parallels to the pejorative use of "un-" in German. – The OED 2nd edition states for "un-" under 2e: "In a small number of nouns *un-* appears with a pejorative in place of a negative sense, as *unǽt* excessive eating, *uncoðu* an evil disease, *uncræft* an evil art, and similarly *undæd, undóm, unlagu, unræd, unsíþ, untíma, unweder.*" *OED*. – The pejorative sense of these nouns thus parallels the ones of their German counterparts, such as "undeed, untime, unweather," mentioned below.

32 An "Un-deed" (die Untat) is an evil deed that goes beyond human understanding. – "[S]tellte das einfach verneinende *un-* den empirischen begriff in frage, so verneint das *un-* improbativum die idee, nicht den gegenstand, wie er ist, sondern wie er sein soll. [...] [S]o gelangt die partikel dazu, das abweichen von der rechten art und beschaffenheit, vom rechten wege, vom brauchbaren, nützlichen, guten, gewöhnlichen, herkömmlichen, relgelmäszigen, hemmung, bezeichnung des unnöthigen, unangenehmen, unheimlichen, unförmlichen, überwältigenden u.s.w. [E]in unmensch ist freilich ein mensch, aber ein solcher, dem alles abgeht, was den menschen zum menschen macht, irrung, entstellung u.s.f. auszudrücken. [...] ergibt sich auch edleres menschenthum, humanität." Grimm and Grimm, "un-," 24–5, Grimm's lowercase nouns, my translation.

33 "[S]o war allmählich das weite gebiet der hauptsächlich durch ungebildeten sprachlichen übergangs- und zwischenbegriffe gewonnen zur bezeichnung von nicht eindeutigen eigenschaften, von jenen mittelzuständen, die J.[akob] Grimm Gr[ammatik] 3 [Band], 684 mit den dämmerungserscheinungen zwischen tag und nacht vergleicht." Grimm and Grimm, "un-," 20–1, Grimm's lowercase nouns, my translation.

34 Cp. the reference to the etymological fallacy and the quote from Kittler in the introduction, p. 26: "In a pun on words Freud equates the uncanny with the secretive, and the secretive with the home; he thus defines childhood as the location of an original [...] uncanniness." Kittler, "Das Phantom unseres Ichs," 149, my translation.

35 "3) aus der bedeutung des heimatlichen und häuslichen flieszt die vorstellung des traulichen und vertrauten. / von einem orte, einer zeit, einem dinge, und den daran sich bildenden gefühlen, in welchem sinne das adjectiv vorzüglich im bair.[ischen] und alemannischen sprachgebiete volksmäszig ist [...]" Jacob Grimm and Wilhelm Grimm, "heimlich," *Deutsches Wörterbuch. Vierter Band. Zweite Abteilung*, ed. Moriz Heyne, vol. 10 (Leipzig: Hirzel, 1877 [1854–1971]) 874, Grimm's lowercase nouns, my translation.

36 "'Heimlich' [...] Die ursprüngliche Bedeutung hatte sich bis in die Neuzeit gehalten, ist aber jetzt völlig veraltet. [...] Schon seit dem 12. Jh. erscheint heimlich dann auch als '(vor Fremden) verborgen' [...]" Alfred Götze, "heimlich," *Trübners Deutsches Wörterbuch*, ed. Im Auftrage der Arbeitsgemeinschaft für deutsche Wortforschung herausgegeben von Alfred Götze, vol. 3 "G-H" (Berlin: Walter de Gruyter, 1939) 389.

37 "[...] dieser hartnäckigen Wiederkehr der einen Zahl eine geheime Bedeutung zuzuschreiben [...]" (GW XII, 250). – We will see that this number has a personal significance for Freud in the discussion of this example in the section on coincidences.

38 Freud uses "geheim" in a similar fashion later in the essay, in his comments on the evil eye: "What is feared is thus a secret intention of doing harm [...]" (SE 17, 240, 15). "Man fürchtet also eine geheime Absicht zu schaden [...]" (GW XII, 255, my emphasis).

39 Freud again uses "geheim" in the sense "secretive in his discussion of the fear of the evil eye": "What is feared is thus a secret intention of doing harm [...]" (SE 17, 240, 15).

40 Freud uses "geheim" again when he draws his first preliminary conclusions, namely, that the uncanny is the recurrence of something repressed. Allegedly, this explains how the meaning of "das Heimliche" (the familiar) has been extended to "das Unheimliche": "[...] if this is indeed the secret nature of the uncanny [...]" (SE 17, 241 13–14); "[...] wenn dies wirklich die geheime Natur des Unheimlichen ist [...]" (GW XII, 254, my emphasis).

41 "[the] uncanny is [...] in reality nothing new or alien, but something which is old-established in the mind" (SE 17, 241, 17–18).

42 In addition, we have already learned that the meaning of *un-* is not restricted to expression opposition. Furthermore, the Grimm entry on "un-" also lists cases in which the pejorative function appears in pairs ("All those 'x' and 'un-x' – they mean nothing to me.").

43 Freud's argument that the merging of opposite meanings influenced the same argumentation, which he employed in Freud, "The Antithetical

205

Meaning of Primal Words" is now discredited by more detailed knowledge of the meaning of Egyptian hieroglyphs.

44 Disavowal will be treated in the following chapter. It needs to be distinguished from repression, because we control this process through a conscious act of volition.

45 Punter re-emphasizes the aspect of secrecy that Freud passes over, thus undertaking the correction implicitly that I propound here: "what is homely and familiar, what is closest to us, becomes also that which we hold as most secret to ourselves, so that by very virtue of being intimately known to ourselves, the uncanny inevitably becomes that also which is not known, which can never be known, because its very identity, bound up as it is with our own, is jealously guarded [...]" Punter, "On Poetry and the Uncanny," 194.

46 This is different from defining the uncanny as the secretly familiar, because the double concealment is not yet made explicit in this definition.

47 "heimlich 1) zugehörig zum Hause [...] in der neueren Sprache zurück-getreten, aber noch bei Goethe [...] [Werther] und mundartlich oberdeutsch bis jetzt geblieben. 2) gewendet zu dem Sinne des fremden Augen Entzogenen Verborgenen (vgl. geheim) [...]" Moriz Heyne, "heimlich," *Deutsches Wörterbuch*, 2nd edn, vol. 2 (Leipig: Hirzel, 1906) 104, my emphasis.

48 Some of the quotations in Sanders and Grimm change their significance in light of a revised definition of the uncanny. Some of this material supports a notion of an uncanny mainly defined by a situation in which a threat is suspected but hidden from view. Compare the example given for "heimlich" ("intimate") in the Sanders entry: "(c) Intimate, [...] comfortable; [...] arousing a sense of agreeable restfulness and security as in one within the four walls of his house. 'Is it still *heimlich* to you in your country where strangers are felling your woods?'" (SE 17, 222, 18–20). When strangers are felling the woods, the feeling of safety as "within the four walls" of the house is disturbed.

49 Grimm lists an example – not included by Freud – for "heimlich" under 3) "familiar, intimate" that already contains the element of protection from enemies, and elements that are introduced in meaning 4). "sheltered from the eyes of strangers etc." Grimm and Grimm, "heimlich," 875. – The place in the following example is cozy because its topography offers physical protection from dangers: "[The place had] [...] two linden trees, whose branches covered a small courtyard in front of the church, a yard enclosed on all sides by farmsteads, barns, and farms – that I cannot recall

having found a place as heimlich anywhere else." – "zwei linden die mit ihren ausgebreiteten ästen den kleinen platz vor der kirche bedecken, der ringsum mit bauerhöfen, scheuern und höfen eingeschlossen ist. so vertraulich, so heimlich hab ich nicht leicht ein plätzchen gefunden" [from Goethe's Werther]." Grimm and Grimm, "heimlich," 874, Grimm's lowercase nouns, my translation.

50 "Homely" [1300–1350, ME] implies an "absence of natural beauty." *The Random House Dictionary of the English Language: The Unabridged Edition* (New York: Random House, 1993).

51 "homey" also suggests "intimate security" and the absence of a threat, as well as "comfortably informal and inviting" [1850–1855] or "homelike," "familiar, warmly comfortable." [1810–1820]. *Random House Dictionary*.

52 As with most Indogermanic roots, the asterix denotes that the form is based on etymological inference.

53 Hence "canny wife": "wise woman, midwife" (Fr. *femme sage*); hence "canny moment": "moment of childbirth" (Scottish, archaic). *OED*, "canny" meaning 3.

54 "Cozy" can be used in the sense "secretively" in English as well. In the movie "The Haunting" (1962), a woman is planning to leave her family, taking the family car against their wishes. Her father says: "I don't know why you're treating this all cozy like that, as if it was a jail-break [...]."

55 "*Unh.[eimlich]* nennt man Alles, was im Geheimnis, im Verborgenen [...] bleiben sollte und hervorgetreten ist [...]" (GW XII, 235; also quoted SE 17, 256).

56 It is possible that Freud senses the enigmatic nature of the quotation himself, and thus speaks of "doubts that can be removed by consulting the Grimm dictionary" (SE 17, 225, 10–11).

57 "Die homerische Götterwelt schließt schweigend ein Mysterium in sich, und ist über einem Mysterium, über einem Abgrund gleichsam errichtet, den sie wie mit Blume zudeckt. [...] Gerade darum hat Griechenland einen Homer, weil es Mysterien hat, d. h. weil es ihm gelungen ist, jenes Princip der Vergangenheit, das in den orientalischen Systemen noch herrschend war, völlig zu besiegen und ins Innere, d.h. in Geheimniß, ins Mysterium (aus dem es ja ursprünglich hervorgetreten war) zurückzusetzen. Der reine Himmel, der über den homerischen Gedichten schwebt, konnte sich erst über Griechenland ausspannen, nachdem die dunkle und verdunkelnde Gewalt jenes unheimlichen Princips (unheimlich nennt man alles, was im Geheimniß, im Verborgnen, in der Latenz bleiben sollte und hervorgetreten ist) – jener Aether, der über Homeros Welt sich wölbt, konnte erst sich

ausspannen, nachdem die Gewalt jenes unheimlichen Princips, das in den früheren Religionen herrschte, in dem Mysterium niedergeschlagen war [...]" Friedrich Wilhelm Joseph von Schelling, "Achtundzwanzigste Vorlesung: Qualitativer Unterschied zwischen dem Charakter der griechischen Religion und dem der früheren Religionen," *Philosophie der Mythologie. Erstes Buch: Der Monotheismus*, ed. Karl Friedrich August Schelling, vol. 2 pt. 2 (Stuttgart und Augsburg: Cotta'scher Verlag, 1856–1861) 649, my translation.

58 Freud is conscious of this conflict, as demonstrated by his motto to the *Interpretation of Dreams*, from Virgil, which implicitly compares the struggle of the repressed to return with the Alecto, one of the goddesses of the older religion, who wished to stir the infernal regions, the river Acheron, because she could not move the new gods who were now in power. Cp. the brilliant essay: Jean Starobinski, "Acheronta Movebo," trans. and ed. Françoise Meltzer, *The Trial(s) of Psychoanalysis* (Chicago: University of Chicago Press, 1987).

59 Cp. footnote 63 in this chapter.

60 The statement illustrates the link between the uncanny and the sacred. Freud himself mentions this connection in *Totem and Taboo*: "The meaning of taboo, as we see it, diverges in two contrary directions. To us it means, on the one hand, 'sacred', 'consecrated', and on the other 'uncanny', 'dangerous', 'forbidden', 'unclean'. The converse of 'taboo' in Polynesian is noa, which means 'common' or 'generally accessible'." Sigmund Freud, "Totem and Taboo," trans. and ed. James Strachey, *The Standard Edition of the Complete Psychological Works*, vol. 13 (London: Hogarth Press/Institute of Psychoanalysis, 1953–1974) 18 [punctuation original].

61 The statement is already made to look as if it were an independent statement, rather than the parenthesis that it is, in the Sanders entry, which capitalizes the first word: "Unh.[eimlich] nennt man Alles, was im Geheimnis, im Verborgenen [...] bleiben sollte und hervorgetreten ist" (GW XII, 235; also quoted SE 17, 256).

62 As these are transcripts of lectures delivered orally, it is possible that the full sentence was not accurately reproduced.

63 This is my translation of "hervorgetreten ist," literally "stepped forward," "noticed by me because of attracting attention to itself." The translation in the SE "come to light" led Terry Castle to use the quotation to support her thesis that the uncanny is the reaction to the enlightenment. Peter L. Rudnytsky mentions this in a letter (TLS, December 29, 1995), in response to Claude Rawson's review of Castle's book (December 15, 1995). Rud-

nytsky overlooks that "come to light" is the wording used in the Standard Edition. It is perhaps a mistranslation, originating in the Standard Edition, but the problem, not addressed in the letter, is whether Castle's argument depends on what is thus reduced to a play on words. A more valid objection, as mentioned in the introduction, is that the uncanny does not originate in the 18th century.

64 The Schelling quotation appears slightly modified in "The Dialectic of Enlightenment," in an attempt by Horkheimer/Adorno to counter Freud's interpretation of the belief in the omnipotence of thoughts, attributed to primitive peoples. Horkheimer/Adorno argue that Freud projects an enlightenment perspective onto primitive peoples with the division into material and spiritual worlds.

65 The asterix indicates that the Schelling quotation is rendered in a form representing a hypothetical alternative to the original.

66 Nevertheless, Freud would have perceived the affinity of his model of repression with Schelling's metaphor of the chasm covered with flowers. The uncanniness of repressed material lies in its concealment. If the repressed is revealed, it is no longer repressed. Freud did not try to clear up the cryptic appearance of the Schelling quotation, because he could apply it to his theory of the uncanny.

67 Schelling, "Achtundzwanzigste Vorlesung," 658, my translation. – "Allerdings sieht man in den Gesichtszügen der ägyptischen Figuren ältere Vorbilder, aber nicht gerade der ägyptischen, sondern jener älteren Kunst überhaupt, welche das Göttliche nur durch entstellte und verdrehte menschliche Züge darstellt, nicht es offen zu zeigen, sondern durch etwas ihnen mitgetheiltes Außermenschliches oder Nichtmenschliches – durch etwas Fremdes – noch zu verhüllen, mit einer gewissen Unheimlichkeit zu umgeben suchten."

68 "Mit dem Worte 'unheimlich' nun scheint unsere deutsche Sprache eine ziemlich glückliche Bildung zu Stande gebracht zu haben. Es scheint dadurch wohl zweifellos ausgedrückt werden zu sollen, dass einer, dem etwas 'unheimlich' vorkommt, in der betreffenden Angelegenheit nicht recht 'zu Hause', nicht 'heimisch' ist, dass ihm die Sache fremd ist oder wenigstens so erscheint [...]" Jentsch, "Zur Psychologie des Unheimlichen," 195, my emphasis, my translation.

69 Kittler calls Jentsch a "psychologist of literature," ("Der Literaturpsychologe Jentsch") which strongly indicates that Kittler has not seen the Jentsch essay. Kittler, "Das Phantom unseres Ichs," 148.

70 Freud also does not mention that Jentsch already refers to E.T.A. Hoffmann's "Der Sandmann."

71 The German word Freud uses for "obviously" is "offenbar" (SE 17, 220, 33). A synonym in German is "anscheinend" (apparently). If Freud had wanted to reveal the aim of his argument from the start, he would have had to use the word "scheinbar" (seemingly), instead of "offenbar/anscheinend" (obviously). He would have had to write (in a hypothetical alternative to the original): "The German word 'unheimlich' is obviously the opposite of what is familiar, but the semantics of the word are misleading, because matters are different in reality than what the word expresses."

72 The SE's somewhat awkward translation of "eine Sache in der man sich nicht auskennt" could also be translated as "a thing one is not familiar with."

73 "[…] kurzum, das Wort will nahe legen, dass mit dem Eindruck der Unheimlichkeit eines Dinges oder Vorkommnisses ein Mangel an Orientirung [sic] verknüpft ist." Jentsch, "Zur Psychologie des Unheimlichen," 195, my emphasis, my translation.

74 "Intellectual certainty is one of the defenses erected in the battle for survival. When it is lacking, it exposes a vulnerable spot in the fight for survival, both in the life of humans and that of other organisms." Jentsch, "Zur Psychologie des Unheimlichen," 205. – Even if "intellectual certainty" prevents the uncanny for Jentsch, its opposite, "intellectual *un*certainty," cannot be inferred as the essence of the uncanny for Jentsch.

75 "[…] entstehen gewisse Regungen von Gefühlen psychischer Unsicherheit besonders dann leicht, wenn entweder die Unkenntnis sehr auffallend oder wenn die subjective [sic] Wahrnehmung des Schwankens abnorm stark ist." Jentsch, "Zur Psychologie des Unheimlichen," 196, my translation.

76 Cixous asks: "Does not Jentsch say more than what Freud wishes to read?" Cixous, "Fiction and its Phantoms," 534.

77 Jentsch, "Zur Psychologie des Unheimlichen," 196. – Magnetism is a similar example, not mentioned by Jentsch, which appears to the uninitiated as if objects were being moved by unseen forces.

78 Cp. the distinction of "Furcht" and "Angst," p. 43.

79 Freud italicizes the noun in his title, acknowledging that it is a neologism, derived from the adjective. Strachey renders the italics as single quotes.

80 The claim that Schelling was the first to use "Das Unheimliche" as a noun in the Grimm entry (originally published 1920) on "unheimlich" is inaccurate. Grimm and Grimm, "unheimlich," 1059. – The entire sentence

in which Schelling allegedly uses the noun was already quoted above on page 61. Schelling uses "Unheimlichkeit" (literally "uncanniness"), never "Das Unheimliche." Schelling, "Achtundzwanzigste Vorlesung," 658. – The word "Unheimlichkeit" (uncanniness) reveals its adjectival origin and expresses a quality of feeling on the part of the observer, not a class of objects causing this feeling. Thus, the word is in agreement with Schelling's notion of the uncanny as characterized by lack of recognition and hidden features. The latter is analogous to Jentsch's emphasis on intellectual uncertainty, and thus Schelling's usage runs counter to Freud's sweeping dismissal of uncertainty.

81   "[...] vielleicht nur darum nicht, weil wir selbst Fremdsprachige sind" (GW XII, 232).

82   Cp. p. 53 above.

83   Freud, "Totem," 22, Freud's emphasis. – Cp. also: "They appear to follow a rule that anything that is uncanny or provokes dread for any reason becomes subject to taboo." Freud, "Totem," 23.

84   In response to Freud's statement "[...] we may expect that a special core of feeling is present which justifies the use of a special conceptual term" (SE 17, 219, 17–19), Cixous comments: "[...] Freud, arguing for the existence of the 'Unheimliche,' wishes to retain the sense, the real, the reality of the sense of things. He thus seeks out 'the basic sense.' Thus the analysis is anchored, at once, in what is denoted [...]. The fact of the matter is that the 'domain' remains indefinite; the concept is without any nucleus: the 'Unheimliche' presents itself, first of all, only on the fringe of something else." Cixous, "Fiction and its Phantoms," 528.

85   Lydenberg adds: "Many literary readings of Freud's 'The Uncanny' follow Cixous and Hertz in attempting to restore the literary qualities of Hoffmann's story and in identifying those neglected aspects as additional sources of uncanniness (cp. Møller, Wright)." Lydenberg, "Uncanny Narratives," 1084, footnote 2. – Lydenberg is referring to Neil Hertz, "Freud and the Sandman," *End of the Line: Essays in Psychoanalysis and the Sublime* (New York: Columbia University Press, 1985), Lis Møller, *The Freudian Reading: Analytical and Fictional Constructions* (Philadelphia: University of Pennsylvania Press, 1991), Wright, *Psychoanalytic Criticism* 142–50. – Nevertheless, many of these readings supply this additional evidence only to further support the Freudian paradigm or variations of it.

86   Freud wrongly believes the ambiguity of this kind in the text are resolved. – I will introduce the term "paranoiac" text for this structure in the Hoffmann chapter.

87   Jacques Offenbach's "Les Contes d'Hoffmann" ("The Tales of Hoffmann") remained unfinished at Offenbach's death (Oct. 5, 1880, Paris) and was first produced on Feb. 10, 1881.

88   Translation follows Freud's summary of Jentsch in SE 17, 227, 10–12. Originally Jentsch, "Zur Psychologie des Unheimlichen," 197. – Jentsch writes: "Einer der sichersten Kunstgriffe, leicht unheimliche Wirkungen durch Erzählungen hervorzurufen, beruht nun darauf, dass man den Leser im Ungewissen darüber lässt, ob er in einer bestimmten Figur eine Person oder etwa einen Automaten vor sich habe, und zwar so, dass diese Unsicherheit nicht direct in den Brennpunkt seiner Aufmerksamkeit tritt [...]. E.T.A. Hoffmann hat in seinen Phantasiestücken dieses psychologische Manöver wiederholt mit Erfolg zur Geltung gebracht." Jentsch, "Zur Psychologie des Unheimlichen," 203.

89   E.T.A. Hoffmann, "Die Automate," *Die Serapions-Brüder: Gesammelte Erzählungen und Märchen. Herausgegeben von E.T.A. Hoffmann*, 5th edn, vol. 2, Winkler Weltliteratur Dünndruck Ausgabe (München: Winkler, 1963/1995). – Hoffmann had seen automata on October 10, 1813 in Dresden (an automatic trumpet player and a piano playing figure). Both automata in Hoffmann's stories perform music. E.T.A. Hoffmann, *Die Serapions-Brüder* 1063. – Jentsch mistakenly groups "Der Sandmann" with Hoffmann's "Fantasy Pieces," whereas "Der Sandmann" was published under the rubric "Night Pieces" in the collection *Fantasie und Nachtstücke (Fantasy and Night Pieces)*. E.T.A. Hoffmann, *Fantasie und Nachstücke*, ed. Walter Müller Seidel (Darmstadt: Wissenschaftliche Buchgesellschaft, 1971).

90   The mistake already appears in the German original of Freud's essay (GW XII, 239). The Standard Edition adapts "Nathaniel," from Freud but also changes the spelling of "Olimpia" to "Olympia." Clara's name is spelled correctly in both GW and the SE.

91   There is no mention in Hoffmann about whether or not Nathanael is happy: "[...] some days ago, namely, on the thirtieth of October, at twelve o'clock at noon, a peddler of weather glasses and thermometers came into my room and wanted to sell me one of his wares. I bought nothing, and threatened to kick him downstairs, whereupon he went away of his own accord." E.T.A. Hoffmann, "The Sandman," trans. and ed. Stanley Appelbaum, *Five Great German Short Stories = Fünf deutsche Meistererzählungen: A Dual-Language Book* (New York: Dover, 1993) 36.

92   Obermeit has remarked that Hoffmann's "Der Sandmann" is the type of story whose meaning, like that of a poem, is lost by a paraphrase of the plot: "A poetical text enables experiences that are closed off to scientific

investigation. This discrepancy has been attributed to literature's comparatively higher receptivity to certain levels of reality than exact science." Werner Obermeit, *Das unsichtbare Ding, das Seele heißt. Die Entdeckung der Psyche im bürgerlichen Zeitalter* (Frankfurt am Main: Syndikat, 1980) 160, my translation. – "Ein poetischer Text hat einige Erfahrungen ermöglicht, die wissenschaftlichen Arbeiten als ihr Ergebnis verwehrt sind. Die Verschiedenheit ist zu einem Teil mit einer vergleichsweise höheren Rezeptivität der Literatur und einer entsprechend größeren Resistenz der Wissenschaft gegenüber einem Wirklichkeitsbereich erklärt worden." – Obermeit interprets "Der Sandmann" in the context of early nineteenth theories of madness. Obermeit, *Das unsichtbare Ding*, 104–26.

93 Feminist critics have attributed this to the ambiguous role of the feminine in the essay, especially in conjunction with the Italian episode, and the topic of womb phantasies. See Lydenberg, "Uncanny Narratives."

94 "a dissociated complex of Nathaniel's which confronts him as a person" (SE 17, 232, n. 1).

95 "It is a common pattern in psychoanalytic experience that a young man [...] who is fixated upon his father by his castration complex [...] becomes incapable of loving a woman [...]" (SE 17, 232, n. 1).

96 Freud's later attempt at introducing a counterpart of the Oedipus complex for little girls, by substituting the fear of castration with the fear of losing the loved object, is not convincing, because that fear is not gender specific. Sigmund Freud, *New Introductory Lectures on Psycho-Analysis.* "Lecture XXXII: Anxiety and Instinctual Life," trans. and ed. James Strachey, *The Standard Edition of the Complete Psychological Works*, vol. 22 (London: Hogarth Press/Institute of Psychoanalysis, 1953–1974) 88.

97 For Huet, the automaton constitutes an example of the uncanniness of the double. I agree with her attempt to find an alternative to Rank's explanation of the double as the "harbinger of death," which Freud adapts. Huet calls the automaton an uncanny monstrosity because it is a perfect imitation of a human being, which deprives the spectator of the ability to tell imitation and original apart. See Marie-Hélène Huet, *Monstrous Imagination* (Cambridge, Mass.: Harvard University Press, 1993) 233–6.

98 Cixous writes: "What if, in looking at [Olimpia], we animated her?" Cixous, "Fiction and its Phantoms," 538.

99 "[...] deception [...] so artfully planned that no one [...] had been aware of it [...]" (SmE 97) – "[...] Betrug, [der] so schlau angelegt worden, daß kein Mensch [...] es gemerkt habe" (SmG 360, 7–9). – The statement is in

the subjunctive in German because it is demanded by the rules governing reported speech, not to express Siegmund's doubt about how many people suspected anything. The statement already separates Olimpia's uncanniness from Nathanael's individual complexes. Her uncanniness manifests itself as an external physical reality, regardless of Nathanael's infatuation.

100 "Uns ist diese Olimpia ganz unheimlich geworden [...]" (SmG 356, 26–34).

101 Kleist expresses similar ideas in "Über das Marionetten Theater" (1810), although he does not use the term uncanniness. The passage in question examines the grace and beauty of puppets, unattainable by humans, because puppets do not have self-consciousness: "[...] human consciousness disrupts the natural grace of man." "[...] welche Unordnung, in der natürlichen Grazie des Menschen das Bewußtsein anrichtet." Heinrich von Kleist, "Über das Marionettentheater," *Kleist: Ein Lesebuch für unsere Zeit*, Goldammer, Peter (Einleitung und Auswahl) (Berlin Weimar: Aufbau, 1986) 365, my translation.

102 Jentsch adds: "The same feelings are aroused when a primitive person sees a locomotive or steamboat for the first time. These impressions have been reported to be more extreme in the dark, and are enhanced by the fact that the object moves on its own accord and makes sounds that are reminiscent of breathing." Jentsch, "Zur Psychologie des Unheimlichen," 197, my translation.

103 "Das erstere [gewisse Regungen von Gefühlen psychischer Unsicherheit wenn die Unkenntnis sehr auffallend ist] beobachtet man leicht bei Kindern: das Kind hat noch so wenig Erfahrung, dass ihm einfache Dinge unerklärlich, nur wenig komplizierte [sic] Situationen bereits dunkle Geheimnisse sein können. Es ist dies eine der wichtigsten Ursachen, warum das Kind meistens so ängstlich ist und so wenig Selbstvertrauen zeigt [...]" Jentsch, "Zur Psychologie des Unheimlichen," 196, my translation.

104 Even if children are not fully conscious of their animating activity, they control it and therefore are not likely to frighten themselves.

105 The process is thus similar to the figures in literary texts, which we bring to life through our imagination. All literary figures are uncanny, seen from this perspective, because they blur the boundary between animate and inanimate beings, like the un-dead figures of the literary uncanny. I expand on this idea in the conclusion.

106 The father's death is not explained, but his death is also accompanied by an odd transformation of his facial expression. The father appears split into a benevolent and a dark side. Ambiguities of causation also produce the uncanniness of the scene in which Nathanael dies. Both issues will be discussed in the Hoffmann chapter.

107 Françoise Meltzer thus presents an alternative explanation for the significance of the eyes, not only in the "Der Sandmann," but also in "Oedipus." The transgression instead of having primarily sexual connotations has to do with science and knowledge. See Meltzer, "The Uncanny Rendered Canny," 222.

108 "[...] a peculiar feeling of uncertainty, which may arise by itself not rarely even in the apprehension of everyday phenomena among more sophisticated persons. This feeling thus perhaps constitutes an important factor for the origin of the scientific urges." – "[...] dann stellt sich wohl manchmal ein eigenthümliches Unsicherheitsgefühl ein, welches bei dem geistig Anspruchsvolleren sich nicht selten von selbst beim Wahrnehmen von alltäglichen Erscheinungen meldet und wahrscheinlich einen wichtigen Entstehungsfactor des wissenschaftlichen Dranges und der Forschertriebe darstellen dürfte." Jentsch, "Zur Psychologie des Unheimlichen," 196, my translation.

109 Todorov, who acknowledges a heavy indebtedness to Freud's essay, also criticizes this argument: "Hoffmann, who was unhappy as a child, describes the fears of childhood. But for this observation to have any explicative value, we must prove either that all writers unhappy in childhood do the same, or that all descriptions of childhood fears are by writers whose childhoods were unhappy." Tzvetan Todorov, "The Uncanny and the Marvelous," *Literature of the Occult. A Collection of Critical Essays*, ed. Peter B. Messent, Twentieth Century Views (Englewood Cliffs, N.J.: Prentice-Hall, 1981) 151.

110 Joan Copjec, "Vampires, Breast-Feeding and Anxiety," *October* 58 (1991). - Quoted following Lydenberg, "Uncanny Narratives," 1078, 84. – Cp. also Huet, *Monstrous Imagination*, 233–6.

111 The term "unreliable narrator" follows Wayne C. Booth, *The Rhetoric of Fiction*, 2nd edn (Chicago: University of Chicago Press, 1983) 159.

112 Hertz has also pointed out this discrepancy: "And yet Freud's second account of the story, offered in a long stunningly condensed footnote (SE 232–3), is precisely that: the sober truth detected behind the products of a madman's imagination, the latent substructure, or what Freud calls the 'original arrangement' of the elements of the story." Hertz, "Freud and the Sandman," 104.

113 According to his hypothesis, the nurse's tale can be still be understood as a determining factor in Nathanael's psyche, without denying the laboratory scene its fantastic reality. Such events are as much symptoms of certain traumatic intrapsychic processes as they are external, albeit fictitious, events.

114 Clara advises Nathanael to stop believing in the identity of Coppola and Coppelius.

115 Cp. the passage on paradoxical ambiguity in the introduction, and the two types of disjunctions that Rimmon distinguishes. See Shlomith Rimmon, *The Concept of Ambiguity: The Example of James* (Chicago and London: The University of Chicago Press, 1977).

116 Instead, this explanation conforms to the idea, which also informs the death drive, namely that all drives are governed by an urge to return to an earlier state.

117 *Interpretation of Dreams* (1900a) opens with the dream of Irma's injection, in which Freud is confronted with the real fear of failing as a doctor. GW II/III 111–12 – Freud, *Interpretation of Dreams*, 106–7.

118 Cixous, "Fiction and its Phantoms," 545. – Death is in itself uncanny because it represents the ultimate secret.

119 "The previously discussed division of the psychical personality has led to a new orientation in regards to anxiety. The Ego is now the primary seat of fear, while it no longer makes sense to speak of an anxiety in the Id." Freud, *New Introductory Lectures*, 85–6.

120 Freud is referring to the castration anxiety that is feared as the direct consequence of the desired union with the mother. Freud, *New Introductory Lectures*, 89.

121 Punishment dreams are still interpreted as disguised wish-fulfilments.

122 Sigmund Freud, *New Introductory Lectures on Psycho-Analysis*. "Lecture XXIX: Revision of the Theory of Dreams," trans. and ed. James Strachey, *The Standard Edition of the Complete Psychological Works*, vol. 22 (London: Hogarth Press/Institute of Psychoanalysis, 1953–1974) 27. – In *Beyond the Pleasure Principle* (1920g), Freud mentions such dreams, but is not prepared to revise his dream theory.

123 Freud, *New Introductory Lectures*, 88, my translation. This passage is translated inaccurately in the Standard Edition as: "In the course of development the old determinants of anxiety should be dropped, since the situations of danger corresponding to them have lost their importance owing to the strengthening of the ego." – "Mit dieser neuen Auffassung ist auch die Funktion der Angst als Signal zur Anzeige einer Gefahr-

situation, die uns ja vorher nicht fremd war, in den Vordergrund getreten, die Frage, aus welchem Stoff die Angst gemacht wird, hat an Interesse verloren [...]."

124 Again, Freud exploits the pun on "home." Considering that neither the fear of being buried alive nor the vagina are very convincing examples of the uncanny, it is possible he discusses these examples only because of the alleged connection to the word "*Heim*," which solidifies Freud's emphasis on the familiar in the uncanny.

125 Would women perceive the female genitals as uncanny? Why does Freud not mention the "horror vacui," the fear associated with absence?

126 "Zum Schlusse dieser [...] Beispielsammlung soll eine Erfahrung aus der psychoanalytischen Arbeit erwähnt werden, die, wenn sie nicht auf einem zufälligen Zusammentreffen beruht, die schönste Bekräftigung unserer Auffassung des Unheimlichen mit sich bringt" (GW XII, 258).

127 Lydenberg has argued that these examples are a symptom of Freud's repression of sexuality that appears is most visible in the Italian episode, discussed below.

128 Cp. Punter's statement footnote 45 in this chapter.

129 Punter strives to correct this shortcoming, and emphasizes the destabilizing character of the uncanny in accordance with the theory presented in this dissertation: "[...] the unnaming, the achievement of anonymity which is akin to the defamiliarising of the uncanny, bound back to back with the inevitability of naming [...] under the insidious, creeping pressure, which is the pressure of writing itself." Punter, "On Poetry and the Uncanny," 199.

130 The topic becomes more relevant in *Beyond the Pleasure Principle*, because it is, for Freud, a symptom of "repetition compulsion." "[...] compulsion to repeat [...] first put us on the track of the death instincts." Freud, *Beyond*, 56.

131 Punter locates the disruptive effect of repression not in the object, but in the sense of a coherent self: "What will we be left with? Déjà vu, a sense that we have been here before; but although we are certain that we hear the echoes, sense the haunting, of a prior state, what is uncertain is not the memory of that state but the memory of the coherence of the self which, perhaps, experienced it." Punter, "On Poetry and the Uncanny," 196. – Nonetheless, it is not entirely clear why the uncertainty about the memory of the "prior state" would not also constitute a disruption of the self.

132 Freud would not accept such an explanation.

133 Lacan more aptly applies the idea of faulty recognition to the subject itself, and uses the term "méconnaissance," which characterizes the ego for Lacan in all its structures. Jacques Lacan, "The Mirror Stage as Formative of the Function of the I," trans. Alan Sheridan, *Écrits: A Selection* (New York and London: Norton, 1977) 6.

134 Sigmund Freud, "A Disturbance of Memory on the Acropolis: An Open Letter to Romain Rolland on the Occasion of his Seventieth Birthday," trans. and ed. James Strachey, *The Standard Edition of the Complete Psychological Works*, vol. 22 (London: Hogarth Press/Institute of Psychoanalysis, 1953–1974) 241, Freud's emphasis. – The visit occurred in 1904. Gay, *Freud*, 158.

135 The remark is also strikingly similar to an anecdote appearing in the study of Jensen's *Gradiva*: "So after all it is true that the dead can come back to life" (SE 9, 71–2; GW VII, 99). – This is Freud's reaction after a woman has come into his office who is the sister of a former, deceased patient of his. The remark not only reveals Freud's own superstitiousness, contrary to the self-image he projects in "The Uncanny," but also his discomfort with this aspect of his character. The latter is visible in his dissociation from the remark, by referring first to a doctor in the third person as the one who had the experience, and adding only at the end that he himself is the man in question. – F. Meltzer mentions the incident in: Françoise Meltzer, "For Your Eyes Only: Ghost Citing," *Questions of Evidence. Proof, Practice, and Persuasion across the Disciplines*, eds James K. Chandler, Arnold Ira Davidson, Harry D. Harootunian and Cass R. Sunstein (Chicago: University of Chicago Press, 1994) 48.

136 It is difficult to distinguish between the two because the revealed component in each case is both familiar and strange, at different points in time.

137 Cixous also refers to the subdued presence of the "death drive" in "The Uncanny," which emerges explicitly only in *Beyond the Pleasure Principle* (1920g).

Chapter 3: E.T.A. Hoffmann's "Der Sandmann" – A Story of Persecution Told by a Persecuted Narrator

1 As mentioned in the introduction, I will not undertake to show how *repetition compulsion* governs both "Der Sandmann" and, as a return of the

repressed, Freud's essay. It is admissible, following Freud, to call any encounter with the unconscious "uncanny," but in this generalization lies the limitation of Freud's definition.

2   Jentsch speaks specifically of a "lack of orientation" – "Mangel an Orientirung" [sic], Jentsch, "Zur Psychologie des Unheimlichen," 195; "psychic uncertainty" – "psychische Unsicherheit" Jentsch, "Zur Psychologie des Unheimlichen," 196.

3   Cp. the discussion of the terms "diegetic" and "extradiegetic" at the end of the introduction, regarding the distinction between the boundaries of the world the characters inhabit in contrast to the totality of information available to the reader.

4   "[…] the holder of point of view." Prince, *A Dictionary of Narratology*, 32.

5   The story thus begins in the style of an epistolary novel, and Nathanael can even be seen as a parody of the protagonist in Goethe's "Die Leiden des jungen Werthers" (1774).

6   The situation is comparable to insane narrators such as the governess in James's *The Turn of the Screw* or Kinbote in Nabokov's *Pale Fire*.

7   The definition thus follows Prince's more general definition of "unreliable narrator": "[…] a narrator, the reliability of whose account is undermined by various features of that account." Prince, *A Dictionary of Narratology*, 101.

8   "paranoiac" as in "possessing attributes of paranoia."

9   See Freud's essay on the Schreber case (1911) and in his two later papers on the topic (1915f/1922b) – Sigmund Freud, "A Case of Paranoia Running Counter to the Psycho-Analytic Theory of the Disease," trans. and ed. James Strachey, *The Standard Edition of the Complete Psychological Works*, vol. 14 (London: Hogarth Press/Institute of Psychoanalysis, 1953–1974). Sigmund Freud, "Some Neurotic Symptoms in Jealousy, Paranoia and Homosexuality," trans and ed. James Strachey, *The Standard Edition of the Complete Psychological Works*, vol. 18 (London: Hogarth Press/Institute of Psychoanalysis, 1953–1974).

10 The definition of paranoid I use is more recent than Freud's. I follow the *Diagnostic and Statistical Manual of Mental Disorders*-IV (1994), which gives the following definition for persecutory delusions: "This subtype [of delusional disorders] applies when the central theme of the delusion involves the person's belief that he or she is being conspired against […] spied on, followed […] harassed, or obstructed in the pursuit of long-term goals. Small slights may be exaggerated and become the focus of a delusional system." *DSM-IV*, under the heading "Schizophrenia and Other Psychotic Disorders," lists a "Paranoid Type": "The essential

feature of the Paranoid Type of Schizophrenia is the presence of prominent delusions [...] in the context of relative preservation of cognitive functioning and affect." The definition appears under the category "Delusional disorders, Persecutory type." *Diagnostic and Statistical Manual of Mental Disorders*, 4th edn (Washington, D.C.: American Psychiatric Association, 1994) 297, 98.

11   Nathanael thinks the man by the name of Coppola trying to sell him glass instruments is the disguised lawyer Coppelius, whom he considers responsible for his father's death.

12   Hoffmann's portrayal of Nathanael's mother also contains an implicit commentary on the oppressed position of women in this Biedermeier household, which will be discussed below.

13   Freud does not focus on the sadistic role of the nanny. He may have been limited in analyzing this role because of a childhood trauma of his own, associated with a nanny. Freud's nanny was expelled from the house and locked up for theft; cp. Ernest Jones, *The Life and Work of Sigmund Freud*, 3 vols (New York and London: Basic, 1953). – This would be another instance of Freud's blind spot, a term Freud himself defines in the following way: "[...] jede ungelöste Verdrängung beim Arzte entspricht nach einem treffenden Worte von W. Stekel einem 'Blinden Fleck' in seiner analytischen Wahrnehmung." Sigmund Freud, "Recommendations to Physicians Practicing Psychonalysis," trans. and ed. James Strachey, *The Standard Edition of the Complete Psychological Works*, vol. 12 (London: Hogarth Press/Institute of Psychoanalysis, 1953–1974) 382.

14   "Sandman, little Sandman – teasing allegory for the sleepiness in children. The Sandman is supposed to come and throw sand into their eyes. Low German: 'sand sower,' Southern German: -> 'tar dwarf.'" ("Sandmann, Sandmännchen – scherzhafte Allegorie für die aufkommende Schläfrigkeit bei Kindern, denen der S[andmann] Sand in die Augen streuen soll. niederdt. Sandsäer, oberdt. -> Pechmännlein"). Entry: "Sandmann," *Meyers Enzyklopädisches Lexikon*, vol. 20 (Mannheim, Wien, Zürich: Bibliographisches Institut / Lexikonverlag, 1977). – The Brockhaus entry reads: "personification of falling asleep" ("Personifizierung des sich einstellenden Schlafs"). *Brockhaus Enzyklopädie: in vierundzwanzig Bänden*, 24 vols. (Mannheim: Brockhaus, 1986). – The belief in the Sandman, even if it is humorous or teasing, contains a slight ambiguity, because it is indeed painful to have sand thrown into one's eyes. The variation recorded in Meyer's Encyclopedia, "Pechmännlein" (tar dwarf) is further proof of this ambiguity, because "Pech haben" also means to have bad luck in German.

It could be a way in which "myth" tries to counteract a basic fear, insofar as sleep is a deathlike state, a form of nonconsciousness.

15   Freud mentions such tales in his *Three Essays*. For Freud the true source of the fear of children is their prematurely developed sexual drive, which is converted into anxiety if it cannot be satisfied. Section 5 of the third of the three essays in: Sigmund Freud, *Three Essays on the Theory of Sexuality*, trans. James Strachey, *The Standard Edition of the Complete Psychological Works*, vol. 7 (London: Hogarth Press/Institute of Psychoanalysis, 1953–1974) 224. – For Freud, the nanny's tale only sticks in Nathanael's memory because it allegorizes a threat of castration. This is based on the substitution of eyes for penis. Cp. the comments below.

16   This has been argued, convincingly, as Coppelius and the father are engaged in an act of procreation. Cp. Kittler, "Das Phantom unseres Ichs," 157.

17   Freud speaks of a "feminine attitude towards his father in infancy." Freud, "The 'Uncanny'," 232.

18   As above, I adopt Todorov's definition, of a story in which the laws that we believe govern reality are broken.

19   Olimpia says more than the words "Ah, Ah!" ("Ach, Ach!") at the end of one of the visits during which Nathanael reads his older and his new literary productions to her. She bids him farewell with the words: "Good night, dear!" (SmE 91) – "Gute Nacht, mein Lieber!" (SmG 357, 33). If we do not suspect that Nathanael imagined this sentence, we must assume that Spalanzani and Coppola have improved Olimpia's speech capabilities.

20   The dictionary by Adelung, having appeared just five years before "Der Sandmann," spells "Der Olymp" with a "y." Johann Christoph Adelung, "Der Olymp," *Grammatisch kritisches Wörterbuch der hochdeutschen Mundart mit beständiger Vergleichung der übrigen Mundarten, besonders des Oberdeutschen*, vol. 3 (Wien: Bauer, 1811). – The standard spelling with "y" is also confirmed by Jakob Heinrich Kaltschmidt, *Gesammt-Wörterbuch der Deutschen Sprache* (Leipzig: Karl Lauchnitz, 1834) 637.

21   The epistolary portion is much longer than is often thought. The third-person perspective begins only two pages short of the halfway point (15 of 33 pages, SmG 343). This division into two almost equal halves, each in a different mode, contributes to the uncertain reality status of the events in Nathanael's childhood. After all, an event is probably more real when several people witness it.

22   Making the everyday world a witness to the fantastical in the manner of science fiction is unique for Hoffmann. This does not, for example,

happen in *Der goldne Topf,* where the world of the crystal Anselmus discovers remains separate from the everyday world. Also, in "Der Sandmann," there is no incident like pulling of a mandrake root as in Tieck's "Der Runenberg," which immediately reveals that, in this story, spirits inhabits the world. Ludwig Tieck, "Der Runenberg," *Phantasus,* ed. Manfred Frank, vol. 6 (Frankfurt am Main: Deutscher Klassiker Verlag, 1985) 186.

Chapter 4: Clues Confirming the Existence of the Sandman

1 This claim seems to contradict logic, because Nathanael still has his eyes. On the other hand, Nathanael's gaze animated Olimpia, so the remark has symbolic meaning. A hypothetical explanation of Spalanzani's remark would be to imagine a fantastical process of animation in which Olimpia accumulates lifelikeness, which is expressed in the eyes, depending on the credibility she achieves in the eyes of her one admirer, Nathanael. His longing eyes then make Olimpia's eyes appear real. However, in this and the other issues cited above, the text does not supply us with conclusive evidence.

2 "Denke Dir einen […] Mann, mit […] Augenbrauen, unter denen […] ein Paar grünliche Katzenaugen stechend hervorfunkeln" (SmG 334, 33–7).

3 "Das schiefe Maul verzieht sich oft zum hämischen Lachen" (SmG 334, 38–9).

4 "[…] frug Coppola mit seiner widerwärtigen heisern Stimme und dem hämischem Lächeln" (SmG 352, 11–13).

5 "sköne Oke – sköne Oke!" (SmG 351, 5).

6 "sköne Glas – sköne Glas!" (SmG 352, 11).

7 His success at calming himself lasts only a short while. Then fear grips him again, and his own words sound to him like a "deep, deathly sigh" (SmE 79) – "war es, als halle ein tiefer Todesseufzer grauenvoll durch das Zimmer" (SmG 352, 19–20). This alienation from his own voice occurs again while he recites his poem to himself before reading it to Clara. Cp. comments p. 126, below.

8 Nathanael is talking about seeing Coppola. The expression indicates that in Nathanael's mind, Coppelius is identical to Coppola.

9   Laplanche and Pontalis define negation thus: "Procedure whereby the subject, while formulating one of his wishes, thoughts or feelings which has been repressed hitherto, contrives, by disowning it, to continue to defend himself against it." J. Pontalis and J.-B. Laplanche, *The Language of Psycho-Analysis*, trans. Donald Nicholson-Smith (New York: Norton, 1973) 261.

10   "'Of course,' Nathanael thought, 'he's laughing at me because I must have paid much too dearly for the little telescope – paid too dearly!'" (SmE 79) – "'Nun ja', meinte Nathanael, 'er lacht mich aus, weil ich ihm das kleine Perspektiv gewiß viel zu teuer bezahlt habe – zu teuer bezahlt!'" (SmG 352, 16–18).

11   Cp. the passage from *DSM-IV*, although this passage appears under the heading "delusions" as one of the criteria for schizophrenia: "Persecutory delusions are most common; the person believes he or she is being tormented, followed, tricked, spied on, or subjected to ridicule." *DSM-IV*, 275.

12   The correct declination in German acknowledges the Latin origin of the word (-us declination), although in colloquial parlance a Germanized genitive ("Coppelius") is frequently used.

13   Cp. the commentary on the elements being assembled in Nathanael's poem.

14   "[…] breiten sich wie schwarze Wolkenschatten über mich aus" (SmG 331, 12–14).

15   "*Peripety* […] The inversion […] from one state of affairs to its opposite. For example, an action seems destined for success and suddenly moves towards failure, or vice versa." Prince, *A Dictionary of Narratology*, 70. – "*Catastrophe* […] The term usually designates the unhappy dénouement of tragedy." Prince, *A Dictionary of Narratology*, 11.

16   Samuel Weber calls it "[…] a repetition and displacement of the horrible face, indeed the eyes, of Coppelius." Samuel Weber, "The Sideshow, or: Remarks on a Canny Moment," *Modern Language Notes* 88.5 (1973): 1122.

17   "unter den grauen, langen Wimpern" (SmG 351, 3).

18   "buschige[n] graue[n] Augenbrauen" (SmG 334, 35–6).

19   The word "bush" signals that it is Coppelius who approaches the tower. This is discussed in more detail below.

20   Cp. the German idiom: "In der Nacht sind alle Katzen grau," literally: "At night all cats are gray." It shows the connection between color and inhibited perception at night. The general significance of color for the uncanny is discussed below.

21 "[…] had walked directly to the marketplace" (SmE 101) – "[…] gerades Weges nach dem Markt geschritten war" (SmG 362, 34–5). This detail is lost in the translation.

22 Cp. quote on p. 110 above.

23 Cp. the passage just quoted: "that actually seems to be walking toward us" (SmE 101).

24 "gerades Weges" (SmG 362, 34), literally: "taking the most direct route."

25 Weber (1973) integrates the gray bush into his Lacanian interpretation and reads it as a representation of the maternal phallus. – Weber draws a parallel between Nathanael's sideways movement when looking through the telescope, perhaps at the bush, and Freud's consideration that aesthetics is an area remote from psychoanalysis. See Weber, "The Sideshow," 1132. – The mother plays a central role in the Hoffmann quotation at the beginning of this chapter. Hoffmann goes beyond Freud's speculations and anticipates Kristeva's speculations about the pre-Oedipal sources of the uncanny in the perception of the child as "abject" status at the moment of birth. Hoffmann's notion of nature as mother and source have a later echo in Kristeva. See Julia Kristeva, *Powers of Horror: An Essay on Abjection*, trans. Leon S. Roudiez (New York: Columbia University Press, 1982).

26 The approaching bush may be intended as an allusion to Macbeth, who, standing on the top of his castle, wonders how "Birnam's wood" can possibly come to Dunsinane, which is also the prophesied sign that his end is near (Macbeth V, iv, 33–5, 43–5). Nathanael swears revenge on Coppelius, like Hamlet on Claudius, the alleged murderer of his father, and does not succeed. However, Hamlet had high currency, especially because of the exposure of the play in Goethe's "Wilhelm Meisters Lehrjahre," which was published in 1795–1796. Hamlet thus became the model for the German Romantic hero in many ways. It would be more appropriate to see Nathanael as Hoffmann's satirical response to the overwrought sensitivity of the protagonists in the novels by Novalis, Schlegel, and Wackenroder, rather than a direct allusion to Hamlet.

27 "wurde den Coppelius gewahr" (SmG 362, 40). – Nathanael sees Coppelius after he looks through the telescope. The meaning of "gewahr werden" is also "to notice," another reason to believe that he sees Clara at first and Coppelius only later.

Chapter 5: Nathanael's Precarious Position as a Writer

1   Samuel Weber in his paraphrase of the text, writes: "Nathanael [...] takes out 'Coppola's glass,' looks *sideways* and sees Clara [...] in front of the lens." Weber, "The Sideshow," 1118, Weber's emphasis and ellipsis marks. – Cp. also Weber, "The Sideshow," 1121–2. – Weber's interest in underscoring his theme of the "sideshow" uses ellipsis points to erase the texts ambiguity. Françoise Meltzer reads the scene like Weber: "Why does Nathanael go mad once again upon staring at Klara's eyes through the telescope?" Meltzer, "The Uncanny Rendered Canny," 234.

2   These aspirations are a variation of his father's search for higher knowledge.

3   Cp. the remarks about the intrinsic uncanniness of the familiar, if the unfamiliar is rigidly excluded.

4   Appelbaum does not translate accurately here: "the fundamental conflicts of his nature" is not the equivalent of "der im Innern zerrissene Nathanael." The German makes no reference to his nature.

5   "When there is no part of the narrative [...] corresponding to [...] narratively pertinent situations and events that took time, ellipsis obtains." Prince, *A Dictionary of Narratology*, 25.

6   "das Phantom unseres eigenen Ichs" (SmG 341, 4).

7   "Klaras Ätiologie des Wahnsinns wird von Hoffmanns ganzem Werk gestützt [...]. Denn dieses Werk errichtet seine Poetologie, indem es den Wahnsinnigen als den negativen Doppelgänger des Dichters bestimmt. Der Wahnsinn produziert zwar auch eine innere Welt, kann sie aber nicht wie die Dichtung reflektieren und damit von der Außenwelt scheiden." Kittler, "Das Phantom unseres Ichs," 142, my translation.

8   "Nathanael blickt ihn Claras Augen; aber es ist der Tod, der mit Claras Augen in freundlich anschaut" (SmG 348, 4–6). – The image also foreshadows Olimpia's lifelessness.

9   "das tolle – unsinnige – wahnsinnige Märchen" (SmG 348, 40).

10   "Du verdammtes lebloses Automat!" (SmG 348, 42).

11   "Holzpüppchen dreh dich" (SmG 359, 26–7; 33–4).

12   Kittler remarks that the only word she speaks is the "Oh" of "Romantic, inward turned sentimentalism" ("das 'Ach' der romantischen Inner- lichkeit." Kittler, "Das Phantom unseres Ichs," 141.) – Nevertheless,

Kittler does not comment on the fact that Hoffmann parodies this very sentimentalism. Cp. also footnote 19.

13 The parallel is further hinted at, because Clara is the only other character who uses "Oh" besides Olimpia. The second paragraph of Clara's letter begins: "Oh, my beloved Nathanael [...]" (SmE 53) – "Ach, mein herzgeliebter Nathanael!" (SmG 339, 12). "Oh, he never loved me [...]" (SmE 73) – "Ach, er hat mich niemals geliebt [...]" (SmG 349, 1–2).

14 Clara is implicitly associated with the ironical smile of reason, while Olimpia is the product of experiments that are the outcome of research conducted in the spirit of enlightened reason. Instead of this unqualified parallel, one might argue that Olimpia personifies "instrumental reason," the application of enlightenment rationality without an ethical foundation, as opposed to practical reason, as defined by Habermas. Nevertheless, Hoffmann's implied critique of the enlightenment does not yet make this distinction.

15 This externalization is foreshadowed at the end of Nathanael's recital of the poem, when he believes the Sandman is speaking. Cp. below p. 126.

16 This emphasizes both the possible identity of the two men, and the similar role the two women play in Nathanael's life, as mentioned above.

17 The word "weissagen" means literally "to prophesize." Thus, the narrator explicitly inserts the idea that the poem has the power to affect the future.

18 While we hear that "Nathanael's productions were indeed very boring" (SmE 69) – "Nathanaels Dichtungen waren in der Tat sehr langweilig" (SmG 347, 15–16), the narrator also tells us that "[h]e had formerly been especially good at pleasant lively stories [...]" (SmE 69) – "Sonst hatte er eine besondere Stärke in anmutigen, lebendigen Erzählungen [...]" (SmG 8–9). "Pleasant" is an early reference to Nathanael's tendency towards sentimental superficiality, which makes him unfit to embark on more serious subject matter.

19 Nevertheless, Kittler does not distinguish clearly between interpretation and text. Nathanael does not identify the Sandman as the speaker when he feels the poem is not spoken by his own voice. Cp. the quotation "whose awful voice is this" on p. 126, below.

20 Although the latter may be due in part to her "prosaic" nature, quoted above on p. 122.

21 The turmoil at the end appears somewhat unmotivated. In comparison to the ending of Hoffmann's story, the clues seem confusing at best.

22 Nathanael's father, Spalanzani, Coppelius and Coppola represent the realm of scientific research. We may interpret the creation of the human

doll Olimpia as a process in the scientific realm that involves some higher principle, because it imitates the life-giving force ordinarily attributed to the divine. We have already stated that there are points of contact between the divine and the uncanny that could become the topic of an anthropological or religious study.

23   "Der Guß der Spiegel geschieht auf sehr dicken, kupfernen Platten [...] wonächst die Masse mit einer metallnen Walze geebnet, und wenn sie im Kühlofen abgekühlt ist, *geschliffen*, polirt [sic] und dann mit der Folie belegt wird." "Spiegel," *Real-Enzyclopädie für die gebildeten Stände (Conversations-Lexikon)*, vol. 9 (Leipzig: Brockhaus, 1824) 361, my emphasis, my translation.

24   Kittler also reads the first portion of the above quoted statement as a paradox, based on the observation that a person cannot appear real if he appears in an image. Kittler, "Das Phantom unseres Ichs," 163. – Kittler overlooks that Hoffmann uses a subjunctive: "that you will in fact feel *as if* you had already seen [...]." Kittler uses this misreading as an opportunity to insert Lacan's mirror phase into his discussion. While Kittler stops short of explicitly identifying Nathanael with Hoffmann, he nevertheless implies that Nathanael is both Hoffmann's and the reader's double in the text: "Nathanael is simply the Hebrew equivalent of Theodor [...]. The signifier 'Nathanael' represents the unconscious subject for the signifier 'Theodor' and vice versa" ("Nathanael ist einfach das hebräische Äquivalent von Theodor [...]. Der Signifikant 'Nathanael' vertritt [das unbewußte Subjekt] für den Signifikanten 'Theodor' und umgekehrt"). Kittler, "Das Phantom unseres Ichs," 165.

25   "Mangel an Orienti[e]rung [...] psychische Unsicherheit." Jentsch, "Zur Psychologie des Unheimlichen," 196, 2. – I thus agree with Cixous, who contests Freud's conviction that the identity of Coppola and Coppelius is no source of uncertainty in the following manner: "[...] decreeing, for example, that [...] Coppola = Coppelius. But this is so by paronomasia. Rhetoric does not create the real." Cixous is referring to Freud's pun on words in the footnote on the same page, regarding the homonyms "coppo" (Ital. "eye-socket") and "coppela" (Ital. "crucible") in the two men's names. Freud, "The 'Uncanny'," 232, footnote. – Nevertheless, Cixous does not base her opposition to Freud's claim on close textual analysis of Hoffmann. – Cixous, "Fiction and its Phantoms," 534.

26   From the passage quoted more extensively above in footnote 9. *DSM-IV*, 298.

27   Freud's claim is repeated by Wright, *Psychoanalytic Criticism* 144. – Also by
      Kittler, "Das Phantom unseres Ichs," 150.
28   Although these conflicts may nevertheless be interpreted as consequences
      of repressed sexuality, there is no explicit reference to sexuality in the
      text's description of the childhood scenario. Nathanael's childhood is
      primarily marked by a lack of communication between the family
      members. Freud's interpretation of the Sandman as representative of
      Nathanael's "feminine attitude towards his father" is inconsistent with the
      Sandman's existence before the first laboratory scene, in which the alleged
      transgression of witnessing the primal scene and the subsequent threat of
      castration take place. Freud, "The 'Uncanny'," 232, note 1.

Chapter 6: Ludwig Tieck's "Der blonde Eckbert" – The Uncanniness of Indifferent Fate

1   Cp. the definition of negation in the Hoffmann chapter.
2   "[...] for this uncanny is in reality nothing new or alien, but something
      which is familiar and old-established in the mind and which has become
      alienated from it only through the process of repression" (SE 17, 241, 14–
      17).
3   Throughout this chapter this being is called "the phantom," rather than
      "the witch," because the figure appears in several incarnations. An
      alternative would have been to call it "the embodiment of the marvelous"
      or "the incarnation of the supernatural." "Phantom" is not to be under-
      stood as "ghost" or "non-material appearance of a deceased person."
4   Although "Kunstmärchen" translates literally as "artistic – or artificial
      fairy tale," it is customarily translated as "literary fairy tale," for example in
      a recent bilingual dictionary of literary terms. James Fanning, *Literatur-
      wissenschaftliches Wörterbuch: Deutsch-Englisch / Englisch-Deutsch* (Frank-
      furt/Main: Peter Lang, 1993). – The same English term also appears in:
      James M. McGlathery, *Grimm's Fairy Tales. A History of Criticism on a Popular
      Classic*, Studies in German Literature, Linguistics, and Culture: Literary
      Criticism in Perspective, ed. James Hardin (Columbia, SC: Camden
      House, 1993).
5   Analogous to the note on the "unreliable narrator" in the Hoffmann
      chapter, I follow Booth, who defines the term in the following way: "For
      lack of better terms, I have called a narrator *reliable* when he speaks for or

acts in accordance with the norms of the work (which is to say, the implied author's norms), *unreliable* when he does not." Booth, *Rhetoric*, 158–9, Booth's emphasis. – Because the "norms of the work" as a reference point does not apply in these examples, I use the term following Prince's more general definition: "[…] a narrator, the reliability of whose account is undermined by various features of that account." Prince, *A Dictionary of Narratology*, 101.

6   I thus agree with Tatar: "If the first part of Tieck's narrative establishes the *coexistence* of two separate domains – one admitting the supernatural, the other knowing only natural laws – the remainder of the text draws us into a middle ground where the two worlds are *copresent*." Maria Tatar, "Unholy Alliances: Narrative Ambiguity in Tieck's 'Der blonde Eckbert'," *MLN* 102.3 (1987): 625, Tatar's emphasis.

7   Rippere repeats this claim: "The incestuous marriage symbolizes the fruitless union of two narcissistic characters who in the other love only themselves." Victoria L. Rippere, "Ludwig Tieck's 'Der blonde Eckbert:' A Psychological Reading," *PMLA: Publications of the Modern Language Association of America* 85.3 (1970).

8   Tatar, "Unholy Alliances," 614. – Tatar constructs a psychoanalytic interpretation based on Freud's essay "The Neuro-psychosis of Defense" (1894a).

9   Cp. the discussion of negation in the Hoffmann chapter.

10   J.M.Q. Davies, "Eckbert the Fair as Paradigm," *Journal of the Australasian Universities Language and Literature Association* 73 (1990): 186. – Davies alludes to Wright's 1984 commentary on Freud's essay. Wright, *Psychoanalytic Criticism* 147. – Davies' article suggests possible approaches to teaching "The Fair-Haired Eckbert," without following through with any particular approach in detail.

11   Davies, "Eckbert the Fair as Paradigm," 185, Davies's emphasis. – It is equally possible to call the phantom Bertha's mother image, however, considering that she does indeed become her surrogate mother.

12   This is also the case in Hoffmann's "Der Sandmann." Comparisons between the two stories are drawn in the conclusion, including the use of meta-narrative structures, letters in Hoffmann, and tale within tale in Tieck.

13   Furthermore, he does not go beyond stating that Tieck's story works through the dialectic of the familiar and the strange. The mere mention of this dialectic, while hinting at the importance of uncertainty, does not accomplish a clear enough position in relation to Freud's point of view.

Martin Swales, "Reading One's Life: An Analysis of Tieck's 'Der blonde Eckbert'," *German Life and Letters* 29 (1975): 174–5.

14   "[…] or when primitive beliefs which have been surmounted seem once more to be confirmed." Freud, "The 'Uncanny'," 249.

15   Cp. the discussion of Freud's concept in the Hoffmann chapter.

16   Cp. the explanation for using the terms "diegetic" and "extradiegetic" in the introduction.

17   "In einer Gegend des Harzes wohnte ein Ritter" (EckG 126, 2). EckE = Eckbert English, numerals indicate page numbers, as noted above in the "Abbreviations," page 13. EckG = Eckbert German, numerals indicate page and line numbers, as noted above in the "Abbreviations."

18   The quotation follows "The Sleeping Beauty in the Wood," *The Classic Fairy Tales*, ed. Iona and Peter Opie (London: Book Club Associates, 1974) 85.

19   We might say that this reinforces the incest motif in a surreal manner, because Bertha as storyteller begets the child that she cannot have as Eckbert's wife.

20   The Brocken Mountain is also the place where witches gather, as illustrated, for example, by the Walpurgisnacht scene in Goethe's "Faust." The location therefore also casts the old woman as a witch, although she is never explicitly called a witch.

21   Carlyle translates "schlicht" as "sleek," but it means "simple" here.

22   Bertha's daydreams come true. During her stay with the old woman, the talking bird's eggs contain pearls. (EckE 28–9; EckG 134, 25–8).

23   Swales identifies the same break with the fairy tale tradition in this description of Eckbert: "With this generalization Tieck establishes the second narrative register of his story: a register that involves a 'modern' awareness of psychological complexity, of paradoxical, indeed neurotic behaviour patterns. Such a passage has no place in the traditional 'Volksmärchen' convention […]" Swales, "Reading One's Life," 167.

24   The Romantic novel of development is a variation on the classical novel of development, the Bildungsroman, exemplified by Goethe's "Wilhelm Meisters Lehrjahre" (1795/96).

25   *DSM-IV* explains: "Delusions […] are erroneous beliefs that usually involve a misinterpretation of perceptions or experiences […]" – "Hallucinations […] may occur in any sensory modality […] but auditory hallucinations are by far the most common. […] Auditory hallucinations are usually experienced as voices, whether familiar or unfamiliar, that are perceived as distinct from the person's own thoughts." *DSM-IV*, 275.

26 Peter Horn uses the terminology of semantics to express the insanity implicit in a talking bird: "The words 'bird' and 'talk' cannot be brought into a sensible syntactic context: 'to talk' has the semantic attribute [plus human], whereas 'bird' has the semantic attribute [minus human]." Peter Horn, "Halluzinierte Vögel oder Wann ist Paranoia literarisch? Zu E.T.A. Hoffmann, Robert Musil und Daniel Paul Schreber," *Acta Germanica: Jahrbuch des Germanistenverbandes im Südlichen Afrika* Supp. 1 (1990): 177, my translation.

27 Under the heading of Schizophrenia, *DSM-IV* explains that "Referential delusions are also common; the person believes that certain gestures, comments [...] or other environmental cues are specifically directed at him or her." *DSM-IV*, 275.

28 My translation. Carlyle translates: "I heard the strangest song, as if coming from the hut, and sung by some bird. It ran thus [...]" (EckE 26). German "also" is an antiquated form of "all so" and is to be read here as "all the time thus," rather than simply "thus."

29 E.T.A. Hoffmann, "Der goldne Topf," Fantasiestücke in Callots Manier, ed. Walter Müller Seidel, vol. Fantasie und Nachtstücke (Darmstadt: Wissenschaftliche Buchgesellschaft, 1971) 182, my translation. – A talking bird also appears in Robert Musil's short story "Die Amsel" (1920): "It is as if you heard whispering, or only a brook murmuring, without being able to tell whether it is the one or the other!" – "Aber es ist, wie wenn du flüstern hörst, oder bloß rauschen, ohne das unterscheiden zu können!" Robert Musil, "Die Amsel," *Deutsche Erzähler*, ed. Marie Luise Kaschnitz, vol. 2 (Frankfurt am Main: Insel, 1971) 255, my translation.

30 Maria Tatar has pointed out that Tieck himself makes this observation in his commentaries on the ghosts in "Macbeth" and "Hamlet." Tatar, "Unholy Alliances," 623.

31 Cp. footnote 25 in this chapter.

32 "[...] der Vogel antwortete mir mit seinem Liede auf alle meine Fragen [...]" (EckG 135, 25–6).

33 In continuation of the passage quoted above in footnote 25 *DSM-IV* states: "Certain types of auditory hallucinations ([...] voices maintaining a running commentary on the person's thoughts or behavior) have been considered to be particularly characteristic of Schizophrenia [...]" *DSM-IV*, 275.

34 V.L. Rippere overlooks the positive connotations of Bertha's impracticality and sees her only as a narcissistic child failing to achieve productive

social adaptation prescribed for her in the world of the work. Rippere, "A Psychological Reading."

35 "[die Alte] sagte, daß ihre Haushaltung, seit ich dazu gehöre, weit ordentlicher geführt werde [...]" (EckG 135, 30–1).

36 The old woman, like her foster parents, asks her to contribute to household work, and while Bertha does not know how to spin wool during her stay at her foster parents' house, she acquires this skill in the woods. However, she is no less prone to delusions as a wool spinner. In fact, the German verb "spinnen" means "to be deranged," possibly to express that a person has "spun a yarn of thought in fantasy that does not stand up to reality."

37 We define uncanny, as mentioned in the Introduction, in the original sense of German "unheimlich," meaning "eerie," "weird," and "strange."

38 "She was dressed almost wholly in black; a black hood covered her head, and the greater part of her face [...]" (EckE 25) – "Sie war fast ganz schwarz gekleidet und eine schwarze kappe bedeckte ihren Kopf und einen großen Teil des Gesichtes" (EckG 131, 19–20).

39 "[...] bei jedem Schritte verzog sie ihr Gesicht so, daß ich im Anfange darüber lachen mußte" (EckG 131, 28–30).

40 These details further undermine the interpretations of forest solitude as a representation of the idyllic. Fries interprets the realm of "Forest Solitude" as a haven of peace that is violated by Bertha. He interprets the old woman as an incarnation of ever changing nature. "It is nature, which knows nothing or does not want to know anything of historicity. [...] [Her] appearance gives her the unmistakable features of a mystification." Thomas Fries, "Ein romantisches Märchen: 'Der blonde Eckbert' von Ludwig Tieck," *MLN*. 88.6 (1973): 1189.

41 The insertion of a poem into the narrative is also typical of the mixing of genres advocated by Schlegel, discussed in the Introduction. Cp. also the subsequent remarks on the folk song structure.

42 Max Reger [1873–1916]. "Waldeinsamkeit" in "Schlichte Weisen," op. 76 (no. 3) 1903–1912. In this song, the loneliness in the forest becomes the secluded space in which the lovers can kiss secretively, with the blackbird being the only witness. "Gestern Abend in der stillen Ruh / Sah ich im Walde einer Amsel zu / Als ich da so saß / Meiner ganz vergaß / Kommt mein Schatz und schleichet sich um mich / Und küsset mich // Soviel Laub als an der Linde ist / Und so viel tausend Mal hat mich mein Schatz geküßt / Denn ich muß gestehn / Es hat uns niemand gesehn / Und die Amsel soll mein Zeuge sein / Wir war'n allein."

43 "Diese Verse geben der aus den Friedensutopien der Zeit hervorwach-
senden Sehnsucht nach einem neuen Paradies und der Goldenen Zeit ein
poetisches Kleid." Gerhard Schulz, *Die deutsche Literatur zwischen französischer Revolution und Restauration. Zweiter Teil. Das Zeitalter der napoleonischen
Kriege und der Restauration: 1806–1830*, vol. 7, 2 (München: Beck, 1989) 389,
my translation.

44 Gail Finney notes that "[…] the Eden analogy has often been noted." Gail
Finney, "Self-Reflexive Siblings: Incest as Narcissism in Tieck, Wagner,
and Thomas Mann," *The German Quarterly* 56.2 (1983): 247–5. – She also
states: "For the child Bertha, the old woman's Eden-like valley embodies a
dream of fairy-tale seclusion […]." In Finney's interpretation, Bertha's and
Eckbert's death is a punishment for their narcissistic solipsism. Finney,
"Self-Reflexive Siblings," 247.

45 "So morgen wie heut / In ewger Zeit" (EckG 132, 22–3).

46 The approximate time of her stay can be inferred from the text: "four
years I had passed in this way […] (I must now have been nearly twelve)"
(EckE 28). The passage describing her departure begins: "I was now
fourteen […]" (EckE 30) which adds two more years to her stay.

47 As mentioned above, "Einsamkeit," in "Waldeinsamkeit," means "loneliness."

48 Cp. the remarks in the conclusion about instances in all three texts
discussed in this dissertation in which repetitions have an uncanny effect.

49 A stanza of the poem "An Tieck" (1802) by Novalis may serve as one of
many examples: "Ein Kind voll Wehmut und voll Treue, / Verstoßen in
ein fremdes Land, / Ließ gern das Glänzende und Neue, / Und blieb dem
Alten zugewandt." Gerhard Hay and Sibylle von Steinsdorff, eds, *Deutsche
Lyrik vom Barock bis zur Gegenwart* (München: Deutscher Taschenbuch
Verlag, 1980) 116. – Heinrich Heine, in his parodies of Romanticism, also
employs the "*Lied*" form.

50 The use of the syllable "freut" in lines 2 and 5 violates the avoidance of
exact repetition, instead of a true rhyme. It might also invoke folklore's
simplicity. Cp. Punter's remark in footnote 51 in this chapter.

51 In his analysis of Coleridge's "Ancient Mariner," Punter (2000) comments:
"[…] rhyme itself has its own uncanny qualities […] Rhyme, we might say,
is always poised between two absurdities: the absurdity of the non-rhyme
where rhyme is expected, and the absurdity of the total rhyme, where the
mere repetition of the same word leads inevitably to the bathetic, as in the
reductio ad absurdum of the limerick." Punter, "On Poetry and the Uncanny," 196.

52   "Den Sinn der von ihnen gesprochenen Worte verstehen sie nicht, haben aber eine natürliche Empfänglichkeit für den Gleichklang der Laute, der kein vollständiger zu sein braucht. Es verschlägt daher für sie wenig, ob man sagt [...] 'Santiago' oder 'Karthago' / 'Chinesentum' oder 'Jesum Christum', / 'Abendrot' oder 'Atemnot', / 'Ariman' oder 'Ackermann' etc. [...]." Sigmund Freud, "Psycho-Analytic Notes on an Autobiographical Account of a Case of Paranoia (Dementia Paranoides)," trans. and ed. James Strachey, *The Standard Edition of the Complete Psychological Works*, vol. 12 (London: Hogarth Press/Institute of Psychoanalysis, 1953–1974) 36.

53   Quoted above on p. 147.

54   The dictionary of superstitions informs us about the significance of the bird as an ill omen: "Birds [...] were anciently regarded as divine or semi-divine beings. [...] Certain types of birds [...] are considered lucky or unlucky, foretellers of the future, or embodiments of the souls of the dead." Christina Hole and Edith M. Horsley, *The Encyclopedia of Superstitions* (New York: Barnes & Noble Books, 1996) "Birds". – Speech is attributed to birds in folklore. According to a Russian tale about Christ on the cross "[...] the kindly swallows tried to protect Him from further torment by crying 'He is dead! He is dead!', but the sparrows retorted 'He is alive! He is alive!', and so urged His persecutors on to still greater cruelties." Hole and Horsley, *Superstitions* "Sparrow." [punctuation original]. – Hole recommends E.A. Armstrong *The Folklore of Birds* (1958) for further research.

55   The doubling of "always again" seems indeed to overwhelm the power of the single word "not," which portrays the relative strength of the repressed to gain consciousness.

56   The letter 'h' in the dog's name "Strohmian" is unusual. "Strohmian" is derived from "Stromer" = "Landstreicher" (tramp, vagabond), the verb "stromern" shares its root with the English "stray," as in "stray animal." A possible explanation for the insertion of the letter "h" into the name may be that it creates a connection between the figures surrounding Eckbert: Bertha, Walther, Hugo, and Strohmian, endowing them all with a mysterious quality through association this silent or whispering sound (the letter "h" is also the first letter of "heimlich" ["secretive"]).

57   Kenneth J. Northcott, "A Note on the Levels of Reality in Tieck's 'Der blonde Eckbert'," *German Life and Letters* 6 (1952–53). – Discussions with Prof. Northcott provided a starting point for this chapter.

58   Martin Swales may well have taken his cue from the label "Kriminalwort" for "Strohmian," used by Bloch. Ernst Bloch refers to his conversation with

Benjamin about "The Fair-Haired Eckbert." Ernst Bloch, "Bilder des Déjà vu," *Verfremdungen*, vol. 1, Bibliothek Suhrkamp, Bd. 85, 120 (Frankfurt a.M.: Suhrkamp, 1962) 34. – Swales makes the following pertinent comment: "The moment [when Walther mentions the dog's name] is a pivotal point in the story, it is both a fantastical and a psychological event, which derives its menacing implications both from its magical import [nourished by one of the oldest magical beliefs that the possession of a name confers power] and from the threatening psychological state of Eckbert and Bertha." Swales, "Reading One's Life," 171.

59   I thus disagree with critics who have claimed that these crimes constitute a violation of a paradise, e.g. Janis L. Gellinek, "'Der Blonde Eckbert:' A Tieckian Fall from Paradise," *Festschrift für Heinrich E.K. Henel. Lebendige Form: Interpretationen zur deutschen Literatur*, ed. Jeffrey L. Sammons and Ernst Schürer (München: Fink, 1970). – Cp. also footnote 60 in this chapter.

60   I therefore disagree with Davies: "In the Christian context Bertha's theft clearly constitutes what Frye would term a 'displaced' secular reenactment of the Fall." Davies, "Eckbert the Fair as Paradigm," 183. – While these events can be seen in light of the narrator commentary "[…] it is the misery of man that he arrives at understanding through the loss of innocence" (EckE 30), the phantom can hardly be seen as an incarnation of the divine.

61   "[…] es ist ein Unglück für den Menschen, daß er seinen Verstand nur darum *bekömmt*, um die Unschuld seiner Seele zu verlieren" (EckG 136, 12–14).

62   Swales has made the absurdity of the phantom's moral demands clear: "[it] is propounding a law which has got to be broken, a law which is expressly designed to produce unavoidable guilt in Bertha." Swales, "Reading One's Life," 169.

63   In this regard I agree with Davies: "[…] one of the most interesting features of this story is that a moral order in the universe is simultaneously affirmed and undermined by the very act of retribution that affirms it." Davies, "Eckbert the Fair as Paradigm," 187.

Chapter 7: Paranoiac Structures of Perception in "Eckbert"

1   Andreas Gailus has recently suggested that the deaths of both protagonists is a consequence of uncovering their secrets, as "blind spots of self-narration" Andreas Gailus, "A Case of Individuality: Karl Philip Moritz and the *Magazine for Empirical Psychology*," *New German Critique* 79 (2000): 103. – The disclosure of these secrets lead to a "psychological dissolution," which is dramatized as a physical destruction. Gailus, "A Case of Individuality: Karl Philip Moritz and the *Magazine for Empirical Psychology*," 105.

2   Henry Fielding's *Tom Jones* is an 18th-century example.

3   The second narrator comment refers to the loss of innocence (EckE 30, quoted below on p. 160). The last two comments concern uncontrolled suspicions (EckE 36, quoted below p. 168; and EckE 40, quoted below p. 169).

4   In his aforementioned article about late 18th-century psychology and Romanticism, Gailus places central importance on the secrets in "Der blonde Eckbert" as the blind spot (the character's unconscious) that defines individuality. Once revealed, the individual disintegrates, thus explaining Bertha's and Eckbert's deaths.

5   These instances are perfect examples of what Freud calls the ability of literature to embody psychoanalytic truths, quoted in the introduction: Freud, *Jensen's "Gradiva,"* 92.

6   "Er nahm seine Armbrust, um sich zu zerstreuen und auf die Jagd zu gehn" (EckG 142, 14–15).

7   Such as gap can be defined as an "ellipsis": "When there is no part of the narrative [...] corresponding to [...] narratively pertinent situations and events that took time, ellipsis obtains." Prince, *A Dictionary of Narratology*, 25.

8   "Eckbert fühlte sich leicht und beruhigt, und doch trieb ihn ein Schauder nach seiner Burg zurück [...]" (EckG 142, 25–6).

9   Even the narrator's comment on Eckbert's qualms about the "murder of his friend" (EckE 38) – "Die Ermordung seines Freundes" (EckG 142, 36), can be interpreted as seen from Eckbert's perspective.

10   *DSM-IV* gives the following definition: "Persecutory delusions are most common; the person believes he or she is being tormented, followed, tricked, spied on, or subjected to ridicule." – "Delusions [...] are

erroneous beliefs that usually involve a misinterpretation of perceptions or experiences. Their content may include a variety of themes (e.g., persecutory, referential [...])" *DSM-IV*, 275.

11   Cp. footnote 3 in this chapter.

12   (EckE 40) – "[Hugo] kannte ihn nicht, wußte seine Geschichte nicht, und [Eckbert] fühlte wieder denselben Drang, sich ihm ganz mitzuteilen, damit er versichert sein könne, ob jener auch wahrhaft sein Freund sei" (EckG 143, 37–9).

13   The reference to the "glitter of the many lights" suggests that Eckbert can better see the truth.

14   *DSM-IV*, under "Delusional disorders – Persecutory Type," includes this process part of persecutory delusion: "Small slights may be exaggerated and become the focus of a delusional system." *DSM-IV*, 298.

15   Insofar as "was convinced" suggests at first that Eckbert is mistaken, but we later find out that he is correct, this is an instance of double irony, because seeming non-literal meaning is itself subjected to irony. Cp. William Empson, *Seven Types of Ambiguity* (New York: New Directions, 1947).

16   Cp. footnote 5 in this chapter.

17   This novella is thus typical of the Romantic obsession with death, Observable in many of the aforementioned examples. The famous exchange between Zulima and Heinrich, in Heinrich von Ofterdingen: "Wo gehen wir denn hin?" "Immer nach Hause." – "Where are we going." "Eternally home." Novalis, "Heinrich von Ofterdingen," Monolog. Die Lehrlinge zu Sais. Die Christenheit oder Europa. Hymnen an die Nacht. Heinrich von Ofterdingen (Hamburg: Rowohlt, 1963) 200, my translation. – The answer expresses the inevitability of death. The religiosity of Novalis is visible in this statement, which distinguishes him from Tieck, who more fittingly might be called a nihilist.

18   "Niemand als Walther" (EckG 144, 20).

19   "Niemand anders als Walther" (EckG 145, 8).

20   "Niemand als ich" (EckG 145, 34).

21   I therefore disagree with Davies, for whom the last scene clearly situates the story in the marvelous world of the fairy tale: "But with the old crone's revelation at the end, it is transposed retroactively into the mode of the marvelous." Davies, "Eckbert the Fair as Paradigm," 184. – Davies uses Todorov's nomenclature, in which the "uncanny" is the supernatural explained (as madness or trick), and the "marvelous" is the supernatural accepted (through suspension of disbelief). As mentioned in the introduc-

tion, Todorov's "fantastic" is much closer to the "uncanny" discussed here, and Tieck's story is part of the genre of the uncanny, because it hovers between the two possible responses to the supernatural and fantastical. The final incident does not "retroactively" undo the ambiguous reality status developed throughout the narrative.

22   This metafictional aspect creates distance to the folk fairy tale and constitutes and additional signal for a literary fairy tale.

23   This latter interpretation deviates from the folk fairy tale convention, because the fantastical appears as hostile to the protagonist. This is untypical of the folk fairy tale, as discussed above.

24   The English translation uses "distracted" (EckE 42), whereas the German more explicitly labels Eckbert "insane": "Eckbert lag wahnsinnig und verscheidend auf dem Boden [...]" (EckG 146, 15).

25   Tatar would agree with me on this issue: "[...] by the time the Old Woman finally appears [...] Eckbert is in the final stages of his descent into madness. [...] when she appears to Eckbert, she may be nothing more than an impalpable figment of his imagination." Tatar, "Unholy Alliances," 625.

26   In Novalis's Heinrich von Ofterdingen (1802), a transmigration of souls is deemed possible. Cp. also stories of doubling, such as Chamisso's "Peter Schlemihl" (1814), and Hoffmann's Die Elixiere des Teufels (1814), "Die Geschichte vom verlornen Spiegelbilde" (1815), although the split is a moral one in these examples.

27   Fries interprets Hugo as a revenant of Walther. For Fries, Eckbert's interpretation of his past does not refer to himself. Instead, Eckbert projects the fact of being a revenant onto the apparitions Hugo and the peasant. Eckbert [and Bertha] are themselves revenants, they have no true life, because they do not fully understand their own story. Fries, "Ein romantisches Märchen," 1197, 201.

28   Cp. the passage above regarding Freud's description, in his commentary on Jensen's Gradiva, of how writers represent unconscious mental processes in literature. Freud, Jensen's "Gradiva," 92.

29   Tatar, "Unholy Alliances," 612.

30   "[...] the sin of adultery was committed by the father." Tatar, "Unholy Alliances," 613.

31   The child given away because of a second marriage also recalls "Cinderella," (Schneewittchen), in which adultery is not the issue. The parallels between this fairy tale and Bertha's account could become the

source for further study, especially considering the role of magic bird in "Cinderella" and the "from rags to riches" scenario.

32 Bertha's story thus contains elements of "Cinderella," in which the heroine loses her favorable position after her widowed father's remarriage. The incest is not intentional, but the result of a curse similar to that of Greek tragedy. Whereas some may view the curse in classical tragedy as carrying out the idea of a divine order, others may see in it an earlier notion of the irrationality and injustice of human fate.

33 I agree with Davies who sees the world of the story as "[...] a universe governed by an implacable and malignant fate. [...] Bertha and Eckbert [...] strike us as the real victims." Davies, "Eckbert the Fair as Paradigm," 187.

34 A Möbius strip is defined in the following way: "[A] one-sided surface that can be constructed by affixing the ends of a rectangular strip after first having given one of the ends a one-half twist. This space exhibits interesting properties, such as having only one side and remaining in one piece when split down the middle. The properties of the strip were discovered independently and almost simultaneously by two German mathematicians, August Ferdinand Möbius and Johann Benedict Listing, in 1858." "Moebius Strip," *The New Encyclopædia Britannica*, 15th edn, Vol. 8 (Chicago: Encyclopaedia Britannica, 1998) 210.

35 Swales expresses this dialectic in the following manner: "Thereby [Tieck] makes us aware of the differing interpretative presuppositions we bring to bear on a given set of experiences according to whether we read them as 'Märchen' or as psychological study. When we attempt to understand 'Der blonde Eckbert,' we find that neither kind of reading is fully satisfying on its own, yet the combination of the two proves to be a peculiarly unacceptable experience because we cannot keep both meanings in focus at the same time." Swales, "Reading One's Life," 174.

36 Fries describes a similar type of interaction between the tale itself and Bertha in regard to Walther's naming of the dog: "[Walther's] superior knowledge is not of a telepathic nature, but the superior knowledge of the narration [the memory of language] in response to the narrating subject." Fries, "Ein romantisches Märchen," 1199. – Fries also points out in the footnote that Benjamin had been working on a theory that distinguishes between epic and reflective memory. Expanding upon Fries/Benjamin, I would see the phantom representing Eckbert's epic memory, in contrast to Bertha's reflective memory. Strangely, when treating this passage, Fries

ignores that the witch later reveals that Walther was one of her disguises. Fries, "Ein romantisches Märchen," 1199, my translation.

37 The name originally meant "ruler of the people" or "leader of the army." Josef Karlmann Brechenmacher, "Walter, 'th,' genet. Waltheri," *Etymologisches Wörterbuch der Deutschen Familiennamen*, vol. 2 (K-Z) (Limburg a.d. Lahn: C.A. Starke, 1957).

38 In the context of the ending, Fries appropriately cites Benjamin, who notes that the phantom represents a law dating from a time before the demons were defeated, where the law governed the relationship, not between human beings, but between man and the gods. Fries, "Ein romantisches Märchen," 1202–3. – Fries also refers to Franz Kafka, where guilt is a mythical, fundamental power, whose origin remains hidden. Fries, "Ein romantisches Märchen," 1204. – This understanding of fate predates that of Greek tragedy, where the death of the hero fulfills a cosmic order that is viewed as just. Cp. also my remarks in the Freud chapter regarding Schelling's commentary on the uncanny. I agree with the now-common critical evaluation of Kafka, in fact, which observes that the inscrutable nature of justice is a chief cause of the uncanny effect of Kafka's fiction. Nevertheless, Fries's interpretation of "Der blonde Eckbert" does not fully account for the text's ambiguity, because he interprets Eckbert's meeting with the old woman as a hallucination.

39 The phantom is also a personification of bad conscience, which reminds us of the impulses that were forbidden.

40 "Certain illusions stem from the ambiguity of visual clues. For example, in a well-known drawing that can be seen either as a vase or as two profiles facing each other, it is uncertain what is the figure and what is the ground against which it is set. Thus, the brain can choose, using the profiles as the ground to perceive the vase, or the vase as the ground to perceive the profiles." "illusion," *The New Encyclopædia Britannica*, 15 edn, Vol. 6 (Chicago: Encyclopaedia Britannica, 1998) 261.

Chapter 8: Conclusion

1 The ties between Romanticism and Modernism are manifold. The affinities between the two periods are visible in direct references within Modernism to Romanticism, such as Mahler's choice to base songs on the

Romantic poems of Friedrich Rückert (1799–1853). See the remarks in the introduction as to how Romanticism prefigures Modernism.

2   Cp. Kleist's discussion at the end of "Über das Marionettentheater" Kleist, "Über das Marionettentheater," 361–8.

3   A similar narrative strategy is still used in more recent examples of the fantastic, such as the episodes of drama series the "Twilight Zone." Each episode begins in a recognizable setting of everyday life that is invaded by the fantastic: "There is a fifth dimension, beyond that which is known to man [...]. It is the middle ground between light and shadow, between science and superstition. It lies between the pit of man's fear and the summit of his knowledge. This is the dimension of imagination, it is an area which we call The Twilight Zone." The introductory text implicitly stresses the importance of cognitive uncertainty.

4   Cp. the first chapter "Freud and Descartes: Dreaming On," in Françoise Meltzer, *Hot Property: The Stakes and Claims of Literary Originality* (Chicago: University of Chicago Press, 1994) 9–42.

5   Cp. F. Meltzer on the importance of this aspect in her response to Terry Castle's essay "Contagious Folly: An Adventure and Its Skeptics" that precedes Meltzer's in the same publication: Meltzer, "Ghost Citing."

6   Cp. Punter's discussions of *Melmoth the Wanderer* (1820), *Caleb Williams* (1794), and *Confessions of a Justified Sinner* (1824). David Punter, *The Literature of Terror: A History of Gothic Fiction from 1765 to the Present Day* (London, New York: Longman, 1980).

7   Punter, *Literature of Terror*, 157.

8   The definition of paranoia I adopt here is more recent than Freud's, who claims that paranoia is caused by repressed homosexual impulses. Cp. his essays on the Schreber case (1911) and two later papers (1915f/1922b): Freud, "Case of Paranoia." – Instead, I follow the *Diagnostic and Statistical Manual of Mental Disorders-IV* (1984): "Delusional disorders [...] Persecutory Type. This subtype applies when the central theme of the delusion involves the person's belief that he or she is being conspired against [...] spied on, followed [...] harassed, or obstructed in the pursuit of long-term goals. Small slights may be exaggerated and become the focus of a delusional system." *DSM-IV*, 297–8.

9   Samuel Taylor Coleridge, *Biographia Literaria, or Biographical Sketches of My Literary Life and Opinions* (New York: Kirk and Mercein, 1817).

10 Punter writes that Coleridge's "Ancient Mariner" "enacts the notion of the word as corpse" and "effects [...] an incarnation of a type of 'life-in-death,' which is the property of every text and demonstrates for us the

problem that there is indeed a sense in which every text might duly be
perceived as uncanny." Punter, "On Poetry and the Uncanny," 196.

11 Richard Langton Gregory, *Eye and Brain: The Psychology of Seeing*, 5th edn
(Princeton: Princeton University Press, 1997).

12 "Ein Gedicht ist mehr als die Summe seiner Interpretationen [...]. Die
Interpretation führt hin an das Gedicht, sie lehrt zunächst einmal genau
lesen. Ganz wie der Betrachter eines Bildes zunächst einmal sehen lernen
muß, was 'da' ist." Hilde Domin, "Über das Interpretieren von
Gedichten," *Doppelinterpretation: Das zeitgenössische deutsche Gedicht zwischen
Autor und Leser*, ed. Hilde Domin (Frankfurt am Main: Fischer, 1969) 19,
my translation.

13 Iser's focus on the "implied reader" has brought his attention to the
foundations of the process of interpretation itself: "The need to decipher
gives us the chance to formulate our own deciphering capacity [...]"
Wolfgang Iser, *The Implied Reader: Patterns of Communication in Prose Fiction from
Bunyan to Beckett* (Baltimore: Johns Hopkins University Press, 1974) 294.

Bibliography

Abrams, M.H. *Natural Supernaturalism: Tradition and Revolution in Romantic Literature*. New York: Norton, 1971.

Adelung, Johann Christoph. "Der Olymp." *Grammatisch kritisches Wörterbuch der hochdeutschen Mundart mit beständiger Vergleichung der übrigen Mundarten, besonders des Oberdeutschen.* Vol. 3. Wien: Bauer, 1811. 605.

Ariès, Philippe. *Centuries of Childhood: A Social History of Family Life.* Enfant et la vie familiale sous l'Ancien Régime. Trans. Robert Baldick. New York: Vintage, 1962.

Barry, Jane Elizabeth. "The Problem of Identity in Ludwig Tieck's Tales from the Phantasus: A Psychoanalytic Interpretation." *Dissertation Abstracts International* 45.6 (1984): 1764A.

Benjamin, Walter. *Der Begriff der Kunstkritik in der deutschen Romantik.* Neue Berner Abhandlungen zur Philosophie und ihrer Geschichte, 5. Ed. Richard Herbertz. Bern: Francke, 1920.

Bloch, Ernst. "Bilder des Déjà vu." *Verfremdungen.* Vol. 1. Bibliothek Suhrkamp, Bd. 85, 120. Frankfurt a.M.: Suhrkamp, 1962. 24–36.

Booth, Wayne C. *The Rhetoric of Fiction.* 2nd edn. Chicago: University of Chicago Press, 1983.

Bordwell, David, and Kristin Thompson. *Film Art: An Introduction.* New York: McGraw-Hill, 1993.

Brechenmacher, Josef Karlmann. "Walter, 'th,' genet. Waltheri." *Etymologisches Wörterbuch der Deutschen Familiennamen.* Vol. 2 (K–Z). Limburg a.d. Lahn: C.A. Starke, 1957. 741.

Brockhaus Enzyklopädie: in vierundzwanzig Bänden. 24 vols. Mannheim: Brockhaus, 1986.

Bronfen, Elisabeth. *Over Her Dead Body: Death, Femininity and the Asthetic.* New York: Routledge, 1994.

Brooks, Peter. "Virtue and Terror: *The Monk.*" *ELH* 40 (1973): 249–63.

Campe, Joachim Heinrich. "unheimlich." *Wörterbuch der Deutschen Sprache.* Vol. 5. Braunschweig: Schulbuchhandlung, 1807–1811. 171.

Castle, Terry. *The Female Thermometer: Eighteenth-Century Culture and the Invention of the Uncanny.* Oxford: Oxford University Press, 1995.

Cixous, Hélène. "Fiction and its Phantoms: A Reading of Freud's 'Das Unheimliche'." *New Literary History* 7.3 (1976): 525–48.

Coleridge, Samuel Taylor. *Biographia Literaria, or Biographical Sketches of My Literary Life and Opinions*. New York: Kirk and Mercein, 1817.

Copjec, Joan. "Vampires, Breast-Feeding and Anxiety." *October* 58 (1991): 25–43.

Curtius, Ernst Robert. *European Literature and the Latin Middle Ages*. Trans. Willard R. Trask. Princeton: Princeton University Press, 1967.

Davies, J.M.Q. "Eckbert the Fair as Paradigm." *Journal of the Australasian Universities Language and Literature Association* 73 (1990): 181–9.

de Man, Paul. *The Resistance to Theory*. Minneapolis: University of Minneapolis Press, 1986.

Diagnostic and Statistical Manual of Mental Disorders. 4th edn. Washington, D.C.: American Psychiatric Association, 1994.

Domin, Hilde. "Über das Interpretieren von Gedichten." *Doppelinterpretation: Das zeitgenössische deutsche Gedicht zwischen Autor und Leser*. Ed. Hilde Domin. Frankfurt am Main: Fischer, 1969. 11–44.

Elias, Norbert. *The Civilizing Process*. Trans. Edmund Jephcott. Vol. 1. 2 vols. Oxford: Blackwell, 1994.

Empson, William. *Seven Types of Ambiguity*. New York: New Directions, 1947.

Falkenberg, Marc. "The Poetical Uncanny: A Study of Early Modern Fantastic Fiction." Ph.D. Diss. University of Chicago, 2000.

Fanning, James. *Literaturwissenschaftliches Wörterbuch: Deutsch-Englisch/Englisch-Deutsch*. Frankfurt/Main: Peter Lang, 1993.

Fickert, Kurt J. "The Relevance of the Incest Motif in 'Der blonde Eckbert'." *Germanic Notes* 13.3 (1982): 33–5.

Finney, Gail. "Self-Reflexive Siblings: Incest as Narcissism in Tieck, Wagner, and Thomas Mann." *The German Quarterly* 56.2 (1983): 243–56.

Freud, Sigmund. "The Antithetical Meaning of Primal Words." Trans. and ed. James Strachey. *The Standard Edition of the Complete Psychological Works*. Vol. 11. London: Hogarth Press/Institute of Psychoanalysis, 1953–1974. 153–61.

— *Beyond the Pleasure Principle*. Trans. and ed. James Strachey. *The Standard Edition of the Complete Psychological Works*. Vol. 18. London: Hogarth Press/Institute of Psychoanalysis, 1953–1974.

— "A Case of Paranoia Running Counter to the Psycho-Analytic Theory of the Disease." Trans. and ed. James Strachey. *The Standard Edition of the Complete Psychological Works*. 1915f. Vol. 14. London: Hogarth Press/Institute of Psychoanalysis, 1953–1974. 263–72.

— *Delusions and Dreams in W. Jensen's "Gradiva."* Trans. and ed. James Strachey. *The Standard Edition of the Complete Psychological Works*. Vol. 9. London: Hogarth Press/Institute of Psychoanalysis, 1953–1974. 1–95.

— "A Disturbance of Memory on the Acropolis: An Open Letter to Romain Rolland on the Occasion of his Seventieth Birthday." Trans. and ed. James Strachey. *The Standard Edition of the Complete Psychological Works.* Vol. 22. London: Hogarth Press/Institute of Psychoanalysis, 1953–1974. 237–48.

— *Inhibitions, Symptoms and Anxiety.* Trans. and ed. James Strachey. *The Standard Edition of the Complete Psychological Works.* Vol. 20. London: Hogarth Press/Institute of Psychoanalysis, 1953–1974. 87–175.

— *The Interpretation of Dreams.* Trans. and ed. James Strachey. *The Standard Edition of the Complete Psychological Works.* Vol. 4/5. London: Hogarth Press/Institute of Psychoanalysis, 1953–1974.

— *Jokes and their Relation to the Unconscious.* Trans. and ed. James Strachey. *The Standard Edition of the Complete Psychological Works.* Vol. 8. London: Hogarth Press/Institute of Psychoanalysis, 1953–1974.

— "Negation." Trans. and ed. James Strachey. *The Standard Edition of the Complete Psychological Works.* Vol. 19. London: Hogarth Press/Institute of Psychoanalysis, 1953–1974. 233–42.

— *New Introductory Lectures on Psycho-Analysis.* "Lecture XXIX: Revision of the Theory of Dreams." Trans. and ed. James Strachey. *The Standard Edition of the Complete Psychological Works.* Vol. 22. London: Hogarth Press/Institute of Psychoanalysis, 1953–1974. 7–30.

— *New Introductory Lectures on Psycho-Analysis.* "Lecture XXXII: Anxiety and Instinctual Life." Trans. and ed. James Strachey. *The Standard Edition of the Complete Psychological Works.* Vol. 22. London: Hogarth Press/Institute of Psychoanalysis, 1953–1974. 81–111.

— "Psycho-Analytic Notes on an Autobiographical Account of a Case of Paranoia (Dementia Paranoides)." Trans. and ed. James Strachey. *The Standard Edition of the Complete Psychological Works.* Vol. 12. London: Hogarth Press/Institute of Psychoanalysis, 1953–1974. 3–83.

— *The Psychopathology of Everyday Life.* Trans. and ed. James Strachey. *The Standard Edition of the Complete Psychological Works.* Vol. 6. London: Hogarth Press/Institute of Psychoanalysis, 1953–1974.

— "Recommendations to Physicians Practicing Psycho-Analysis." Trans. and ed. James Strachey. *The Standard Edition of the Complete Psychological Works.* Vol. 12. London: Hogarth Press/Institute of Psychoanalysis, 1953–1974. 109–20.

— "Some Neurotic Symptoms in Jealousy, Paranoia and Homosexuality." Trans. and ed. James Strachey. *The Standard Edition of the Complete Psychological Works.* Vol. 18. Gesammelte Werke; Chronologisch geordnet, Vols. I-XVIII. London: Hogarth Press/Institute of Psychoanalysis, 1953–1974. 225–30.

— *Studies in Hysteria.* Trans. and ed. James Strachey. *The Standard Edition of the Complete Psychological Works.* Vol. 2. 24 vols. London: Hogarth Press/Institute of Psychoanalysis, 1953–1974.

— *Three Essays on the Theory of Sexuality.* Trans. and ed. James Strachey. *The Standard Edition of the Complete Psychological Works.* Vol. 7. London: Hogarth Press/Institute of Psychoanalysis, 1953–1974. 123–243.

— "Totem and Taboo." Trans. and ed. James Strachey. *The Standard Edition of the Complete Psychological Works.* Vol. 13. London: Hogarth Press/Institute of Psychoanalysis, 1953–1974. 1–161.

— "The Uncanny." Trans. and ed. James Strachey. *The Standard Edition of the Complete Psychological Works.* Vol. 17. London: Hogarth Press/Institute of Psychoanalysis, 1953–1974. 217–56.

Fries, Thomas. "Ein romantisches Märchen: 'Der blonde Eckbert' von Ludwig Tieck." *MLN* 88.6 (1973): 1180–211.

Gailus, Andreas. "A Case of Individuality: Karl Philip Moritz and the *Magazine for Empirical Psychology.*" *New German Critique* 79 (2000): 67–105.

Gay, Peter. *Freud: A Life For Our Time.* New York and London: Norton, 1998.

Gellinek, Janis L. "'Der Blonde Eckbert:' A Tieckian Fall from Paradise." *Festschrift für Heinrich E.K. Henel. Lebendige Form: Interpretationen zur deutschen Literatur.* Ed. Jeffrey L. Sammons and Ernst Schürer. München: Fink, 1970. 147–66.

Genette, Gérard. "Frontiers of Narrative." Trans. Alan Sheridan. *Figures of Literary Discourse.* New York: Columbia University Press, 1982. 127–44.

Ginsburg, Ruth. "A Primal Scene of Reading: Freud and Hoffmann." *Literature and Psychology* 38.3 (1992): 24–46.

Götze, Alfred. "heimlich." *Trübners Deutsches Wörterbuch.* Ed. Im Auftrage der Arbeitsgemeinschaft für deutsche Wortforschung herausgegeben von Alfred Götze. Vol. 3 "G–H." Berlin: Walter de Gruyter, 1939. 388–9.

Gregory, Richard Langton. *Eye and Brain: The Psychology of Seeing.* 5th edn. Princeton: Princeton University Press, 1997.

Grimm, Jacob and Wilhelm. "Hänsel und Gretel." *Kinder und Hausmärchen gesammelt durch die Brüder Grimm.* München: Winkler, 1971. 116–25.

— "Von dem Machandelbaum." *Kinder und Hausmärchen gesammelt durch die Brüder Grimm.* München: Winkler Verlag, 1971. 260–73.

— "heimlich." *Deutsches Wörterbuch. Vierter Band. Zweite Abteilung.* Ed. Moriz Heyne. Vol. 10. Leipzig: Hirzel, 1877 [1854–1971]. 873–9.

— "un-." *Deutsches Wörterbuch. Elfter Band. III. Abteilung. Un-Uzvogel.* Ed. Karl Euling. Vol. 11. Leipzig: S. Hirzel, 1936 [1854–1971]. 1–33.

— "ungeheuer." *Deutsches Wörterbuch.* Ed. Karl Euling. Vol. 11. Leipzig: Hirzel, 1936. 691–706.

— "unheimlich." *Deutsches Wörterbuch. Elfter Band. III. Abteilung. Un-Uzvogel.* Ed. Karl Euling. Vol. 11. Leipzig: S. Hirzel, 1936. 1055–9.

Hay, Gerhard and Sibylle von Steinsdorff, eds *Deutsche Lyrik vom Barock bis zur Gegenwart.* München: Deutscher Taschenbuch Verlag, 1980.

Hertz, Neil. "Freud and the Sandman." *End of the Line: Essays in Psychoanalysis and the Sublime.* New York: Columbia University Press, 1985. 97–121. "Freud and the Sandman." In *Textual Strategies: Perspectives in Post-Structuralist Criticism,* edited by Josué V. Harari, 296–321. Ithaca: Cornell University Press, 1979.

Heyne, Moriz. "heimlich." *Deutsches Wörterbuch.* 2nd edn. Vol. 2. Leipig: Hirzel, 1906. 104–5.

Hoffmann, E.T.A. "Der goldne Topf." *Fantasiestücke in Callots Manier.* Ed. Walter Müller Seidel. Vol. Fantasie und Nachtstücke. Darmstadt: Wissenschaftliche Buchgesellschaft, 1971. 179–255.

— "Der Sandmann." *Fantasie und Nachtstücke.* Ed. Walter Müller Seidel. Darmstadt: Wissenschaftliche Buchgesellschaft, 1971. 331–63.

— "Die Automate." *Die Serapions-Brüder: Gesammelte Erzählungen und Märchen. Herausgegeben von E.T.A. Hoffmann.* 5th edn. Vol. 2. Winkler Weltliteratur Dünndruck Ausgabe. München: Winkler, 1963/1995. 328–55.

— *Die Serapions-Brüder: Gesammelte Erzählungen und Märchen. Herausgegeben von E.T.A. Hoffmann.* Winkler Weltliteratur Dünndruck Ausgabe. 5th edn. München: Winkler, 1963/1995.

— *Fantasie und Nachtstücke.* Ed. Walter Müller Seidel. Darmstadt: Wissenschaftliche Buchgesellschaft, 1971.

— "The Sandman." Trans. and ed. Stanley Appelbaum. *Five Great German Short Stories = Fünf deutsche Meistererzählungen: A Dual-Language Book.* New York: Dover, 1993. 36–103.

Hofmannsthal, Hugo von, ed. *Deutsche Erzähler.* Vol. 1. 2 vols. Darmstadt: Insel, 1971.

Hole, Christina and Edith M. Horsley. *The Encyclopedia of Superstitions.* 1961 Helicon Publishing Ltd. New York: Barnes & Noble Books, 1996.

Horkheimer, Max, and Theodor W. Adorno. *Dialectic of Enlightenment.* Trans. John Cumming. New York: Seabury, 1972.

Horn, Peter. "Halluzinierte Vögel oder Wann ist Paranoia literarisch? Zu E.T.A. Hoffmann, Robert Musil und Daniel Paul Schreber." *Acta Germanica: Jahrbuch des Germanistenverbandes im Südlichen Afrika* Supp. 1 (1990): 97–122.

Huet, Marie-Hélène. *Monstrous Imagination.* Cambridge, Mass.: Harvard University Press, 1993.

"illusion." *The New Encyclopædia Britannica.* 15th edn. Vol. 6. Chicago: Encyclopaedia Britannica, 1998. 261.

Iser, Wolfgang. *The Implied Reader: Patterns of Communication in Prose Fiction from Bunyan to Beckett.* Baltimore: Johns Hopkins University Press, 1974.

Jastrow, Joseph. *Fact and Fable in Psychology.* Boston: Houghton Mifflin, 1900.

Jentsch, Ernst. "Zur Psychologie des Unheimlichen." *Psychiatrisch-Neurologische Wochenschrift* 22, 23 (1906): 195–98, 203–5.

Jones, Ernest. *The Life and Work of Sigmund Freud.* 3 vols. New York and London: Basic, 1953.

Kaltschmidt, Jakob Heinrich. *Gesammt-Wörterbuch der Deutschen Sprache.* Leipzig: Karl Lauchnitz, 1834.

Kant, Immanuel. *Critique of Pure Reason.* Trans. J.M.D. Meiklejohn. New York: Willey Book Co., 1943.

Kittler, Friedrich. "'Das Phantom unseres Ichs' und die Literaturpsychologie: E.T.A. Hoffmann—Freud—Lacan." *Urszenen.* Ed. Horst Turk Friedrich Kittler. Frankfurt am Main: Suhrkamp, 1977. 139–66.

Kleist, Heinrich von. "[Letter dated March 22, 1801]." *Sämtliche Werke.* Eds Roland Reuß and Peter Staengle. Vol. 4 part 1. Brandenburger Ausgabe: Stroemfeld/Roter Stern, 1988. 498–509.

—. "Über das Marionettentheater." *Kleist: Ein Lesebuch für unsere Zeit.* Goldammer, Peter (Einleitung und Auswahl). Berlin Weimar: Aufbau, 1986. 361–8.

Kristeva, Julia. *Powers of Horror: An Essay on Abjection.* Trans. Leon S. Roudiez. New York: Columbia University Press, 1982.

Lacan, Jacques. "The Function and Field of Speech and Language in Psychoanalysis." Trans. Alan Sheridan. *Écrits: A Selection.* New York and London: Norton, 1977. 30–113.

—. "The Mirror Stage as Formative of the Function of the I." Trans. Alan Sheridan. *Écrits: A Selection.* New York and London: Norton, 1977. 1–7.

Laplanche, J. and J.-B. Pontalis. *The Language of Psycho-Analysis.* Trans. Donald Nicholson-Smith. New York: Norton, 1973.

Lenz, Barbara. *un-Affigierung: unrealisierbare Argumente, unausweichliche Fragen, nicht unplausible Antworten.* Studien zur deutschen Grammatik, 50. Ed. et al. Werner Abraham. Tübingen: Gunter Narr, 1995.

Lonitz, Henri, ed. *Adorno Benjamin Briefwechsel 1928–1940.* Frankfurt: Suhrkamp, 1994.

Lydenberg, Robin. "Freud's Uncanny Narratives." *Publications of the Modern Language Association* 112.5 (1997): 1072–86.

McCaffrey, Phillip. "Freud's Uncanny Woman." *Reading Freud's Reading.* Ed. Sander L. Gilman et al. New York: New York University Press, 1994. 91–108.

McGlathery, James M. *Grimm's Fairy Tales: A History of Criticism on a Popular Classic*. Studies in German Literature, Linguistics, and Culture: Literary Criticism in Perspective. Ed. James Hardin. Columbia, SC: Camden House, 1993.

Meltzer, Françoise. "For Your Eyes Only: Ghost Citing." *Questions of Evidence. Proof, Practice, and Persuasion across the Disciplines*. Eds James K. Chandler et al. Chicago: University of Chicago Press, 1994. 43–9.

— *Hot Property: The Stakes and Claims of Literary Originality*. Chicago: University of Chicago Press, 1994.

— "The Uncanny Rendered Canny: Freud's Blind Spot in Reading Hoffmann's 'Sandman'." *Introducing Psychoanalytic Theory*. Ed. Sander L. Gilman. New York: Brunner/Mazel, 1982. 218–39.

"Moebius Strip." *The New Encyclopædia Britannica*. 15th edn. Vol. 8. Chicago: Encyclopaedia Britannica, 1998. 210.

Møller, Lis. *The Freudian Reading: Analytical and Fictional Constructions*. Philadelphia: University of Pennsylvania Press, 1991.

Musil, Robert. "Die Amsel." *Deutsche Erzähler*. Ed. Marie Luise Kaschnitz. Vol. 2. Frankfurt am Main: Insel, 1971. 237–55.

Northcott, Kenneth J. "A Note on the Levels of Reality in Tiecks 'Der blonde Eckbert'." *German Life and Letters* 6 (1952–53): 292–4.

Novalis. "Heinrich von Ofterdingen." *Monolog. Die Lehrlinge zu Sais. Die Christenheit oder Europa. Hymnen an die Nacht. Heinrich von Ofterdingen*. Hamburg: Rowohlt, 1963. 87–218.

Obermeit, Werner. *Das unsichtbare Ding, das Seele heißt: Die Entdeckung der Psyche im bürgerlichen Zeitalter*. Frankfurt am Main: Syndikat, 1980.

Orlowsky, Ursula. *Literarische Subversion bei E.T.A. Hoffmann: Nouvelles vom "Sandmann"*. Probleme der Dichtung, Heidelberg, Germany (PdD); 20. Heidelberg: Carl Winter Universitätsverlag, 1988.

The Oxford English Dictionary. 2nd edn. Oxford: Clarendon Press, 1989.

Poe, Edgar Allan. "The Philosophy of Composition." *Selected Writings*. Graham's Magazine. Harmondsworth: Penguin Books, 1979. 480–92.

Prince, Gerald. *A Dictionary of Narratology*. Lincoln: University of Nebraska Press, 1987.

Punter, David. *The Literature of Terror: A History of Gothic Fiction from 1765 to the Present Day*. London, New York: Longman, 1980.

— "Shape and Shadow: On Poetry and the Uncanny." *A Companion to the Gothic*. Ed. David Punter. Blackwell Companions to Literature and Culture. Oxford: Blackwell, 2000. 193–205.

The Random House Dictionary of the English Language: The Unabridged Edition. New York: Random House, 1993.

Random House Webster's College Dictionary. New York: Random House, 1991.

Rimmon, Shlomith. *The Concept of Ambiguity: The Example of James.* Chicago and London: The University of Chicago Press, 1977.

Rippere, Victoria L. "Ludwig Tieck's 'Der blonde Eckbert:' A Psychological Reading." *PMLA: Publications of the Modern Language Association of America* 85.3 (1970): 473–86.

Roget's II. The New Thesaurus. 3rd edn. Boston: Hougthon Mifflin, 1996.

Royle, Nicholas. *The Uncanny.* New York: Routledge, 2003.

Rubin, Bernard. "Freud and Hoffmann: 'The Sandmann'." *Introducing Psychoanalytic Theory.* Ed. Sander L. Gilman. New York: Brunner/Mazel, 1982. 205–17.

"Sandmann." *Meyers Enzyklopädisches Lexikon.* Vol. 20. Mannheim, Wien, Zürich: Bibliographische Institut / Lexikonverlag, 1977.

Schelling, Friedrich Wilhelm Joseph von. "Achtundzwanzigste Vorlesung: Qualitativer Unterschied zwischen dem Charakter der griechischen Religion und dem der früheren Religionen." *Philosophie der Mythologie. Erstes Buch: Der Monotheismus.* Ed. Karl Friedrich August Schelling. Vol. 2 pt. 2. Stuttgart und Augsburg: Cotta'scher Verlag, 1856–1861. 645–60.

Schelling, Karl Wilhelm Joseph von. *System des transzendentalen Idealismus.* Eds Horst D. Brandt and Peter Müller. Hamburg: F. Meiner, 1992.

Schlegel, Friedrich von. "Athenäums-Fragment 116." *Charakteristiken und Kritiken I, 1796–1801.* Ed. Ernst Behler. Vol. 2. München, Paderborn, Wien, Zürich: Ferdinand Schöningh, 1967. 182–3.

— "Athenäums-Fragment 299." *Charakteristiken und Kritiken I, 1796–1801.* Ed. Ernst Behler. Vol. 2. München, Paderborn, Wien, Zürich: Ferdinand Schöningh, 1967. 215.

Schulz, Gerhard. *Die deutsche Literatur zwischen französischer Revolution und Restauration. Zweiter Teil. Das Zeitalter der napoleonischen Kriege und der Restauration: 1806–1830.* Vol. 7, 2. München: Beck, 1989.

"The Sleeping Beauty in the Wood." *The Classic Fairy Tales.* Eds Iona and Peter Opie. London: Book Club Associates, 1974. 85–92.

"Spiegel." *Real-Enzyclopädie für die gebildeten Stände (Conversations-Lexikon).* Vol. 9. Leipzig: Brockhaus, 1824.

Starobinski, Jean. "'Acheronta Movebo.'" Trans. and ed. Françoise Meltzer. *The Trial(s) of Psychoanalysis.* Chicago: University of Chicago Press, 1987. 273–86.

Swales, Martin. "Reading One's Life: An Analysis of Tieck's 'Der blonde Eckbert'." *German Life and Letters* 29 (1975): 165–75.

Tatar, Maria. "Unholy Alliances: Narrative Ambiguity in Tieck's 'Der blonde Eckbert'." *MLN* 102.3 (1987): 608–26.

Tieck, Ludwig. "Der blonde Eckbert." *Phantasus.* Ed. Manfred Frank. Vol. 6. Frankfurt am Main: Deutscher Klassiker Verlag, 1985. 126–48.

— "Der Runenberg." *Phantasus.* Ed. Manfred Frank. Vol. 6. Frankfurt am Main: Deutscher Klassiker Verlag, 1985. 184–209.

— "The Fair-Haired Eckbert." *Novellas of Ludwig Tieck and E.T.A. Hoffmann: Translated by Thomas Carlyle.* Ed. Eitel Timm. 1st edn. Studies in German Literature, Linguistics, and Culture, 51. Columbia, SC: Camden House, 1991. 18–42.

"Tiecks Redaktion der Erstfassung." *Bibliothek deutscher Klassiker.* Ed. Manfred Frank. Vol. 6. Frankfurt am Main: Deutscher Klassiker Verlag, 1985. 1254–5.

Todorov, Tzvetan. *The Fantastic: A Structural Approach to a Literary Genre.* Trans. Richard Howard. Ithaca, NY: Cornell University Press, 1973.

— "The Uncanny and the Marvelous." *Literature of the Occult. A Collection of Critical Essays.* Ed. Peter B. Messent. Twentieth Century Views. Englewood Cliffs, N.J.: Prentice-Hall, 1981.

"unheimlich." *Duden: Das große Wörterbuch der deutschen Sprache in acht Bänden.* Ed. Wissenschaftlicher Rat und die Mitarbeiter der Dudenredaktion unter der Leitung von Günther Drosdowski. 2nd edn. Vol. 7: Sil–Urh. Mannheim, Leipzig, Wien, Zürich: Dudenverlag, 1993.

Weber, Samuel. "The Sideshow, or: Remarks on a Canny Moment." *Modern Language Notes* 88.5 (1973): 1102–33.

Williams, Anne. *Art of Darkness: A Poetics of Gothic.* Chicago: University of Chicago Press, 1995.

Wittgenstein, Ludwig. *Philosophical Investigations.* Trans. G.E.M. Anscombe. London, New York: Macmillan, 1953.

Wolfreys, Julian. *Victorian Hauntings: Spectrality, Gothic, the Uncanny and Literature.* Houndmills, Basingstoke, Hampshire, New York: Palgrave, 2002.

Wright, Elisabeth. *Psychoanalytic Criticism: Theory in Practice.* New Accents. London and New York: Methuen, 1984.

Index

Studies in Modern German Literature

Peter D. G. Brown
General Editor

22 Joachim Warmbold, *Germania in Africa: Germany's Colonial Literature.* 1989.

23 Ernst Schürer, *Franz Jung: Leben und Werk eines Rebellen.* 1994.

24 David B. Dickens, *Negative Spring: Crisis Imagery in the Works of Brentano, Lenau, Rilke, and T.S. Eliot.* 1989.

25 Ernest M. Wolf, *Magnum Opus: Studies in the Narrative Fiction of Thomas Mann.* 1989.

26 Roger Gerhild Brueggemann, *Das Romanwerk von Ingeborg Drewitz.* 1989.

27 Margaret Devinney, *The Legends of Gertrud von Le Fort: Text and Audience.* 1989.

28 Jürgen Kleist, *Das Dilemma der Kunst. Zur Kunst- und Künstlerproblematik in der deutschsprachigen Prosa nach 1945.* 1989.

29 Frederick Amrine (ed.), *Goethe in the History of Science: Bibliography, 1776–1949. Volume I.* 1996.

30 Frederick Amrine (ed.), *Goethe in the History of Science: Bibliography, 1950–1990. Volume II.* 1996.

32 Christina E. Brantner, *Robert Schumann und das Tonkünstler-Bild der Romantiker.* 1991.

33 Brenda Keiser, *Deadly Dishonor: The Duel and the Honor Code in the Works of Arthur Schnitzler.* 1990.

34 Claus Reschke, *Life as a Man: Contemporary Male-Female Relationships in the Novels of Max Frisch.* 1990.

35 Bernhard H. Decker, *Gewalt und Zärtlichkeit. Einführung in die Militärbelletristik der DDR 1956–1986.* 1990.

36 Kathy Brzovic, *Bonaventura's "Nachtwachen": A Satirical Novel.* 1990.

37 Jozef A. Modzelewski, *Das Pandämonium der achtziger Jahre. Kurzprosa des Jahres 1983.* 1990.

38 Jürgen Fröhlich, *Liebe im Expressionismus. Eine Untersuchung der Lyrik in den Zeitschriften "Die Aktion" und "Der Sturm" von 1910–1914.* 1991.

39 Richard A. Weber, *Color and Light in the Writings of Eduard von Keyserling.* 1990.

40 Ingeborg C. Walther, *The Theater of Franz Xaver Kroetz.* 1990.

41 Ralph W. Büchler, *Science, Satire and Wit: The Essays of Georg Christoph Lichtenberg.* 1990.

42 Peter J. Schroeck, *Character Transition in the Writings of Hans Erich Nossack.* 1991.

43 William Grange, *Partnership in the German Theatre: Zuckmayer and Hilpert, 1925–1961.* 1991.

44 Mary Rhiel, *Re-Viewing Kleist: The Discursive Construction of Authorial Subjectivity in West German Kleist Films.* 1991.

45 Hülya Ünlü, *Das Ghasel des islamischen Orients in der deutschen Dichtung.* 1991.

46 Russel Christensen, *The Virility Complex: A Casebook of National Socialist Practice.* Forthcoming.

47 Klaus-Jürgen Röhm, *Polyphonie und Improvisation. Zur offenen Form in Günter Grass' "Die Rättin"*. 1992.

48 Kevin G. Kennedy, *Der junge Goethe in der Tradition des Petrarkismus*. 1995.

49 Thomas Mann, *Thomas Mann – Félix Bertaux: Correspondence 1923-1948. Edited by Biruta Cap*. 1993.

50 Ilse-Rose Warg, *"Doch ich krümm mich um alles, was lebt". Wolfdietrich Schnurres lyrisches Schaffen*. 1993.

51 Muriel W. Stiffler, *The German Ghost Story as Genre*. 1993.

52 Roger F. Cook, *The Demise of the Author: Autonomy and the German Writer, 1770–1848*. 1993.

53 Gisela Moffit, *Bonds and Bondage: Daughter-Father Relationships in the Father Memoirs of German-Speaking Women Writers of the 1970s*. 1993.

55 Margo R. Bosker, *Sechs Stücke nach Stücken. Zu den Bearbeitungen von Peter Hacks*. 1994.

56 Calvin N. Jones, *Negation and Utopia: The German Volksstück from Raimund to Kroetz*. 1993.

57 Alan John Swensen, *Gods, Angels, and Narrators: A Metaphysics of Narrative in Thomas Mann's "Joseph und seine Brüder"*. 1994.

58 Karl-Heinz Finken, *Die Wahrheit der Literatur. Studien zur Literaturtheorie des 18. Jahrhunderts*. 1993.

59 Marina Foschi Albert, *Friedrich Schlegels Theorie des Witzes und sein Roman "Lucinde"*. 1995.

60 Johann Wolfgang Goethe, *Correspondence between Goethe and Schiller 1794–1805: Translated by Liselotte Dieckmann*. 1994.

61 Timothy Torno, *Finding Time: Reading for Temporality in Hölderlin and Heidegger*. 1995.

62 Steven Fuller, *The Nazis' Literary Grandfather: Adolf Bartels and Cultural Extremism, 1871–1945*. 1996.

63 Cordelia Stroinigg, *Sudermann's "Frau Sorge": Jugendstil, Archetype, Fairy Tale*. 1995.

64 Jean H. Leventhal, *Echoes in the Text: Musical Citation in German Narratives from Theodor Fontane to Martin Walser*. 1995.

66 Cordula Drossel-Brown, *Zeit und Zeiterfahrung in der deutschsprachigen Lyrik der Fünfziger Jahre. Marie Luise Kaschnitz, Ingeborg Bachmann und Christine Lavant*. 1995.

67 Marianne & Martin Löschmann, *Einander verstehen. Ein deutsches literarisches Lesebuch*. 1997.

68 Caroline Kreide, *Lou Andreas-Salomé. Feministin oder Antifeministin? Eine Standortbestimmung zur wilhelminischen Frauenbewegung*. 1996.

69 Fredric S. Steussy, *Eighteenth-Century German Autobiography: The Emergence of Individuality*. 1996.

70 Aminia M. Brueggemann, *Chronotopos Amerika bei Max Frisch, Peter Handke, Günter Kunert und Martin Walser*. 1996.

71 Norgard Klages, *Look Back in Anger: Mother-Daughter and Father-Daughter Relationships in Women's Autobiographical Writings of the 1970s and 1980s*. 1995.

72 Romey Sabalius, *Die Romane Hugo Loetschers im Spannungsfeld von Fremde und Vertrautheit*. 1995.

73 Bianca Rosenthal, *Pathways to Paul Celan: A History of Critical Responses as a Chorus of Discordant Voices*. 1995.

74 Lilian Ramos, *Peter Rosegger: Pedagogue of Passion*. Forthcoming.

75 Sandra L. Singer, *Free Soul, Free Woman? A Study of Selected Fictional Works by Hedwig Dohm, Isolde Kurz, and Helene Böhlau*. 1995.

76 Brigitta O'Regan, *Self and Existence: J.M.R. Lenz's Subjective Point of View*. 1997.

77 Elke Matijevich, *The "Zeitroman" of the Late Weimar Republic*. 1995.

78 Vera B. Profit, *Menschlich. Gespräche mit Karl Krolow*. 1996.

79 Schürer/Keune/Jenkins (eds.), *The Berlin Wall: Representations and Perspectives*. 1996.

80 Frank Schlossbauer, *Literatur als Gegenwelt. Zur Geschichtlichkeit literarischer Komik am Beispiel Fischarts und Lessings*. 1998.

81 Cara M. Horwich, *Survival in "Simplicissimus" and "Mutter Courage"*. 1997.

82 Catherine O'Brien, *Women's Fictional Responses to the First World War: A Comparative Study of Selected Texts by French and German Writers*. 1997.

83 Heather I. Sullivan, *The Intercontextuality of Self and Nature in Ludwig Tieck's Early Works*. 1997.

85 Jean Wotschke, *From the Home Fires to the Battlefield: Mothers in German Expressionist Drama*. 1998.

86 Ellen M. Nagy, *Women in Germanics, 1850–1950*. 1997.

87 Mary R. Strand, *I/You: Paradoxical Constructions of Self and Other in Early German Romanticism*. 1998.

88 Hildegard F. Glass, *Future Cities in Wilhelminian Utopian Literature*. 1997.

89 Irene B. Compton, *Kritik des Kritikers. Bölls "Ansichten eines Clowns" und Kleists "Marionettentheater"*. 1998.

90 Heide Witthoeft, *Von Angesicht zu Angesicht. Literarische Spiegelszenen*. 1998.

91 Peter Yang, *Theater ist Theater. Ein Vergleich der Kreidekreisstücke Bertolt Brechts und Li Xingdaos*. 1998.

92 Hartmut Heep (ed.), *Unreading Rilke: Unorthodox Approaches to a Cultural Myth*. 2001.

93 Wendy Wagner, *Georg Büchners Religionsunterricht 1821–1831. Christlich-Protestantische Wurzeln sozialrevolutionären Engagements*. 2000.

94 Kevin F. Yee, *Aesthetic Homosociality in Wackenroder and Tieck*. 2000.

95 Gary Schmidt, *The Nazi Abduction of Ganymede: Representations of Male Homosexuality in Postwar German Literature*. 2003.

96 Susan Ray, *Beyond Nihilism: Gottfried Benn's Postmodernist Poetics*. 2003.
97 W. Scott Hoerle, *Hans Friedrich Blunck: Poet and Nazi Collaborator, 1888–1961*. 2003.
98 Olivia G. Gabor, *The Stage as "Der Spielraum Gottes"*. 2005.
99 Forthcoming.
100 Marc Falkenberg, *Rethinking the Uncanny in Hoffmann and Tieck*. 2005.
101 Erika M. Nelson, *Reading Rilke's Orphic Identity*. 2005.
102 Forthcoming
103 Bennett Irving Enowitch, *Eros and Thanatos: A Psycho-Literary Investigation of Walter Vogt's Life and Works*. 2005.